D0871991

Milton the Dramatist

Medieval & Renaissance Literary Studies

Timothy J. Burbery

Milton

THE DRAMATIST

 Duquesne
University
Press

Published in the United States of America by
DUQUESNE UNIVERSITY PRESS
600 Forbes Avenue
Pittsburgh, Pennsylvania 15282

Library of Congress Cataloging-in-Publication Data

Burbery, Timothy J., 1963–
   Milton the dramatist / Timothy J. Burbery.
      p. cm. — (Medieval & Renaissance literary studies)
   Includes bibliographical references (p.   ) and index.
   ISBN-13: 978-0-8207-0387-9 (acid-free paper)
   ISBN-10: 0-8207-0387-7 (acid-free paper)
   1. Milton, John, 1608–1674—Criticism and interpretation. 2. Milton, John,
1608–1674—Dramatic works. 3. English drama—17th century—History and
criticism. 4. Literary form—History—17th century. I. Title.
   PR3588.B87 2007
   822'.4—dc22

                                                      2006032803

∞ Printed on acid-free paper.

To Hannah, Peter, and Claire

CONTENTS

ACKNOWLEDGMENTS

It is a pleasure to record the numerous debts to colleagues, students, and friends incurred during the writing of this book. Albert Labriola suggested the topic, while Joseph Pequigney supervised my doctoral thesis on the subject. Lee Erickson supplied excellent advice during the project's early phases, as well as learned scrutiny of chapter 1. The entire manuscript benefited considerably from Michele Schiavone's vigilant proofreading. Thanks are due, besides, to my sister Kathleen for editorial aid and assistance with the Hebrew text of Judges. And I am very grateful to Kathy McLaughlin and Ryan Pfahl for their help in preparing the manuscript for publication. Needless to say, any remaining errors in the text are my own.

Marshall University generously awarded me several research grants, course releases, and a semester's leave to work on the book, which has profited as well from my conversations with my honors and English students.

A portion of chapter 1 appeared in volume 10 of the *Ben Jonson Journal*, nearly the whole of chapter 5 was printed in the March 2004 *Milton Quarterly*, and a part of chapter 4 was published in *English Language Notes*. I wish to thank these journals for their kind permission to reprint the essays.

Introduction

One of the most striking enigmas of literary history concerns the
ambiguity of John Milton's status as a dramatist. On the one hand,
his tragedy *Samson Agonistes* has been highly esteemed by generations of critics and readers. James Russell Lowell was the first
of many to remark that *Samson* constitutes the best re-creation of
a Greek tragedy in English. Coleridge went further, declaring that
the play is the finest "Greek" drama in any modern language, a
judgment seconded in our day by George Steiner. Classicist Watson
Kirkconnell stated that the tragedy "may fairly challenge most of
the surviving dramas of Athens' greatest period," and the eminent
Miltonist William R. Parker accorded it the highest praise, claiming that *Samson* "is more than an imitation of Attic drama, in the
same sense that *The Aeneid* is more than an imitation of Homer.
It is . . . so truly an individual work of art that we are justified now
in adding the name of John Milton to the brief catalogue of 'Tragic
poets unequalled yet by any,'" which is Milton's own description
of Aeschylus, Sophocles, and Euripides.[1]

On the other hand, despite such acclaim Milton is seldom
regarded as a dramatist. Neither Frank Magill's *Critical Survey of
Drama* nor Frederick Link's *English Drama: 1660–1800* even mentions Milton. (Link's omission seems especially puzzling, given his
otherwise exhaustive catalogue, which extends to obscure figures
such as Moses Mendez and Gabriel Odingsells.) William Adams's
Dictionary of English Literature refers to Milton as a "poet and prose-
writer," the *New Century Handbook of English Literature* calls him

an "English poet," *Webster's New World Companion to English and American Literature* labels him a "poet and controversialist," and both the *Dictionary of Literary Biography* and the *Cambridge Guide to Literature in English* denominate him a poet. Moreover, *Samson* is hardly ever included in drama anthologies. So while Parker wished to include Milton in the company of the great Athenian dramatists, and while Alfred Harbage's *Annals of English Drama* lists him as a playwright, such assessments are indeed rare.[2]

In a 1966 *PMLA* article, Roger Wilkenfeld pointed out that the reluctance of the professoriate to view Milton as a dramatist had become something of a truism: "In the long history of Milton commentary a single axiom has survived for generations as a critical touchstone. . . . Simply stated it reads: *Milton was not a dramatist and his poems are not dramatic.*"[3] Some 40 years later, that assessment remains the dominant one. It is founded primarily, perhaps, on the belief that neither *Comus* nor *Samson* constitutes successful drama. Samuel Johnson seems to have initiated this critique, claiming in *Lives of the English Poets* that the speeches of *Comus*, though poetic, are too long to be dramatically effective. Johnson also argued that the tragedy fails to provide any significant causal action between Samson's entrance and exit that either hastens or delays the catastrophe.[4]

The present study contests the prevailing view, arguing that in addition to being a superb writer of epic and lyric, Milton was also a dramatist, and a considerable one at that. Though he composed but one play, it is an undisputed masterpiece. Moreover, as I demonstrate in chapter 5, *Samson* has a surprisingly extensive stage history. And if *Comus* is not a play, it is nonetheless very close to being one, much more so than any other masque. What is more, *Paradise Lost* was originally conceived of as a tragedy, not as an epic. In the early 1640s Milton completed four detailed outlines for a Fall tragedy, as well as at least one speech for the projected tragedy, a 10-line soliloquy by Satan that was later transferred wholesale into *Paradise Lost* 4. Even in its present form, *Paradise Lost* retains other dramatic vestiges, including what appear to be stage directions in book 9. In fact, as I argue in chapter 3, it is even possible that Milton completed the projected Fall tragedy. I also make the case in chapter 1 that his passion for drama was deep and lifelong, evidenced not only by his dramas and dramatic plans, but also by his extensive annotations of Euripides and by his firsthand experience with, and published defense of, the public theater.

Regarding Milton as a dramatist restores a better balance to the totality of his literary achievement and sheds light on some of the most critical questions about his corpus, including the Satan controversy and the questionable implications of Samson's relation to terrorism. Yet many common objections remain as obstacles to affirming Milton's dramatic accomplishments. For instance, against both Johnson's characterization of the Ludlow masque, as well as Johnsonian interpretations, I argue in chapter 3 that the work is, in fact, considerably dramatic. Unlike the vast majority of court masques, *Comus* offers a plot, character development, and, most strikingly, conflict between the masquers and antimasquers. Milton certainly was obligated to conform to the requirements of the Bridgewater family when he composed the masque, yet he appears to have seen the commission as a chance to develop his skills as a dramatist. He had already mastered the conventions of the masque form in the exquisite and compact *Arcades,* so when he was called upon to compose the longer *Comus* a year later, he transcended the masque form to create something more akin to drama. The result is a daring innovation that pushes the essentially inert masque form closer to drama than it had ever gone before. Moreover, when Milton revised *Comus* for publication in 1645 he added certain stage directions while expanding on others. The poet also provided 27 new lines (779–806), including the Lady's rebuke of the temptation scene, which enhanced characterization and clarified stage business.[5]

My fourth chapter contends that while *Samson* is a poem, it is also a genuine play. Although Milton refers to it as a "dramatic poem" in his preface to this tragedy, Anthony Low has demonstrated that the preface employs the term inclusively to refer both to staged and non-staged works. Low also points out that when Milton argues in his commonplace book in favor of staging plays, he utilizes the same phrase he applies to *Samson:* "poema dramaticum," that is, dramatic poem.[6] Moreover, while the preface claims that the tragedy was "never intended" for the theater, that remark may refer only to the Restoration stage. Some critics argue that Milton disapproved of that theater for offering bawdy comedies such as Etheredge's *She Would If She Could* (1668) and Wycherly's *Love in a Wood* (1671), and they may be correct. However, theater historian Robert Hume has recently argued that the lewdness often ascribed to the Restoration stage has been exaggerated by scholars.[7] Furthermore, Milton's own feelings about that theater seem not to have been wholly unfavorable, for he granted John Dryden permission to compose an opera based on *Paradise Lost;* it was registered in 1677 as *The State of Innocence.* It may be that *Samson* was never intended for the Restoration stage mainly because of the poet's isolation in the 1660s: after all, he was completely blind by 1652, and following the Act of Oblivion rarely ventured out in public. It is therefore unlikely that he even attended any commercial plays during this time in his life, let alone considered writing one.

Nonetheless, Milton kept staging matters in mind while composing his tragedy. The preface states that his chief models were Aeschylus, Sophocles, and Euripides, three playwrights who wrote for the Athenian theater. A concern for performance is also evident in the play's dialogue, which embeds an abundance of "stage" directions about the body language, costumes, and gestures of the personae. For instance, most scholars recognize the theatricality of the Chorus's detailed, vivid portrait of Dalila's entrance, yet they tend to overlook similarly dramatic moments elsewhere in the play, with the result that the work often strikes them, overall, as static or undramatic. I contend that by regarding *Samson Agonistes* as a true play, the impression of stasis is dispelled. Such an approach also helps to resolve some of the ongoing arguments swirling about the tragedy. My study thus engages recent, influential accounts of *Samson Agonistes* and its relation to terrorism, including the work of Joseph Wittreich, Stanley Fish, and Feisal Mohamed. In addition, as mentioned earlier, my fifth chapter demonstrates that while scholars have been slow to recognize the stage qualities of Milton's tragedy, the theater world has not: The twentieth century saw dozens of successful performances of the tragedy, many of them in theaters and in full dress. The largely successful production history of the play confirms *Samson's* inherent theatricality.

The poet's Puritanism may also tend to prevent scholars from regarding him as a true dramatist. However, our picture of early modern Puritanism has been expanded by the research of Margot Heinemann, Laura Knoppers, and others. Heinemann, for instance, has demonstrated that a significant minority of Puritans enjoyed and regularly attended the theater.[8] Milton, I believe, appears to have been one of them. As I point out in chapter 3, his best-known pamphlet, *The Reason of Church-Government,* was published in 1642, just as Parliament was about to close the theaters. In it he boldly — though unsuccessfully — argues that, rather than shutting the playhouses to forestall unruly or subversive behavior, the government should allow them to remain open. What ought to be changed is the fare being shown to the people. Neoclassical drama, such as works that emulate Euripides and Sophocles, will not foment rebellion — on the contrary, it will induce catharsis, and thus "allay the perturbations of the mind, and set the affections in right tune"[9] (YP 1:816–17).

Chapter 1 also suggests that while Milton never wrote for the commercial stage, he may have had some familiarity with its productions. Building on Herbert Berry's 1992 discovery that the poet's father was a co-trustee of the Blackfriars, the winter home of the King's Men, I explore the possibility that Milton himself attended this theater and propose that he alludes to the experience in his first elegy as well as, perhaps, in *L'Allegro*.[10] I also suggest that that exposure may have contributed to his portrait of Dalila's entrance in the tragedy. In like manner, Comus's famous speech on how Nature's bounty is to be relished ("Wherefore did Nature pour her bounties forth") may be indebted to a commercial production, namely, Thomas Randolph's play *The Muses' Looking-Glass (The Entertainment)*, staged in 1630. Chapter 1 also explores the possibility that Milton witnessed the performance of his own early masque-like *Arcades*, and suggests that its composition and dramatization had a critical influence on his later work — not only on the Ludlow masque, but also on the depiction of Satan's self-revelation on the throne of Pandaemonium in book 10 of *Paradise Lost*. In short, though Milton was never employed as a commercial playwright, two major passages in his dramas may have been considerably influenced by the professional stage, and a third might be based on an actual production.

Some see Milton's egoism as an insuperable obstacle to his being taken seriously as a dramatist. William Hazlitt was perhaps the first to offer such a critique. Reviewing an 1815 performance of *Comus*, he claimed that "The genius of Milton was essentially undramatic: he saw all objects from his own point of view, and with certain exclusive preferences." He extended this analysis by comparing him unfavorably with Shakespeare. Both Leigh Hunt and John Keats seized on the comparison, and it has since become a staple of literary history: Shakespeare is a chameleon who disappears into each of his characters, while Milton is fatally self-conscious, at best a playwright manqué whose voice in the dramas can be detected all too easily. Wilkenfeld, for instance, states, "although the authorial 'I' is patently absent in *Comus* and *Samson Agonistes*, many critics assume that it is indirectly present and that its presence can be felt or 'discovered' in the illegitimate control Milton exercises over his characters."[11] Such a view, however, neglects the fact that the poet possessed an abundance of imaginative sympathy, awarding some of his best lines to his villains. Hence, a substantial number of readers feel that these characters seem as compelling as their opponents, making it difficult to discern who, if anyone, truly speaks for the author. It is possible, too, that as *Samson* continues to be produced in the twenty-first century, the charge that it is a thinly veiled autobiography may diminish. We may witness more comments like those of Terence Spencer, who remarked on a 1951 dramatization that "the impression from this performance was that the play was written with far more dramatic objectivity than is commonly supposed by readers."[12]

Still, even assuming that Milton's dramas really *are* dramas, not merely poetry, and that his Puritanism and personality do not necessarily disqualify him as a dramatist, a considerable challenge to my thesis remains: a gap of some 40 years exists between the first appearance of Milton's chief dramatic works (*Comus*, 1634; *Samson*, 1671). The gap would seemingly make it difficult to study this author as a dramatist, to trace any growth or development in his skills as a playwright. But although *Arcades* comes early in his career, Milton apparently returned to that masque's processional structure and its employment of an illuminated throne when composing the scene of Satan's self-revelation in *Paradise Lost*. Furthermore, the gap between *Comus* and *Samson* is also spanned by the plans for tragedies in the Trinity manuscript. As I demonstrate in my third chapter, Milton probably began setting down entries in this notebook in 1638, added to them until as late as 1652, when total blindness set in, and may have had amanuenses read from them as he composed *Samson Agonistes*, probably in the late 1660s. He eventually jotted down approximately 100 titles for potential tragedies, wrote out several long sketches of tragedies respectively based on the Fall and Sodom narratives, and may have composed all or part of a tragedy that formed the basis for the epic *Paradise Lost*. These plans are not well-known to scholars, and the few studies that treat them focus on how they forecast *Paradise Lost*, but in fact they also tell us much about this writer's abiding commitment to drama during the 1640s and 1650s. They suggest that he worked on ideas for plays, outlined plots, and clarified staging issues throughout these years. As such, they constitute a major intermediary step in Milton's growth as a dramatist, and thus enable us to study his progress as one.

Milton the Dramatist is eclectic in its critical methodology, combining author-contextual criticism, reader-response theory, and new historicism. According to Derek Wood, contextual interpretation has occasioned some of the best recent criticism of the play. Yet this approach has been rightly criticized for often failing to limit the contexts under consideration. As J. Martin Evans remarks, "by their very nature contexts are infinitely expandable." Knowing where to draw the line, to accept one contextual layer while excluding another, is the primary challenge of this method. Joseph Wittreich sums up the matter well when he notes that "the problem of contextualization is one of locating the relevant contexts for criticism; it is finally a problem of value."[13]

The issue might seem particularly daunting in regard to Milton, for one could argue that the essence of his genius was dramatic, and that a dramatic quality suffuses all his work. Hence, I have chosen to examine only those texts by him that *are* dramas (or latent dramas) in the traditional sense, and that were undoubtedly written by him: *Arcades, Comus,* the Trinity manuscript plans, and *Samson Agonistes.* I briefly consider the Fall tragedy he may have written, as well as possible dramatic roots of *Paradise Lost,* yet I do not investigate *Tyrannicall-Government Anatomized,* the anonymous 1642 English translation of *Baptistes sive Calumnia,* George Buchanan's Latin closet drama, composed in 1578. (Francis Peck was the first to suggest, in 1740, that Milton translated the play, but this view has never been accepted by the majority of scholars.)[14]

My study also deploys a particular type of reader-response theory, one that Robert Hume deems "historical reader-response criticism," which he and others have formulated in reaction to what they regard as the ahistorical nature of much reception theory. As Hume puts it, "Most reader-response theories tell us (broadly) how readers must respond in the abstract, but say very little about how to determine how readers did respond to a given text at a particular time. . . . What I am trying to propose here amounts to . . . a kind of historicization of Stanley Fish."[15] I employ Hume's method often. For instance, the opening chapter surveys Milton's consumption of drama, both read and staged, throughout his life. I then explore how other readers and spectators have reacted to his work. One example is Sir Henry Wotton, who in a 1638 letter to the poet praised *Comus* and labeled it a tragedy. That assessment has impelled scholars to consider to what extent, if any, the structure of the Ludlow masque may be regarded as tragic. Another instance of Hume's approach is my account of the performance history of *Samson Agonistes* and the questions that survey raises such as, What did William Poel, the tragedy's first producer, see in this text that compelled him to mount the play in 1900? How did the *London Times'* review of Michael Redgrave's 1965 production of *Samson* anticipate the current debate over whether the protagonist is a terrorist? These and related questions constitute the kind of historically inflected reception theory I believe Hume is rightly advocating.

The present volume also shares affinities with new historical scholarship. However, while recent new historicist research in Milton studies has contextualized the poet within the time frame of the 1660s and early 1670s, I believe that the 1620s and 1630s present an equally fertile site for inquiry. In fact, one advantage to historicizing Milton in the context of the Jacobean and Stuart periods is that we possess solid evidence of this author's public persona — as a man-about-town, an avid walker in the countryside, and a Cambridge undergraduate. By contrast, as previously noted, in the 1660s he seems to have been confined for the most part to his cottage in Chalfont St. Giles. Hence, as critics continue to demystify the image of Milton handed down to them by previous generations of scholars, namely, that of a poetic soul set apart, removed from the hurly-burly of real life, the 1620s and 1630s may prove to be one of the most productive areas of investigation. Remarkable pieces of biographical evidence from this period have emerged since the mid-1990s. For instance, Gordon Campbell has confirmed the Milton-Blackfriars link with documentary proof, and argued plausibly that the poet's father may have composed one of the tribute poems to Shakespeare in the First Folio, published in 1623. That poem may explain how the younger Milton came to be commissioned to tender his own contribution — "On Shakespeare" — to the Second Folio.[16]

This is not to deny the considerable progress that has been made with historicizing Milton in the context of later decades, of course. Indeed, *Milton the Dramatist* may be seen as a contribution to that phase of the historicist project, with its account of the composition of *Paradise Lost* and *Samson Agonistes*. Similarly, the present book's conclusion historicizes Milton's overall achievement as a dramatist by comparing him to one of his near-contemporaries, Jean Racine, who during the 1670s and 1680s composed both biblical and neoclassical plays.

ONE

Milton as Spectator, Reader, and Editor of Drama

One of the first tasks in making the case for Milton the dramatist is to demonstrate that he had significant exposure to staged drama. The point matters because if his experience with the dramatic genre was essentially literary, limited to his reading of plays or, at most, supplemented by rudimentary academic productions, then it becomes difficult to regard him as a dramatist in the traditional sense. If, however, he attended at least one full-scale production and found it sufficiently engaging, then he could not have helped being affected when crafting his own dramas. A single afternoon at the theater could furnish copious inspiration for writing a drama, as well as more information on staging and costumes than he could infer from reading scores of plays.

I. *Milton as Blackfriars Theatre Spectator?*

Milton's birth in 1608 meant that his early boyhood coincided with Shakespeare's final seven years, and of course the Milton family home on Bread Street was a stone's throw from the Mermaid Tavern and well within walking distance of the Blackfriars Theatre. Images of the young scamp colliding with his great predecessor on the street might seem no more than the stuff Hollywood scripts are made on, given that Shakespeare probably lived out his last years at New Place, in Stratford. However, recent scholarship has established several key ties between the Milton family and Shakespeare, including the Blackfriars trusteeship, as well as Gordon Campbell's suggestion that John Milton senior may have composed one of the tributes to Shakespeare for the First Folio (1623). That contribution may help to explain something that has long puzzled literary historians, namely, the inclusion of the younger Milton's first published poem, "On Shakespeare," in the Second Folio (1630).

Still, it is hard to say which commercial play productions, if any, he might have witnessed. The problem is a vexing one for a variety of reasons. One is that there are only three references to play-going in Milton's entire corpus: some lines in *"Elegia Prima"* (1626), an allusion in *L'Allegro* (1631?–38), and a description of his (negative) reaction to college theatricals in *An Apology for Smectymnuus*. Moreover, each of these references is problematic. While the lines in the elegy seem to indicate attendance at a theater, they appear to catalog stock plots and personae that also could have come from Milton's reading of New Comedy. And *L'Allegro* may be autobiographical, or it may simply catalog the pleasures of a typical "happy man." At first glance, the *Apology* reference provides a firmer ground, yet it shows Milton as anything but pleased to be at this performance. What is more, he cites this attendance at college plays to *counter* the accusation that he frequented commercial playhouses.

Scholarship has never been able to say definitively if Milton ever took in any commercial plays. Early in the twentieth century, Harris Fletcher, James Holly Hanford, and Denis Saurat, among others, claimed that he was familiar with the London stage; subsequently, in their influential histories of early modern theater audiences, both published in the 1980s, Andrew Gurr and Ann Cook seconded that claim. Yet no scholar or theater historian was able to prove that the references to play-going in Milton's poetry were anything more than poetic embellishments based on his reading of drama. In fact, in 1997, T. H. Howard-Hill published a trenchant critique of the alleged link between Milton and the stage. After reviewing primary documents for the Caroline plays and the records of theatrical performances at Cambridge, he concluded, "there is no substantial evidence that Milton either experienced the theater of his time or valued its products." Roy Flannagan concurs, citing Howard-Hill's article in *The Riverside Milton*'s preface to *"Elegia Prima,"* and adding, "Milton may never have gone near a theater in London."[1] Nonetheless, Berry's discovery of the link between the Milton family and the Blackfriars tempts us to think that he did attend the theater. And yet, as remarkable as the finding is, it offers no evidence that the young man may have actually taken advantage of his father's trusteeship. I propose to furnish such evidence by arguing that the play-going references in the first elegy and *L'Allegro* may well be factual, and could be based on Milton's attendance at a 1626 showing of Jonson's comedy *The Staple of News*.

Milton had gone to Cambridge in 1625, but in the spring of 1626 was temporarily expelled, perhaps over a quarrel with his tutor, William Chappell. He returned to London, remaining there for at least several weeks. During this time, the seventeen-year-old poet composed his first elegy, a Latin verse-letter to his closest friend, Charles Diodati. In it, Milton claims to be enjoying his unexpected holiday by reading, girl-watching, and attending the theater. Scholars have never reached consensus about his claims of attending plays, for while the young man speaks as a spectator, the plots and characters he mentions — these include comic types such as a crafty old man and a spendthrift heir, as well as tragic personages and situations such as the attempt of Creon's house to atone for its incest — seem more characteristic of classical drama than anything presented in the commercial playhouses. Nevertheless, a significant number of editors take the claim literally, though none have been able to identify any specific plays to which Milton could be referring. A second group of editors and scholars contends that he was simply imagining scenes based on his play-reading.[2]

The latter group is almost certainly correct about the elegy's references to tragic figures, for no Greek tragedy was mounted in the period of 1620–27, either in London or in Cambridge.[3] They may also be right about his allusions to comic personages, for New Comedy abounds in stock characters such as sly geezers and prodigals, and Milton of course was an avid reader of such drama from his early youth. Moreover, he wanted to make a good impression on Diodati, and to prevent awkward questions about why he was not in school at a time when his friend was (at Oxford). If he presented himself as a mere bookworm rather than a sophisticated man-about-town, the letter would have been far less effective. Hence, it is not difficult to believe that Milton simply invented the play-going scenario, basing it on his reading.[4]

We could leave the matter there were it not for Berry's finding. Using it as a point of departure, I shall argue, first, that there is a good possibility that Milton was referring to the Blackfriars in *Elegia Prima*; second, that five of the comic figures cataloged in the poem could have been inspired by his attendance at the King's Players' 1626 presentation of Jonson's comedy; and third, that this experience of seeing *Staple* may have also had a significant influence on the composition of *Samson Agonistes*.

According to Berry, in 1597 James Burbage, owner of the Blackfriars and father of two sons (Cuthbert, the elder, and Richard, the eminent Shakespearean actor), willed the property to Cuthbert. Richard, however, became the *de facto* owner of the playhouse, and in 1599 rented the theater to Henry Evans, who managed a company of child actors. At Richard's death in 1619, the Burbage family decided that his heirs, his widow, Winifred, and their two children William and Sarah, would be given official ownership of the theater and thus receive the rents paid on the playhouse, while the King's Men would take the play profits. Berry adds, however, that

> Because Winifred and her children could lose control of their property if she should make an unfortunate marriage, that property had to be conveyed to [her and the children] as a trusteeship. In a three part contract dated July 4, 1620, the [Burbage] family assigned the

playhouse to . . . four men who would hold them in trust for Winifred and the children. The parties to the contract were Cuthbert in the first part, Winifred and her children in the second, and the four trustees in the third.

According to Berry, the four trustees were listed as follows: "Edward Raymond, gentleman; Henry Hodge, ale brewer; Robert Hunt, ale brewer; and John Milton, gentleman." Berry admits that John Milton was a common name in the period; also, the poet's father was a scrivener, not a gentleman. However, Berry points out that writing and managing trusteeships was a staple component of a scrivener's job in this period. He also states that Milton senior had become wealthy as a scrivener; thus, "the Burbages could have preferred to think of him as a gentleman rather than a man who tended a scrivener's shop." In 1999 Campbell corroborated Berry's hunch, declaring that "Milton's father is described as a gentleman in a series of Chancery documents drawn up in 1634 and 1645, so the term is not an obstacle to the identification of this John Milton with the poet's father." Furthermore, Berry's most telling piece of evidence is the fact that Edward Raymond is listed along with John Milton, for the poet's biographers have long known that Milton's father was associated with a man by this name in another context: he lent him 50 pounds on February 9, 1622.[5]

I would add that certain aspects of the Blackfriars Theatre might have made it less objectionable to a sound Puritan like Milton senior. According to Andrew Gurr, it was the most reputable of all the playhouses in this period, in part because it alone was within the city walls. Two other upscale, private theaters, the Whitefriars and the Phoenix (also known as Cockpit), were situated not far outside the city walls, while the open-air amphitheaters, such as the Globe, were built further off in the suburbs. Also, the Blackfriars had the highest ticket prices of any playhouse; the cheapest seat there cost the same as the most expensive one at the Globe. Gurr notes that while these high prices did not prevent lower-class "stinkards" from taking in plays at the Blackfriars it relegated them to the highest tiers in the house.[6] As noted, the theater was within walking distance of the Milton home on Bread Street. Hence, any member of the family who wished to see a play — possibly at no cost — while avoiding unwelcome contact with lower-class spectators probably could have done so more conveniently at the Blackfriars than anywhere else. Finally, it is worth noting that the Blackfriars had a reputation for attracting Puritan spectators; that reputation is lampooned in Thomas Randolph's 1630 play *The Muses' Looking-Glass*, which is set in the Blackfriars, and in two Jonson plays, *Bartholomew Fair* (5.3) and in the opening scene of *The Alchemist*.

In light of his father's connection with this playhouse, its ability to attract well-to-do Puritans, and its proximity to his family's home, it is possible that Milton witnessed the King's Players' presentations of Shakespeare, Fletcher, Jonson, Massinger, and Middleton, among others. He could have continued to do so throughout the 1620s and into the 1630s; indeed, Campbell speculates that his father's trusteeship could have continued until 1647, the year of Milton senior's death, at which point Milton himself would have taken it on.

Elegia Prima, I believe, alludes to at least one such visit. The letter's opening 24 lines consist of a sketch of Milton's current situation: he is in London, savoring his time away from Cambridge. In order to show how much he is enjoying himself, he segues into a detailed account of his leisure activities:

> Tempora nam licet hic placidis dare libera Musis,
>   Et totum rapiunt me mea vita libri.
> Excipit hinc fessum sinuosi pompa theatri,
>   Et vocat ad plausus garrula scena suos.
> Seu catus auditur senior, seu prodigus haeres,
>   Seu procus, aut posita casside miles adest,
> Sive decennali fecundus lite patronus
>   Detonat inculto barbara verba foro,
> Saepe vafer gnato succurrit servus amanti,
>   Et nasum rigidi fallit ubique patris;
> Saepe novos illic virgo mirata calores
>   Quid sit amor nescit, dum quoque nescit, amat.

Sive cruentatum furiosa Tragoedia sceptrum
   Quassat, et effusis crinibus ora rotat;
   Et dolet, et specto, iuvat et spectasse dolendo;
   Interdum et lacrimis dulcis amaror inest:
   Seu puer infelix indelibata reliquit
   Gaudia, et abrupto flendus amore cadit;
   Seu ferus e tenebris iterat Styga criminis ultor,
   Conscia funereo pectora torre movens;
   Seu maeret Pelopeia domus, seu nobilis Ili,
   Aut luit incestos aula Creontis avos.
   Sed neque sub tecto semper nec in urbe latemus,
   Irrita nec nobis tempora veris eunt.
   Nos quoque lucus habet vicina consitus ulmo
   Atque suburbani nobilis umbra loci.
   Saepius hic blandas spirantia sidera flammas
   Virgineos videas praeteriisse choros.

[Here I am permitted to devote my spare hours to the gentle Muses, and books (which are my whole life) completely carry me away. *When I am tired, the splendor of the round theatre draws me out,* and the babbling stage invites my applause. Sometimes I listen to a crafty old man, sometimes a spendthrift heir; sometimes a suitor appears, or a soldier with doffed helm. Sometimes a lawyer, grown rich on a ten-year-old case, thunders out his barbarous jargon to an uncouth court. Often a cunning slave comes to the aid of a love-struck son, and cheats the stern father at every turn — right under his nose. There, often a virgin girl, marvelling at the strange fire within her, does not know what love is, and loves without knowing it.

Sometimes raging Tragedy brandishes her bloodstained sceptre, with dishevelled hair and rolling eyes. The sight pains me, but I look, and there is pleasure in the pain. Sometimes there is sweet bitterness even in tears: as when an unfortunate youth leaves joys untasted, and is torn from his love to perish and be mourned; or when a cruel avenger of crime returns from the shades across the Styx, tormenting guilty souls with a deadly torch; or when the house of Pelops or of noble Ilus mourns, or Creon's palace atones for incestuous forebears.

But I am not always confined under a roof, or in the city. Springtime does not pass me by in vain. I also frequent a dense grove of elms nearby, and a glorious shady spot *just outside the city.* Here you may often see groups of maidens passing by — stars breathing out seductive flames.] (25–52; my emphases)[7]

These lines list three distinct activities — reading, play-going, and girl-watching — as well as two apparently physical transitions, which I have italicized: the movement from study to theater when Milton tires of his books, and from the theater, located within the city walls, to a grove outside them.[8] The fact that the play-going occurs in London proper suggests that the playhouse is the Blackfriars, for as we saw, it alone stood within the city limits.

The poet's description of the theater is "sinuosi pompa theatri" (29), a conflation of Ovid's "curvis . . . theatris" (*Amores* 1.89), and Propertius's "sinuosa cavo pendebant vela theatro," his reference to the flowing curtains in the Roman theaters (4.1.15).[9] Most editors are in agreement about "pompa," interpreting it as "splendour" or "magnificence." Translations of "sinuosi" vary, and include "the rounded theater" (thus Flannagan, Hosley, Patterson, Carey, and Fowler) and Leonard's similar "the round theater," "the curved theater" (Gurr, Shawcross), "the serpentine theater" (Perkins), "the winding theater" (Campbell), "the intricate theater" (Berry), "the changing theater" (Orgel and Goldberg), and "the arched theater" (Hughes).[10]

His emphasis on the curvature or roundedness of the building might seem to indicate that Milton alludes here to one of the open-air amphitheaters or playhouses rather than the rectangular Blackfriars, and indeed, Flannagan and Hosley have interpreted it as such, though again, the Globe was in Southwark, not London proper. Yet even if Milton refers to some feature of the Blackfriars, it is not clear which one he meant. That theater offered a curtained discovery space at the back of the stage, but the curtain was not large or grand enough to elicit Milton's description, which is fairly general. Another possibility is that Milton was pointing out the set of ornate, winding stairs that led up to the Blackfriars' entrance. Such an interpretation would accord with those who interpret "sinuosi" as "winding" or "serpentine," yet although the staircase was a well-known feature of the Blackfriars, it was at the opposite (north) end from where the stage was, and thus not integral to the theater's architecture.

I wish to offer a fourth possibility, namely, that Milton was alluding to the curve of the Blackfriars' auditorium. For years, scholarly reproductions of the auditorium depicted it as rectangular, with galleries parallel to its walls. Yet such reproductions have been challenged by both Gurr and John Orrell. In an essay on the Blackfriars' interior, Orrell declares that theater historians G. Topham Forest, Irwin Smith, Richard Hosley, and Michael Shapiro have all made the mistake of assuming that the seats within the Blackfriars' interior followed the external rectangular shape of the building. He contends that this theater, as well as similar halls from this period, might well have been equipped with seats placed in a rounded arrangement, or at least a segmented one imitating a round shape. Orrell examines contemporary references to the actual designs of the private theaters, and concludes, correctly, that

> It is time . . . to make a fundamental reappraisal of the shape and origins of the Blackfriars, [and the other two private theaters] the Phoenix, and the Salisbury Court. The evidence . . . positively indicates that they were rounded in plan, and not rectilinear. . . . While the Phoenix galleries and benches were actually made to a semi-circular plan, those at the Blackfriars appear to have been polygonal.[11]

The polygon design, he adds, was chosen for "practical reasons of construction" since it provided a cost-effective illusion of curved galleries. Such a design, it seems to me, could account for Milton's representation of the interior as rounded or curved. While we may never know precisely what he meant, the Blackfriars' auditorium is our best guess, for it alone would have been large and striking enough to elicit Milton's response.

Still, whether he was representing that theater's auditorium, its staircase, or some other feature in the hall, it is possible that Milton knew of these items simply from his father's descriptions of them, or from glancing inside the building during off-hours. One good look at the interior would have furnished his vivid imagination with enough material to "see" the drama he was reading on the Blackfriars' boards. Yet I believe the elegy offers evidence that he witnessed a play there. To explore this possibility, we must consider approximately when and how long Milton was home in London.

According to John Leonard, the young man's suspension from Cambridge began at some point during the Lent term of 1626, which lasted from January 13 to March 31.[12] As we saw, Milton goes to considerable lengths in the elegy to prove to Diodati how much he is enjoying London, and to avoid awkward questions about why he is at home during term. In fact, Milton prefaces his description of his London activities by claiming that "At present I do not care to revisit the reedy Cam; I do not yearn for my rooms, recently forbidden to me. . . . Nor is it pleasing constantly to have to put up with the threats of a stern tutor, and other things besides that my spirit cannot bear" (15–16). It is unlikely that he would speak in this way if school were out of session. Thus, Milton must have read, girl-watched, and attended the theater during term, that is, somewhere between mid-January and late March. Another clue to the time frame is the allusion to his enjoyment of springtime ("veris"), in line 48; the phrase suggests that at least his walks outside the city were taken in late March or early April. The elegy's closing lines, which refer to the plan that the young man would soon return to Cambridge, seem to indicate that the actual writing of the poem occurred not long before the beginning of the Easter term, which in 1626 began on April 19. Hence, it appears that Milton's rustication could have lasted for several weeks or even over a period of a month or two, starting in the late winter and ending in the early spring. It seems likely that he would have found the Blackfriars a welcome, and perhaps familiar, diversion from his reading. Indeed, it would be peculiar for such a young man *not* to attend a theater, especially one so near his home.

What was playing at Blackfriars in Lent 1626, which in that year started on February 21?[13] Harbage and Schoenbaum indicate that Jonson's *The Staple of News* began running in February, and Herford and Simpson declare that *Staple* was shown in 1626 "during Lent," citing internal evidence that indicates that the playwright deliberately sets the comedy's action in that season in contemporary

London.[14] For instance, at one point, while Mirth discusses the play with Expectation, Tattle and Censure, the other three choric members, Censure tells her companions, who have been critical of the drama thus far, that perhaps it will still "prove right, seasonable, salt butter," and Mirth corrects her by saying "Or to the time of year, in Lent, delicate almond butter" (2 Int. 64–65). Also, at 3.2.84 Dutch eel boats are described as being tied up at Queenhithe, a quay on the bank of the Thames where such boats traditionally moored during Lent.[15]

It is possible, of course, that Jonson was being optimistic, hoping for a long run extending throughout the 40 days of Lent, that is, from February 21 to April 2, but which in fact never materialized. And indeed Anthony Parr, editor of the definitive New Cambridge edition of *Staple*, notes that only two performances of the comedy are certain — a Blackfriars staging at some point in February 1626, and a court production on February 19, 1626.[16] Moreover, Parr recognizes that Jonson's note "To the Readers" in the published version could imply that the play was not successful, for in it Jonson complains that a "sinister" interpretation has been foisted on the work. Parr contends, however, "There may have been further performances during [the 1626] season, for . . . the play was a topical one, and registered sufficiently in certain circles to give currency to the 'sinister' interpretation of its meaning which Jonson tried to quell in 'To the Readers.'"[17] Moreover, Richard Levin has pointed out that "even if *Staple* was unsuccessful, it would still have had a number of performances. . . . There were no opening night (afternoon) closings in the Jacobean theater."[18] Perhaps most telling is the fact that *Staple* was regarded highly enough to be imitated by at least four other plays — Thomas Randolph's *The Drinking Academy*, William Davenant's *News from Plymouth*, William Cartwright's *The Ordinary*, and John Fletcher's *Rollo, Duke of Normandy*. Moreover, *The Drinking Academy* was composed in the 1620s, well before *Staple* was first published (in 1631), suggesting that Randolph saw a performance of it.

It is plausible, then, that the comedy was shown at least several times throughout Spring 1626, from late February until early April, when its Lenten allusions would still feel current. Milton may have been motivated to see it in part because he already knew Jonson's work, having first encountered his poetry at St. Paul's School, where he studied *Logonomia Anglica,* an English grammar written by the headmaster Alexander Gill senior. The textbook drilled students in translating from English to Latin by using examples from Jonson, Samuel Daniel, Thomas Campion, and others. Moreover, in his 1623 masque *Time Vindicated to Himself and to his Honours,* Jonson satirized the dread felt by students at St. Paul's when confronted with the formidable *Logonomia.* Like the masque, *Staple* is a highly topical satire — it skewers the fledgling news industry. If Milton received any advance notice about it, he might have felt compelled to go, perhaps fearing — or hoping — to hear his own school roasted on the public stage.

Staple offers a cast of some thirty characters, five of whom may have inspired the poet as he penned the elegy. The protagonist, Pennyboy Junior, and his father, Pennyboy Canter, may correspond to the first two personages mentioned in the verse-letter, namely, the "catus senior" and the "prodigus haeres" (29), usually translated, respectively, as "the crafty (or cunning) old man" and "the spendthrift heir." "Crafty old man" is an apt description of Pennyboy Canter since he is often referred to as an old man by the other characters (for example, 5.1.101), and before the play starts he fakes his own death, then disguises himself as a beggar to inform his son of the inheritance. This disguise enables Canter to observe his son's mishandling of the fortune, and thus sets up his later unveiling (in act 4) to mete out judgment on the wastrel. Likewise, Pennyboy Junior is described on the drama's original title page as "the son, the heir, and suitor," and the play's action occurs during his twenty-first birthday when he begins squandering the inheritance of 60,000 pounds. Hence, he certainly qualifies as a spendthrift heir. Furthermore, he is also a suitor — one of the key actions in the play is his wooing of the princess Pecunia — so he could be the source of both the "prodigus haeres" and the third figure noted in the poem, the "procus."

Milton describes the fourth character with the following phrase: "posita casside miles adest." Most editors translate this literally to suggest that this person is a soldier with a "doffed helmet," or a "helmet set aside," yet the phrase may also be interpreted figuratively. Thus, he could be one who has set aside, or foregone, warfare itself. Turning to *Staple*, we find a (supposed) military officer named Captain Shunfield, who, as his name suggests, avoids the battlefield, and indeed, who proves to be a coward in the play. (He is, in fact, one of the parasites who try to gull Pennyboy Junior.) It is feasible, then, that Milton alludes to this pretender.

Picklock, the comedy's lawyer, could have inspired the fifth personage sketched in the elegy, namely, the "lawyer grown rich on a ten-year-old case, [who] thunders out a ten-year-old case to an uncouth court." While there is no suggestion in the play that Picklock has prospered from a decade-long suit, he is a master at spouting legalese. For example, in 4.4, when Pennyboy Junior wonders if Picklock has the ability to "cant," that is, to utilize the language of his profession, the lawyer replies that in fact he can,

> In all the languages in Westminster Hall,
> Pleas, Bench, or Chancery; *fee-farm, fee-tail,*
> *Tenant in dower, at will, for term of life,*
> By *copy of court roll, knights' service, homage,*
> *Fealty, escuage, soccage,* or *frank almoigne,*
> *Grand sergeanty,* or *burgage.*   (103–08)

Picklock's on-stage audience, which consists of Pennyboy Junior, Captain Shunfield, and three of Shunfield's cronies (Fitton, Almanac, and Madrigal), could correspond to the "uncouth" or "unlearned" court mentioned in the elegy, in two ways: All but Pennyboy are parasites, seeking to fleece the young man, and all are ignorant not only of Picklock's jargon, but also of the professions they supposedly represent. (In fact, all are former prodigals.) Furthermore, Picklock's style of delivery throughout the play leads Pennyboy Canter to characterize him as a "stentor" (5.6.49), a phrase that could have suggested to Milton the image of a lawyer "thundering out" his argot.[19]

Princess Pecunia is both the play's leading female character and a personification of money. When Pennyboy Junior first meets her, he tells her how much he has longed to see her; she replies,

> And I have my desire, sir, to behold
> That youth and shape which in my dreams and wakes
> I have so oft contemplated and felt
> *Warm in my veins* and native as my blood.
> When I was told of your arrival here,
> I felt my heart beat as it would leap out
> In speech, and all my face it was a flame,
> *But how it came to pass I do not know.* (2.5.50–57; my emphases)

This passage could have provided Milton with images used in his elegy, such as line 53 suggesting a girl marveling at a "strange fire" within her, and line 57, the image of a maiden loving despite not knowing what love is.

The other figures listed among the comic types in the elegy include a slave, a lovelorn son and his father. No such persons appear in *Staple*. They could have been inspired by another comedy staged by the King's Men at the Blackfriars, although no extant play staged there during the first half of the 1620s offers such personages.[20] Yet since many of Jonson's comic figures are derived from Roman drama it is possible that seeing *Staple* on stage reminded Milton of such characters from his reading. Thus, these last comic figures could be based on a New Comedy such as Terence's *The Self-Tormentor*.

As noted at the outset, the tragic figures cataloged in the elegy seem based entirely on Milton's reading of Greek tragedy, with the possible exception of John Ford's *The Broken Heart*, which was mounted at the Blackfriars at some point between 1625 to 1633.[21] It also seems significant that he prefaces his descriptions of the comedies with details reminiscent of an actual theater: there the "babbling stage invites [his] applause," and on it a suitor "appears"; moreover, he listens to a "crafty old man," and the lawyer "thunders

out his barbarous jargon" (28–29, 32). By contrast, while the personification of Tragedy signals a visual transition to his description of tragic plots in lines 37–46, none of these representations
is enhanced by sound or sight effects, reinforcing the basic impression that the comedies Milton mentions were witnessed on stage,
while the tragedies were read.

While we cannot prove that Milton saw *Staple*, Dalila's entrance
in *Samson Agonistes* seems to owe something to Lady Pecunia's
arrival in act 2.5 of *Staple* — for both women are compared to
ships, both are dressed quite lavishly, and both are seconded by a
retinue. Several scholars of Milton's tragedy have adduced *Staple*
in relation to this scene, though for different reasons than the ones
I have suggested. In a 1950 article Pete Ure suggested that Pecunia's
entrance could have provided a print inspiration for Milton, who
might have read *Staple* in Jonson's Second Folio (1640). Merritt
Hughes adduced Ure's note in his own edition of the poet's works,
though he did so to emphasize that the ship/woman parallel is part
of a long satirical tradition. John Leonard's 1998 edition of Milton
cites Hughes's note to make the same point.[22]

What has yet to be considered is how Milton's experience of seeing Lady Pecunia in performance might have influenced his representation of Dalila's approach. To explore this possibility it is
necessary to quote her entrance as it is described by the Danite
Chorus to the blind Samson:

> But who is this, what thing of sea or land?
> Female of sex it seems,
> That so bedecked, ornate, and gay,
> Comes this way sailing
> Like a stately ship
> Of Tarsus, bound for th' isles
> Of Javan or Gadire
> With all her bravery on, and tackle trim,
> Sails filled, and streamers waving,
> Courted by all the winds that hold them play,
> An amber scent of odorous perfume
> Her harbinger, a damsel train behind;

> Some rich Philistian matron she may seem,
> And now at nearer view, no other certain
> Than Dálila thy wife.   (710–24)

G. M. Young suggests that certain images here are probably based on John Harrington's 1659 pamphlet, "A Word Concerning the House of Peers," a work that Milton refutes in his own tract written the same year, *The Ready and Easy Way to Establish a Free Commonwealth*. Young quotes Harrington, who personifies the commonwealth as a vessel entering "with all its tackling, full sail, displaying its streamers, and flourishing with top and top-gallant," lines which seem paralleled by the Chorus's remarks, "With all her bravery on, and tackle trim, / Sails filled, and streamers waving."[23] Yet Harrington does not assign gender to this approaching ship, nor does he explicitly associate it with wealth. Such details could have been provided by Jonson's play. In 2.5 of *Staple*, Pennyboy Junior visits Pennyboy Senior, Pecunia's guardian, and asks to have a look at the lady, who is hiding in the study with her attendants. While the two men wait for her to get ready, Pennyboy Junior remarks, "Your fortunate princess, uncle, is long a-coming" (41), to which Pennyboy Senior replies, "She is not rigg'd, sir. Setting forth some lady / Will cost as much as furnishing a fleet. / Here she's come at last, and like a galley / Gilt i' the prow" (42–45).

It is not clear how this scene was staged. In the 1640 Folio a margin note says, "The study is open'd where she sits in state." According to this scenario, the discovery space would have been uncurtained, revealing Pecunia with her entourage. However, this folio is regarded by most editors as an inferior version of the 1616 First Folio. Among its drawbacks are the numerous and often obtrusive margin notes, many of which simply restate the action or the dialogue. Scholars are not sure if these annotations are Jonson's, for as Devra Kifer points out, while his "usual practice was to place a few explanatory notes and stage directions in the margins of his plays. . . . *The Staple of News* [has] a great number of side notes." William Gifford deleted these marginalia in his 1816 edition of Jonson's works, not regarding them as authoritative, and the Third Folio (1692) omitted this particular direction, replacing it with the following: "Enter Pecunia in state, attended by Broker, Statute, Band, Wax, and Mortgage" (320).

This revision, it seems to me, reflects what actually happened in performance, for it makes better sense of the characters' speeches and actions. For instance, when Pennyboy Senior remarks, "Here she's come at last," he implies that Pecunia and her train actually walk in, from the direction of the study. Also, upon her arrival Pennyboy Senior tells her to give the young man her hand. She refuses the command and instead kisses the prodigal, who then returns the favor to her ladies-in-waiting. These actions constitute a piece of stage business that would be much easier if all the actors were already up and about instead of seated. Perhaps most importantly, if Pecunia did indeed come in from the study with a slow, stately gate, followed by her train, the effect would have been reminiscent of an approaching ship; if she were seated, however, such an image would seem incongruous. Assuming that the princess did enter from the study, such a vivid performance could have made a lasting impression on a young man like Milton. While she appears earlier in the play, this entrance is the first time the off-stage audience sees Pecunia fully dressed up. In light of Pennyboy Senior's remark that "setting forth" the lady costs as much as "furnishing a fleet," it seems probable that the actor playing her was lavishly costumed, with her followers perhaps even carrying the princess's train.

Such an image could have influenced Milton, consciously or not, when he composed his tragedy, for Dalila also enters from afar, dressed "with all her bravery on," walking slowly and proudly, and seconded by damsels. It also seems significant that her arrival constitutes the one moment in the tragedy often singled out as theatrical. That impression of theatricality may testify to the scene's origins in an actual stage production.

II. *Examples of Milton's Spectatorship*

If I am correct in arguing that Milton was telling the truth about his play-going in the first elegy, then the similar claim in *L'Allegro* also deserves to be regarded as truthful and as autobiographical. In the poem, after a walk in the country, the happy man repairs to the city where knights and barons discuss the fate of the country and contend for the attention of courtly ladies. From court he proceeds to take in the "well-trod stage . . . / If Jonson's learned sock be on, / Or sweetest Shakespeare, Fancy's child, / Warble his native wood-notes wild" (131–34). There are four periods during which the poem may have been composed: the summer of 1631, when Milton was on his last long vacation from Cambridge; the Christmas season of that year; the period when he lived in Hammersmith, between 1632 and 1635; or during his residence at the family home in Horton, between 1635 and 1638. Throughout the 1630s, while he usually stayed indoors to study, Milton would take walks to relieve his tedium, and occasionally went to the city where he would visit friends, buy books, and, perhaps, take in plays. *L'Allegro* would seem to allude to the last-mentioned activity.

However, not all scholars regard the poem as autobiographical; William R. Parker, for instance, contends that "neither [this poem nor *Il Penseroso*] is intended as a self-portrait, and neither should be taken as such. The poet nowhere calls attention to himself as an individual, and for good reason — he is trying to express moods which all of us, at one time or another, have experienced." Roy Flannagan sees them as biographical, yet he suggests that Diodati is the happy man, Milton the melancholic.[24] I contend, however, that the poem's references to the consumption of drama — L'Allegro sees comedies, while Il Penseroso reads tragedy — may well be autobiographical because they echo Milton's verse-letter to Diodati quite closely. In both the elegy and *Il Penseroso*, for example, Tragedy is personified as a majestic woman who introduces the plays. Moreover, in both works she presents the same personage, namely, Pelops, patriarch of the family of Agamemnon, as well as the same places, Thebes and Troy (see *Elegia Prima* 35–45; *Il Penseroso* 97–100). It seems telling, too, that both preserve a clear distinction between seeing comedy on stage and reading tragedy in the study.

Commentators do agree that *L'Allegro* refers to Jonson's comedies, and it is possible that Milton is recollecting here the performance of *Staple* he witnessed in 1626. On the other hand, *L'Allegro* was composed anywhere from five to twelve years after the elegy, so it seems more likely that he is alluding to a newer, more recent performance(s) of Jonson at either the Blackfriars or Globe. Flannagan observes that "the 'native woodnotes' seem to refer to the bucolic settings of [Shakespeare's] comedies."[25] Although the happy man does not specify any particular playhouse, the works of both Jonson and Shakespeare were premiered and revived throughout the 1630s by the King's Men. *Pericles* was mounted at the Globe in June 1631; *The Alchemist* was revived at the Blackfriars in December 1631; *Richard II* was revived at the Globe that same month; *Othello* was put on at Blackfriars in 1635; and *Volpone* was performed there in October 1638.[26] Each of these plays was mounted during the years when Milton could have composed *L'Allegro* and *Il Penseroso*. There were other plays as well, undoubtedly, for which specific records are not extant. For instance, we have the journals of spectators such as Herbert Mildmay, which sometimes mention plays while failing to specify the names of them. And of course, a number of performances were never recorded at all. Hence, it seems quite plausible that Milton could have seen the works of both Jonson and Shakespeare on stage in the 1630s, and drew on these experiences when writing *L'Allegro*.

Our knowledge of the Blackfriars' trusteeship also suggests that in 1630 Milton may have witnessed a performance of Thomas Randolph's *The Muses' Looking-Glass (The Entertainment)*. Although *Muses'* was produced at the Salisbury Theatre, it is set in the Blackfriars Theatre, and depicts two Puritans, Mistress Flowerdew, a haberdasher, and Bird, a feather-maker, who have come to the theater to condemn the day's performance. For most of the play they sit on stage and watch a series of paired characters enter and debate. These pairs represent the extremes of particular virtues. For instance, in 3.4 the two extremes of Truth enter: Alazon, who, according to the stage directions, "arrogates that to himself which is not his," and Eiron, who, "out of an itch to be thought modest, dissembles his qualities." In nearly every scene, after the two figures have debated for some time, they are joined by a flatterer named Colax, who echoes the views of each character and then proceeds to dismiss each figure, one at a time, telling them that a certain mirror off-stage (the looking-glass of the play's title) will show them what they really are. Each character, once dismissed, eagerly exits, and is then cured of his extremism by being transformed into a moderate embodiment of the virtue.

Several scholars have argued that a speech in 2.3 of *Muses'* influenced Comus's famous reply to the Lady. In fact, the entirety of 2.3 may constitute a source for the well-known debate scene in Milton's masque, for it features an epicurean (Acolastus) trying to sway an ascetic (Anaisthetus) to indulge in pleasure. After about 100 lines of debate, Colax intervenes, commends Anaisthetus's temperance, then sends him away, promising that the looking-glass backstage will show him "all the dismal groves and caves: / The horrid vaults, dark cells, and barren deserts, / With what in hell can dismal be." Given that Anaisthetus is, according to the stage directions, a "mere anchorite . . . that delights in nothing," he finds such a prospect alluring, and promptly departs. Colax then turns to Acolastus, and presents a speech that echoes Acolastus's hedonism.

The speech is remarkably similar to Comus's response to the Lady. Both speeches employ the same logic, namely, that Nature's riches are to be eagerly consumed, not partaken of modestly. There are also numerous striking verbal echoes between the two speeches. For instance, Colax's opening words, "Nature has been bountiful," resembles Comus's opening question, "Wherefore did Nature pour her bounties forth . . . ?" (710). Similarly, Colax asks, "Shall we be niggards / At plenteous boards?" while Comus argues that if we eschewed the Creator's gifts "we should serve him as a grudging master, / As a penurious niggard of his wealth" (725–26). Just so, while Colax notes that Nature "gave so many different odours / Of spices, unguents, and all sorts of flowers," Comus makes the very similar claim that Nature covered "the earth with odors, fruits, and flocks" (712). As well, Colax asserts that "when nature thought the earth alone too little / To find us meat, [she] therefore stored the air / With winged creatures," while Comus refers to the "winged air darked with plumes" (730) that would result if temperance ruled the world. He also seems to echo Colax's assertion here by stating that Nature "hutched th' all-worshipping ore, and precious gems / To store her children with" (719–20). Henry Todd seems to have been the first scholar to notice the similarities, citing *Muses'* as a source for Comus's speech in his 1798 edition of the masque. In 1917, C. B. Cooper revived the point, as did G. C. Moore Smith, in 1922, who also suggested that *Muses'* may have been produced at Cambridge while Milton was a student there.[27]

I believe that our new knowledge of the Blackfriars' trusteeship sheds further light on this source. *Pace* Smith, there are no recorded presentations of the play at Cambridge. According to Gerald Bentley, it was first acted in the summer of 1630 on the road, then taken to London, where it was licensed on November 25, 1630, shortly before its London debut. The reason it was licensed this late in the season is that 1630 was a plague year; the theaters were closed from April 17, 1630 to November 12, 1630. The universities were also shut down for much of that year. William R. Parker states that in April 1630 "[Cambridge University] abandoned all activities . . . and the colleges did not begin to reassemble until November or December [1630]." He also notes that "Milton's whereabouts during most of the year 1630 are a mystery," then speculates that "If Milton went to Cambridge at the beginning of the Lent term [which began in mid-January] of 1630, he probably returned home in March and remained there until the threat of plague — which for once had struck Cambridge before it menaced London — drove him and his family to some haven in the country."[28] Given that the theaters reopened in mid-November 1630, it seems reasonable that well-off families like the Miltons probably began returning to London around this time. If John Milton was among the returnees, he would have had ample time to see a performance of *Muses'*, especially if Christ's College were only starting to reconvene in November or December, and if the Christmas holiday was about to begin.

Other facts about its performance render this conjecture more plausible. The Salisbury Theatre was an upscale, private playhouse built just outside the city walls, north of the Thames. Given that *Muses'* spoofs the Blackfriars audiences, it seems possible that Milton would have wished to see how "his" theater was roasted, especially if the play was written by a schoolmate. (Both he and Randolph [1605–35] were at Cambridge at the same time; Randolph attended Trinity College.) *Muses'* seems to have enjoyed a successful run, if we are to believe Sir Aston Cokain's poetic tribute to Randolph; Cokain notes that "Thy Entertainment had so good a fate, / That whosoe'er doth not admire therat, / Discloseth his own ignorance."[29] Also, while the Salisbury Theatre was not quite within the city walls, socially it was a vast distance from Southwark and the public playhouses. A respectable young man could have attended a play there without feeling compromised. Furthermore, one of the play's main characters, Roscius, helps to convince the two Puritan figures, Bird and Mistress Flowerdew, that the stage may help inculcate virtue, a view that Milton shared, for by the end they realize that they have been overly critical, and resolve to take in plays for their own moral instruction.

Muses,' moreover, was not published until 1638, four years after *Comus* was written. True, Milton could have read it in manuscript form before 1634; however, the history of the publication of Randolph's play casts doubt on this scenario. It is worth noting that copies of a volume of Randolph's work entitled *Poems with the Muses Looking-Glasse: and Amyntas,* along with Milton's masque, were sent by a certain "Mr. R." to Sir Henry Wotton, provost of Eton, several years before Milton donated a second copy of the masque to Wotton, in 1638. Milton donated the second copy, apparently, in hopes of furthering his career, and without realizing that

Wotton had already received the first one, for in Wotton's written reply to Milton, he tells him that "the work it self, I had view'd som good while before, with singular delight, having receiv'd it from our common Friend Mr. R." (Wotton did not thank Milton for the first gift because Milton's name was not on it.) He adds that in the earlier gift, the masque was appended to a copy of "the late R's Poems, Printed at *Oxford,* whereunto it was added (as I now suppose) that the Accessory might help out the Principal, according to the Art of *Stationers.*"[30]

Douglas Bush believes that the double gift was tendered to Wotton by Randolph's literary executor, his younger brother Robert, and suggests that if Robert were the donor, that is, the "common friend" referred to by Wotton, then "Milton might well have seen [the play] in MS." However, William R. Parker points out that "there is no reason to suppose that either Wotton or Milton knew [Robert] Randolph, and it is improbable that Randolph would have bound his brother's poems with the work of another poet." Moreover, if Robert Randolph and Milton were indeed friends, it would be peculiar for Randolph to send a copy of Milton's masque to Wotton without telling Milton. Parker adds that Wotton's thank-you note to Milton suggests that he believed that "a bookseller had had the two works bound together." He suggests that "Mr. R." was Humphrey Robinson, who published both *Comus* and Wotton's own work, *Ad Regem e Scotia reducem plausus et vota,* in 1633.[31] If Parker is correct, then it would seem likely that the echoes of Colax's speech in Milton's masque were based on his seeing the play in performance rather than in manuscript. If so, that would mean that while Milton never composed drama for the commercial stage, two key scenes in his dramas — the debate between Comus and the Lady, and the entrance of Dalila — are significantly indebted to plays shown in the theater.

Returning to the questionable autobiographical status of *L'Allegro,* and the possible evidence that it provides for Milton's own activities, it is also important to note that the narrator claims to take in masques. Following his time in the country, he remarks that

> Towered cities please us then,
> And the busy hum of men,
> Where throngs of knights and barons bold,
> In weeds of peace high triumphs hold
> With store of ladies, whose bright eyes
> Rain influence, and judge the prize
> Of wit or arms . . .
> There let Hymen oft appear
> In saffron robe, with taper clear,
> And pomp, and feast, and revelry,
> With masque and antique pageantry;
> Such sights as youthful poets dream
> On summer eves by haunted stream.   (117–23, 125–30)

In *A Variorum Commentary on the Poems of John Milton*, Douglas Bush initiated a debate among Miltonists by asking whether the happy man witnesses these sights or simply reads and fantasizes about them, lying by a haunted stream. Critics and editors remain divided on the issue. Bush contends that the happy man is physically present at the events "since throughout the poem, L'Allegro is assumed to be an observer of the scenes he describes (that, as Verity says, is part of his social character), and there is no reason to make this passage exceptional."[32] But is the passage autobiographical? We have no evidence, apart from this reference, that Milton attended any court masque — yet, not all masques were in court. In September 1632, according to Gerald Bentley, the Queen danced in a masque put on "in a country village not far from London."[33] It is possible that Milton might have witnessed this or a similar performance.

In fact, he may have attended the production of his own masque-like *Arcades*, which was performed around 1632. Milton, as we saw, was still residing at Hammersmith in this period, and the piece was staged on the estate of the Dowager of Derby, in Harefield at Middlesex, just a few miles from Hammersmith. Stephen Dobranski points out, "Milton's letters and publications suggest that even while living in Hammersmith . . . he traveled frequently and socialized often. In *Defensio Secunda* he fondly remembers traveling to

London, 'exchanging the country for the city.' . . . Living with his family in the country posed little difficulty for such journeys." Furthermore, both Charles Osgood and William R. Parker point out, in separate discussions, several lines in the text suggesting familiarity with the terrain, such as references to the estate's oak-groves (45), a local mountain (55), and the walkway to the house, which was roofed with thick-leaved elms (89). Parker concludes that "it is almost inconceivable that [Milton] did not travel to Harefield to be graciously thanked for his verses by the aging Countess. . . . Possibly [he] was present at the entertainment itself."[34] Granted, Milton could have relied solely on others' descriptions of the area as he composed *Arcades,* and even if he had visited it before the production, that does not mean he was at the performance. Barbara Lewalski contends that in *Arcades* "Milton seeks both to confirm and to educate [his audience] in [the virtues of Protestant aristocracy]. . . . There is no evidence, however, that he had any personal contact with them, nor is it at all likely that he saw *Arcades* presented at Harefield."[35] Though we may never know for certain where Milton was on the night *Arcades* was performed, it is interesting that the masque significantly influenced two of the poet's later works. Not only did it provide structural underpinnings for the Ludlow masque, composed about a year later, it also appears to have served as a model for Satan's stunning manifestation on the throne of hell in book 10 of *Paradise Lost.*

III. *Milton's Other Exposure to Drama*

Yet even if Milton had seen *Arcades, The Staple of News, The Muses' Looking-Glass,* or any other theatrical production, what are we to make of his apparent disclaimer in *An Apology for Smectymnuus?* This tract was published in 1642, three years before *Elegia Prima, L'Allegro,* and *Il Penseroso* appeared in print. Milton's remarks there need to be understood in the context of the tract wars of the early 1640s. Milton himself helped to initiate this conflict with the 1641 publication of his first pamphlet, *Of Reformation in England,*

and the Causes that hitherto have hindered it, which argues that
prelacy and civil liberty are fundamentally incompatible. Bishops
Hall and Ussher responded to this tract, and to similar attacks by
other writers, with a treatise entitled *An Humble Remonstrance
to the High Court of Parliament.* In July 1641, Milton counter-
attacked by writing a pamphlet in dialogue format, entitled
*Animadversions, upon The Remonstrants' Defence, Against Smec-
tymnuus.* In it he deploys various theater terms such as "vizards"
(masks), "old cloaks," and "false beards." Someone, perhaps Hall
or one of his sons, then composed a response to *Animadversions,*
seizing on these passages as proof that in his youth, Milton was a
profligate who frequented, among other things, playhouses. Milton
answers these charges in *Apology for Smectymnuus,* claiming that
he had ample opportunity to learn these terms from the college dramas he attended while at Cambridge. He claims that "There while
they acted, and overacted, among other young scholars, I was a spectator; they thought themselves gallant men, and I thought them
fools, they made sport, and I laughed, they mispronounced and I
misliked, and to make up the atticism, they were out, and I hissed."
As a spectator, Milton was particularly distressed that so many of
his fellow students, who were in training for the ministry, were
acting in these plays. He then points out, "if it be unlawful to sit
and behold a mercenary Comedian personating that which is least
unseemly for a hireling to do, how much more blameful is it to
endure the sight of as vile things acted by persons either entered,
or presently to enter, into the ministry, and how much more foul
and ignominious for them to be the actors."[36]

It is not known which university play(s) he witnessed. From
1603–32 Milton's Christ's College, a Puritan stronghold, did not
mount any drama. Christ's Puritan influences were felt throughout the university, and after 1622–23 only Trinity and Queens colleges staged plays.[37] Perhaps it was one of these Milton recounts
in *An Apology.* In any event, the crucial point is that he never *denies*
that he attended the public playhouses; instead, he simply mentions that he watched plays in college, then asks his readers to
"Judge . . . whether so many good text men [the college actors]

were not sufficient to instruct me of false beards and vizards, without more expositors."[38] The answer, of course, is yes — yet he could have learned about them from the Blackfriars Theatre or Salisbury Court as well, or, alternatively, from seeing one or both of the productions of *Arcades* and *Comus*. In the former, for instance, the actors playing the shepherds wore masks. As noted earlier, the Blackfriars was the poshest theater in the early seventeenth century. Its audiences were characterized by the antiquarian James Wright in 1699: looking back on the Caroline period, he claimed that those who attended the Blackfriars were "men of grave and sober Behaviour." Andrew Gurr notes, "Most of the evidence for the composition of audiences at these various playhouses supports Wright's description."[39] Consequently, it is possible that Milton might have regarded his youthful attendance there as categorically different from attendance at other playhouses, and thus felt no need to mention it in *An Apology*.

One known performance that Milton saw in person was during his 1639 tour of the Continent, where he attended a dramatization in Rome at the palace of Cardinal Francesco Barberini, the pope's nephew. The production was probably Giulio Rospigiliosi's comic opera *Chi Soffre Speri* ("Let the Sufferer Beware"), a five-hour extravaganza showcasing a large cast and dazzling sets, with 3,500 spectators in attendance. John Arthos describes its basic plot:

> Egisto, an impoverished gentleman, is in love with a young widow, Alvida, who does not believe in men's love. But by many sacrifices he convinces her of his affection, and finally he overcomes her reluctance and gains her consent to be his bride. There are many intertwined episodes, and several intermezzi, one including the famous *fiera* — with street vendors, merchants, singers, charlatans, men on horseback, knights, and ladies.

We do not know what Milton thought of the entertainment, since the only comment from him is his surprised gratitude at being singled out by Cardinal Barberini at the door upon entering the theater.[40]

Milton may have attended puppet shows as a child. These shows are of importance because they contained residual elements of the defunct mystery play genre and thereby could have given Milton some idea of what these plays were like. The mysteries had ceased to be performed in London a generation before his birth: The York cycle was staged for the last time in 1569, the Chester in 1575, and the Wakefield plays were officially condemned in 1576 by the Diocesan court, yet productions of the mysteries were not entirely eliminated. Alfred Harbage lists several early seventeenth century performances, including a neo-miracle play entitled *St. Christopher* that was mounted in 1609; a Cornish mystery called *The Creation of the World, with Noah's Flood*, put on in 1611; and *Christ's Passion*, performed at Ely House in or around 1618. Milton was too young to witness the first two, and probably did not see the Ely House production, yet the themes and characterizations of the mysteries may have been familiar to him through oral tradition as well as puppet shows, also known as "motions." The motions, which remained popular throughout his lifetime, often presented the same characters and plots shown in the mysteries, and Milton could have witnessed them at venues such as Sturbridge Fair, held every year near Cambridge since the 1400s. His well-known remark in *Areopagitica* (1644) on Adam's freedom of choice — "when God gave [mankind] reason, he gave him freedom to choose, for reason is but choosing; he had else been a mere artificial Adam, such an Adam as he is in the motions" — may be based on a puppet show he saw or heard about. A motion entitled *The Creation of the World* was licensed in 1619, and might have included a segment on the Fall. Milton would have been eleven at this time, and quite possibly could have seen it.[41]

As far as we know, Milton had no access to any English manuscripts of the biblical dramas. If he did have a chance to read any, one suspects that he would have disapproved of their lively mixture of sacred and profane, comic and sublime, particularly in light of the preface to *Samson Agonistes*, which censures playwrights who try to combine comedy and tragedy. Yet certain items in his poetry suggest some familiarity with the stage conventions of medieval popular drama. Roy Flannagan, for instance, points out that the depiction of the open gates of hell in *Paradise Lost* 2:888–89 as a mouth belching forth smoke and flame may owe something to the "Hell mouth" popular on the medieval stage. Also, Satan's serpentization in book 10 of the epic ("his arms clung to his ribs, his legs entwining / Each other, till supplanted down he fell / A monstrous serpent on his belly prone" [512–14]) is reminiscent of the way mystery actors playing Lucifer would fall on their bellies and crawl away after being cursed by God. Moreover, if John Leonard is right in claiming that Milton considered using flesh-colored robes to costume Adam and Eve in the first draft of his Fall tragedy, it may be that the poet intuited this bit of stagecraft from what he knew of mystery plays. His use of personifications like Sin and Death might owe something to morality plays such as *Everyman*, which was first printed by John Skot about 1530. While we do not know if he ever read this work, W. R. Ramsay suggests that Milton's fourteenth sonnet ("When Faith and Love"), which features a group of personifications, including Faith and Love, accompanying a recently deceased woman to heaven, may be influenced by *Everyman*, since the play concludes with Good Deeds escorting Everyman to his death.[42]

Milton's other reading in drama is not hard to tally, in part because he incorporates dramatists into his own work so often, and in part because of his classical education. We know, for instance, that he loved Euripides, whom he first encountered at St. Paul's at about age 14; that he edited a volume of the Athenian's plays over a period of nearly 20 years; and, according to Deborah Milton, that he esteemed Euripides (along with Ovid) as his second-favorite writer, after Homer. He also loved Aeschylus and Sophocles, and read Aristophanes. Although he refers to Aristophanes' plays in *Areopagitica* (1644) as "trash" and as "books of grossest infamy," in *Of Education* (1643) he recommends the reading of certain "choice comedies" by Aristophanes, provided that students are warned in advance about the possible effects of lasciviousness on them. Milton owned a copy of Terence's comedies as well. Contemporary dramatists whose work he read include Jonson and

Shakespeare, both of whom he frequently echoes; John Marston, whose *Scourge of Villanie* almost certainly influenced L'Allegro's banishment of Melancholy and summoning of Mirth (1–24); and, Hugo Grotius, author of *Adamus Exul*.

Of the drama he read, Euripides' work seems to have had the greatest impact on him. He quotes him 18 times throughout his prose and poetry. (Sophocles and Aeschylus, the other two poets "unequalled yet by any," according to the prefatory statement to *Samson Agonistes*, are cited eight times and once, respectively, in Milton's corpus.) In fact, he implicitly compares himself to Euripides in "Captain or Colonel, or Knight in Arms," for just as Athens was saved from destruction when one of its inhabitants recited a chorus from *Electra* to the invaders, so Milton hopes that his sonnet will sway any Royalist captain or colonel who comes to destroy his house as Charles's army retakes the city from the Parliamentary forces. (As it turned out, the feared invasion by the King never took place.) And in "Methought I Saw My Late Espoused Saint" he has a dream-vision of his wife, who appears to him like Alcestis at the end of Euripides' play.

In 1634, while studying independently at the family home in Hammersmith, Milton bought a complete, two-volume edition of Euripides' plays. First printed in Geneva in 1602, the edition contains the playwright's entire corpus in Greek, as well as a Latin translation, commentary by Johann Broadaeus, Wilhelm Canter, and Gaspar Stiblinus, and a subject index. The text contained a fairly high number of errors, so from 1634 until 1652, the year he went completely blind, Milton edited the text by transposing letters, correcting misspelled words, adding and subtracting syllables to smooth out the meter, commenting on translations, disputing with the commentators, and reassigning speeches whenever he saw fit. He read the entire edition through at least twice, according to Maurice Kelley and Samuel Atkins, making it one of the most-read books in his personal library.[43] His intensive reading and correcting of these plays undoubtedly shaped his growth as a dramatist. Certain annotations suggest that he scanned the text as he read, perhaps declaiming the speeches as he did so.[44] Other corrections evince a keen awareness of staging matters.

In the 1990s, John Hale published two helpful essays on Milton's Euripides marginalia, and the following brief discussion of two of Milton's alterations of the stage directions is substantially indebted to him. At the beginning of the *Bacchae*, Tiresias and Cadmus, two old men, enter and present themselves as votaries of Dionysius. They are appropriately dressed to take part in the wild dancing characteristic of the cult. Hale explains Milton's remarkable emendation at this point in the text:

> At line 188 the received text had read, "Being old men, we have forgotten about glad things"; that is, "glad things" (*hedeos*) was governed directly by the verb, giving a remark suitable enough to old men resigned to decrepitude. But Milton, in his 1640s hand, writes alongside "perhaps *pleasurably* (for *hedeos*)," thus changing the sense to "we have glad*ly* forgotten that we are old men." Instead of an elderly remark about the deprivations of old age, Cadmus says the new rites of Bacchus make them forget their old age.

Hale goes on to point out that Milton made the change — which has been accepted by most editors of the play — to highlight "the amazing stage spectacle, the old made youthful." He also notes that out of Milton's 700 annotations, two of his proposals have been accepted in a modern edition, the Oxford Classical Texts series, and he adds that "If that does not seem a great number . . . the acceptance ratio of the immortal Richard Bentley in his Horace edition [i.e., over 700 suggestions, with just one or two finding acceptance] does not differ greatly." Hale points out, further, that Milton's own text of Euripides was so poor that in many cases he was often correcting an error that had already been fixed in authoritative editions. Another alteration evidences Milton's sensitivity to speech assignments. In *Supplices* 754–71, the traditional speakers were the Chorus and Messenger, with the former interrogating the latter. Milton, however, realized that although the scene does indeed begin as such, at line 734, King Adrastus begins asking the questions, and editors since have given Milton credit for the correction.[45]

IV. *Miltonic Drama: Its Relation to Puritan Views of Theater and to Shakespeare*

Having considered Milton as a reader, spectator, and editor of plays, we are now in a position to examine, first, his views of drama vis-à-vis his fellow Puritans, and second, his probable opinion of Shakespeare's work. Let us return once more to *L'Allegro*, whose narrator, as mentioned earlier, associates court masques with chivalry and "Hymen" (125), that is, with marriage. In doing so he parts company with many of his Puritan contemporaries. As noted in the introduction, Margot Heinemann has demonstrated that not all members of the sect disapproved of the stage.[46] Nevertheless, many Puritans were critical of the masque because of its links with the court and because it tended to feature women as dancers. Moreover, masque costumes were sometimes quite risqué; those featured in Jonson's *Masque of Blackness* were condemned by one spectator as "courtesan-like," and other masques featured bare-breasted women.[47] William Prynne's *Histriomastix; or, The Player's Scourge and Actor's Tragedy*, first published in 1633, constitutes a lengthy, vitriolic attack on masques and the stage, and by implication, on the court of Charles I, for both the king and his queen, Henrietta Maria, were ardent masquers. While Prynne's book represents the extreme wing of the Puritan view, others of his party held similar views, albeit less strictly.

Milton, however, was not one of them, at least not in the 1630s. As we saw, it seems doubtful that he ever attended any court masques, though he probably read them: Jonson's *Works*, which included several masques, was published in 1616, and echoes of Jonson's masques in Milton's early compositions show that he had access to the *Works*. Two indicators of Milton's opinion of masque in this period are *Arcades* and *Comus*. By accepting the commissions to compose these two pieces, he effectively disagreed with the masque's critics. Yet he probably was aware of their censures; one of Prynne's ears was cropped for writing *Histriomastix* — he received the same penalty on the other ear for attacking the bishops in 1637 — and Milton may allude to this punishment in an early draft of his sonnet "On the New Forcers of Conscience." Ethyn Kirby, in fact, holds that *Comus* was written to protest the views espoused by Prynne, and while there is no firm evidence that this is the case, Parker acknowledges that Kirby's hypothesis may be true.[48] Milton's high regard for the masque is also evident in the fact that he consented to the 1637, 1645, and 1673 publications of *Comus*, and projected an inset masque of "all the evils of this life and world" in the sketches for his Fall play.

His favorite dramatic genre, however, was tragedy. His hopes of composing one were first adumbrated in 1637 in an entry in his commonplace book. In it, he quotes Tertullian's censure of the public theater, from *De Spectaculis*, then observes that "in the book which he wrote on public shows, [Tertullian] condemns their use and closes them to Christians." Yet this church father, he adds, was not completely antithetical to drama, for Tertullian "stirs up the mind of the Christian to better plays, that is, divine and heavenly plays, which, in great number and in great value, the Christian can anticipate concerning the coming of Christ and the Last Judgment." While agreeing that "corruptions in the theater deservedly should be removed," Milton contests Tertullian's declaration that play performances should be banned altogether. Such a prohibition, he declares, "would be absurd beyond measure. For what in all philosophy is more important or more sacred or more exalted than a tragedy rightly produced, what more useful for seeing at a single view the events and changes of human life?" (YP 1:491)

In early 1642, prior to the closing of all theaters, which took place in September of that year, Milton went public with his minority view in *The Reason of Church-Government*. In a sustained autobiographical digression in the pamphlet's second book, he sketches out his plans for future literary projects and contemplates the respective merits of epic, tragedy, ode, and lyric. His primary concern is to decide which of these genres might prove the most "doctrinal and exemplary to a nation," that is, which would most effectively inculcate moral and spiritual virtue in its audiences.

Literature, he believes, has the potential to supplement preaching since it is capable of "inbreed[ing] and cherish[ing] in a great people the seeds of virtue and public civility" (YP 1:815 passim). To this end, he recommends that literary works be presented and recited in pulpits, in front of church gates, and in theaters.

When considering tragedy, Milton cites Sophocles and Euripides because he regards their works, which he calls "dramatic constitutions," as the supreme exemplars of the genre. He also expresses the hope that the current authorities will imitate "those famous governments of old" — that is, of fifth century Athens — and assume greater control over public sports and pastimes by holding "paneguries," that is, solemn, quasi-religious assemblies. (He coined the term from the Greek *panegyrikos*, which denotes a religious festival.) By recommending that such works be presented in the theaters, Milton implicitly counters the current proposal to shut the playhouses, and does so with considerable ingenuity. The reason the Puritans wanted to close them was to help prevent plague, and to prevent rowdy behavior by the spectators. Milton proposes that the theaters can be redeemed, however, if the fare they present is changed. Instead of stirring up the public to licentiousness and drunkenness, classical drama will teach the public virtue through catharsis; in his words, it will "allay the perturbations of the mind, and set the affections in right tune" (YP 1:816).

Despite Milton's plea, the theaters were shut in September, and the closings were intended, apparently, to be permanent: Alfred Harbage notes that the Globe was torn down in 1644, the Cockpit's interior was razed in 1649, and the Blackfriars was dismantled in 1655. Moreover, David Kastan points out that Parliament reiterated the closing order in 1647 and 1648.[49] Nonetheless, Milton's hopes for writing a tragic drama remained strong well into the 1640s. Perhaps the relatively late disassembling of the Blackfriars preserved his hopes of composing a work that could be staged with the blessing of the Puritan authorities. And Gordon Campbell notes that "it is possible, though arguably unlikely, that [Milton's father's trusteeship of that theater] was still in effect when he died in

March 1647, in which case Milton would have become a trustee and retained that position until the Blackfriars was sold by William Burbage in 1651."[50] Such a possibility would indicate that Milton's request to the authorities to keep the theaters open was based on his (partial) ownership of one of those theaters.

Milton's view of tragedy seems to have remained fairly consistent from the 1640s to the 1660s (most scholars believe *Samson Agonistes* was probably written in the late 1660s). For instance, he always seems to have felt that comedy and tragedy should be kept separate. As mentioned earlier, though L'Allegro dreams of masques and attends stage comedies, his alter ego consumes only tragedy alone in his tower. What the latter envisions is the personification of Tragedy serving as a prologue. She introduces Thebes, which is Oedipus's city, of course, and, like Troy, the scene of many classical tragedies, and also ushers in "Pelops's line" (99), that is, characters such as Agamemnon, Electra, and Iphigeneia, all of whom appear in tragedies by Aeschylus, Sophocles, Euripides, and Seneca. The thoughtful man also reads contemporary tragedy even though genuinely edifying examples of it are unusual.

The fact that Milton presents *L'Allegro* and *Il Penseroso* as representing two separate tastes would seem to indicate his basic agreement with the ancients' practice of sharply distinguishing between the two genres. This assumption is also implicit in his first elegy, for as we have seen, whenever the elegist turns from comedy to tragedy, Tragedy herself, a grand lady with a blood-stained scepter, appears in his mind's eye to ring in the change. In the prefatory epistle to *Samson* Milton denounces the blending of comedy and tragedy. Annette Flower suggests that in making this statement the poet may have been weighing in on the debate that took place in the mid-1660s between John Dryden and Robert Howard. Milton was friends with both writers and almost certainly contributed to their earlier dispute over the use of rhyme in his prefatory note to *Paradise Lost*, published in 1658. In that note, Milton claims that "the best English tragedies" use blank verse, not rhyme, thus supporting Dryden's perspective. Regarding mixed genres, however, Milton sides with Howard, who allowed for comic relief in tragedies.[51]

Milton's other prose works also evince his high regard for "pure" tragedy. *Of Education* (1643), for instance, recommends that students read tragedies that "treat of houshold matters," including Euripides' *Alcestis,* which focuses on domestic affairs related to one family (Admetus's), as well as those that offer the "statliest, and most regal argument, with all the famous Politicall orations." He also stipulates that young men study Aristotle's *Poetics* as well as commentaries on it, such as Castlevetro's *Poetic d'Aristotle* (1570).[52] By reflecting on these commentaries Milton believes that students will come to see "what despicable creatures our common rhymers and playwrights be" (YP, 2:398 passim). Though he does not mention any contemporary dramatists by name, he may have in mind those writers who flout the Aristotelian unities (of place, action, and time) — which would, of course, include nearly all Elizabethan playwrights, as well as Shakespeare. Milton mentions his great predecessor twice in his poetry, in *L'Allegro* and in his tribute poem for the Second Folio (1632). Both references are positive: *L'Allegro* calls him "Sweetest Shakespeare" (133), and the Folio encomium develops the idea set forth in *L'Allegro* that the Bard's genius is essentially spontaneous and shames writers who rely on "slow-endeavoring art" (9).

It is possible that Milton approved of Shakespeare's comedies but not his tragedies. Not only would he have condemned him for ignoring the unities in his tragedies, he also would have censured him for introducing into the tragedies comic characters such as the Porter and the Gravedigger. In his Trinity manuscript plans, Milton contemplated a Macbeth tragedy that would begin "at the arrival of Malcolm at Macduff," and adds that "the matter of Duncan may be expressed by the appearing of his ghost." Milton does not mention Shakespeare's play; in fact, he lists Holinshed's *Chronicles* as his only source. If Milton knew of Shakespeare's *Macbeth,* the fact that he was planning his own version could indicate his tacit disapproval of it. His single prose reference to Shakespeare, in

Eikonoklastes (1651), clearly censures one of Shakespeare's tragedies. In it, Milton accuses Charles of reading *Richard III* on his deathbed, intimating that the king should have been, instead, meditating on something edifying.

Two

Mastering Masque, Engaging Drama

ARCADES AND COMUS

For the examination of Milton's evolution as a dramatist it is apt to begin with *Arcades* (1632?), a short (109-line), masquelike entertainment, and *A Masque Presented at Ludlow Castle*, first produced in 1634. It is essential to see these two pieces in relation to one another, for in *Arcades* Milton mastered key demands of the masque form: the work evinces his familiarity with masque conventions such as the deployment of illuminated thrones and the approach of the masquers to compliment a seated dignitary. Hence, when he was commissioned to write *Comus* a year or so after *Arcades* was mounted, it is conceivable that Milton was less interested in simply writing another masque than in trying to stretch himself artistically. To be sure, the young man was, no doubt, under fairly strict guidelines from his patrons about what to write, yet he may have seen the commission as an opportunity to essay something in a more dramatic vein. The result is a composition that, unlike court masques, offers a plot, speaking roles for the noble actors, and conflict between the masquers and the villain. Such a combination of masque and play items has led the critical tradition to debate whether *Comus* is a true masque. I believe it is, based

39

on its original title and its inclusion of songs and dances. However, as I shall demonstrate, its dramatic components are considerable, and at times seem to overwhelm the masque features.

I. Arcades *in Performance*

The first stage direction of *Arcades,* which also appears to function as a subtitle, is "Part of an entertainment presented to the Countess Dowager of Derby at Harefield, by some noble persons of her family, who appear on the scene in pastoral habits, moving toward the seat of state with this song." The precise reason for the tribute is not clear, though in the early 1630s, the Countess was in her seventies, a venerable and distinguished lady and the recipient of many literary accolades, including one by Spenser, who dedicated *The Tears of the Muses* to her. Cedric Brown, one of the most influential interpreters of *Arcades,* has plausibly argued that its tribute celebrates the Countess's hospitality that she extended to the younger members of her family who had come to live with her, seeking shelter from the turmoil surrounding the trial and execution of the Earl of Castlehaven, one of her sons-in-law.[1] Yet *Arcades* honors the visitors as well as the Dowager, so it seems that the work was commissioned as a kind of double compliment to her and her guests. Milton thus needed to create a piece that would pay homage to both parties, and did so by combining elements of entertainment and masque genres.[2]

His earliest draft of *Arcades,* set down in the Trinity manuscript, was initially titled "part of a maske" and, subsequently, "part of an entertainment." Although entertainment structures varied, they tended to offer an official greeting to the visiting monarchs or aristocrats as they entered the main gates of the estate; an escort(s) who would refer to features of the local grounds and the main house; and, a finale in which the visitors were officially brought into the house. Entertainments were often episodic and drawn-out because the pathways up to the houses were usually long and the visitors had to be amused as they traveled up the path. Hence, dances, speeches, presentations — even, in the case of Ben Jonson's "Entertainment at Althrope," the shooting of live deer — were provided for the guests' enjoyment as they proceeded.[3]

Yet *Arcades* is influenced by the masque as well. Milton never crossed out his first title "part of a maske" in the Trinity manuscript, which suggests that he kept both genres in mind while composing the work. As I shall demonstrate, *Arcades* offers the following composite structure: (a) an opening discovery more reminiscent of those found in court masques than in typical entertainments (1–25); (b) a welcome that is clearly modeled on those found in traditional entertainments (26–73); and (c) an invitation to approach the throne (74–109), which recalls the approach of masquers to a seat of state.

In the beginning sequence, a group of nymphs and shepherds is surprised by a "sudden blaze of majesty" (2) emanating from the rural queen's throne, which suggests that in performance the state was illuminated instantaneously, perhaps as a curtain was whisked away. The light continued to shine, apparently, for as they near the Countess the visitors urge one another to "Mark what radiant state she spreads / In circle round her shining throne, / Shooting her beams like silver threads" (14–16). Because nearly all entertainments were produced outdoors, such effects were normally impossible. Also, no entertainment offered its visitors a lavish seat of state, for their purpose was to bring guests into the great house, not to keep them outside. Even Queen Elizabeth, who had an entertainment put on for her in 1602 at Harefield, simply watched the production while seated on her horse, under a tree. Hence, it would seem that the throne in *Arcades* would have required an indoor setting.

For years, however, editors followed David Masson's assumption that *Arcades* had been put on *al fresco*, in large part because of the Genius's various references to the landscape and great house. For instance, he appears to point to the house at line 36 when he calls it "yon princely shrine," to the surrounding forests at line 45 ("this fair Wood"), and, at line 89, to the elms shading the walkway up to the house. Cedric Brown, however, has disputed the claim that *Arcades* was shown outdoors, and John Leonard, Roy Flannagan, and co-editors Stephen Orgel and Jonathan Goldberg have seconded his contention. The detailed allusions to the lighting would also appear to support Brown. In addition to those mentioned, the Arcadians describe the Countess as "Sitting like a goddess bright / In the center of her light" (18–19), one "Whose luster leads us" (76), and the Genius subsequently invites them to approach "her glittering state" (81). It may be that these effects were merely implied by the poetry, but the abundance of references would seem to indicate a literal enactment, one that would require the celebration to be indoors. There, the seat of state could be set up, decorated as a relatively elaborate throne, perhaps even canopied;[4] such an arrangement would allow for a truly startling revelation of the Countess. An outdoor performance might permit some of the lighting effects if it were staged in the evening, but a "sudden blaze of majesty" would be difficult to produce.

Even so, the Genius's references to objects outside the great house are hard to ignore. A. S. P. Woodhouse attempted to solve the problem by surmising that "this preliminary part of the Entertainment [i.e., the approach by the nymphs and shepherds] . . . may have been set out of doors. . . . Here the Countess's seat of State, whether itself set indoors or out, must have been visible from within." Yet his proposal raises an additional difficulty, namely, that of the Countess not being able to fully hear what was going on outside if she were indoors. Brown's response to Woodhouse is convincing: he remarks that the actors were engaged in a "*pretense* that they are outside in the park." Brown also argues that "the use of the word 'scene' [in the opening stage direction] might . . . be thought to be technical, to mean in this case a single standing set or playing place, however modest or perfunctory. It may have signified simply a part of the room in which the initial dramatic action took place."[5]

Though they were probably inside, the actors were able to maintain this fiction of being outdoors. For instance, while the on-stage audience (the shepherds and nymphs) is impressed by the Countess's throne and its light, it is also baffled by the fact that such a manifestly glorious queen reigns in such an unpromising place. (Like many early moderns, Milton believed that northern climates were inhospitable to creative genius.) Their opening song, in fact, climaxes with the query, "Who had thought this clime had held / A deity so unparalleled?" (24–25). Hence, a hint of dramatic motivation is provided for their approach: they are astounded at her presence and move forward in hopes of solving the riddle. The Genius's welcome speech answers the visitors' question. He admits that the area is not perfect; it is afflicted with "nightly ill / Of noisome winds, and blasting vapors chill" (48–49), as well as "evil dew" (50) and "thunder blue" (51), smitten by "the cross dire-looking planet" (52), and plagued by the "hurtful worm with cankered venom" (53). He has, however, been commissioned by Jove to protect the place, a task he performs avidly, and so the rural queen is allowed to rule in safety and peace. His speech is clearly indebted to entertainment welcome episodes, for allusions to the local scenery are typical of such events.

After stopping to listen to the welcome, the visitors, now escorted by the Genius, begin once more to proceed to the throne. At this point, *Arcades* reverts to masque mode, for as Orgel and Goldberg point out, their movement forward echoes the "customary [moment] at the conclusion of a masque."[6] A masquing tone is also created by the fact that in performance the shepherds were masked (26–27), while the young women probably wore buskins, that is, knee boots, whose silver coloring would have helped reflect lighting effects in the hall (33).

It is not clear if there was dancing in *Arcades*. Neither stage direction mentions dance, although the work's second song, which consists of the Genius's invitation to the travelers to follow him "O'er the smooth enamelled green / Where no print of step hath been" (84–85), could allude to the green carpet sometimes laid out for dances. His third song, which begins "Nymphs and shepherds dance no more / By sandy Ladon's lillied banks. / On old Lycaeus or Cyllene hoar / Trip no more in twilight ranks" (96–99), is ambiguous. Either the Genius is telling them to cease dancing back in Arcadia, and to come and live with the queen, or urging them to stop dancing at the present moment. Parker believes that dancing is implied in the second song, and argues that the approach to the throne may have consisted of the participants moving forward with "measured steps, [since that] song is made up of varied and dancing rhythms."[7] For Brown, however, the lack of references to dancing in the stage directions indicates that none was offered.

He may be right, although I am not sure we can dismiss the possibility that dances are implied by the poetry. It does seem unlikely that revels were presented, for although the Dowager was seated on a throne of state and approached by masque-like figures, it would have been indecorous, even impossible, for them to take her off that throne and lead her out to dance, given her age and the solemnity of the occasion. Perhaps instead of dancing, the climax of *Arcades* occurred when the noble children approached and kissed her hem. Incidentally, lines 82–83 — "Where ye may all that are of noble stem / Approach, and kiss her sacred vesture's hem" — suggest that in the group of visitors there were certain non-nobles, perhaps even Milton, who stayed back as the aristocrats approached their queen. The sequence leading up to the climax, beginning with the invitation to the nobility, might have continued through the second song ("O'er the smooth enamelled green") as it accompanied the visitors up to the seat; then perhaps after a brief pause, the third song followed ("Nymphs and shepherds dance no more"), as the Genius stopped to invite the visitors to remain in this place. Their decision to stay would have been indicated by the kissing of her hem.

At any rate, even if dances were not performed, the work's costuming, scenery, and seat of state would have been recognized as masque elements by the spectators. Yet the audience might have been surprised by Milton's combination of elements of masque and entertainment, for while entertainment structures varied considerably, his fusion of masque and entertainment conventions in

Arcades is virtually unprecedented.[8] Some entertainments were fol-lowed by masques, with the latter being performed after the visi-tors had entered the house, but none incorporated masque elements into their structure. Despite its composite nature, however, *Arcades* is remarkably unified. Such unity results in a concentrated effect that is somewhat dramatic, especially compared to typical enter-tainments, which, as I mentioned earlier, were loose and episodic.

His creative blending of masque and entertainment in *Arcades* testifies to Milton's familiarity with the two genres. As we saw, he almost certainly read Jonson's 1616 Folio, which published both masques and entertainments, and various acquaintances of Milton's, including Alexander Gill Jr., Henry Lawes, and Charles Diodati, may have witnessed entertainments and could have described them to Milton. *Arcades* thus demonstrates that at this point the poet had sufficient awareness of entertainment and masque con-ventions to be able to join them artistically. This felicitous unification of two genres normally kept separate may have inspired Milton to attempt a similar experiment in the Ludlow masque.

II. *The Primacy of Drama over Masque in* Comus

A Masque Presented at Ludlow Castle was first staged on September 29, 1634, to celebrate the installation of the Earl of Bridgewater as Lord President of Wales and the Marches. The Earl served on Charles I's Privy Council, and he and his wife had fifteen children, at least four of whom sang, acted, or danced in court masques. He was both stepson and son-in-law of the Countess of Derby, and it seems probable that the success of *Arcades* led him to commis-sion Milton to write a second work for him. The Ludlow masque featured the youngest three children playing themselves, more or less: Lady Alice Egerton, 15, Lord John Brackley, 11, and Lord Thomas Egerton, 9. Lawes composed the music for the masque's five songs and acted the part of the Attendant Spirit.

One ongoing debate over *Comus* is whether or not it constitutes a true masque. Samuel Johnson called it a "drama in the epic style" and censured it according to play standards. For instance, he contended that its speeches were too long and lacking in stichomythia, and its action often implausible. Johnson's argument has been persuasively answered by numerous scholars, including John Demaray and Stephen Orgel, who adduce the work's original title and emphasize its masque features, including songs and dances. Demaray also argues that *A Masque* was intended to be a sequel to Aurelian Townshend's *Tempe Restored*, a court masque in which both Lawes and some of the Bridgewater children participated.[9]

As is often the case, however, Johnson's evaluation in this matter cannot be completely set aside. For instance, he rightly points out that *Comus* offers unmistakably dramatic features, which, I believe, tend to outweigh its masque elements in quantity and significance. This imbalance is perhaps most obvious in *Comus*'s songs, which were normally an integral part of a masque: many court masques commenced with one, and nearly all had them interspersed through the performance, since singing and music served to showcase the performers' talents. Barbara Lewalski claims that songs "have special prominence" in the Ludlow masque, but in fact four of its five songs are deferred until nearly the end of the piece, where they follow one another in rapid succession.[10] While the entire work is 1023 lines in length, the second song ("Sabrina fair") begins at line 859, the third ("By the rushy-fringèd bank") at line 890, the fourth ("Back shepherds, back, enough your play") at line 958, and the fifth ("Noble Lord, and Lady bright") at line 966. Only the first one, "Sweet Echo," sung by the Lady, occurs near the beginning, at line 230. Moreover, Lawes took 20 lines from the Attendant Spirit's epilogue (lines 976–83, 988–99), which was originally written to be spoken, and turned them into an opening song in the Ludlow performance. This transfer underscores the scarcity of songs in the first half of the text, and in a sense, constitutes one of the first commentaries on the inequity of genres of *A Masque*. Also, it is worth emphasizing that *Arcades*, though just 109 lines, contains three full songs.

A Masque also seems to have minimized dance to some extent. Like the songs, its dances were concentrated near the end of the production. Apparently there were at least three, and possibly four, in the original performance: the wild, grotesque dancing of Comus and his crew, performed until the Lady approaches (143–44); the country dances that usher in the third scene, set in "Ludlow Town and the President's Castle"; the dances performed by the Egerton children when presented to their parents; and the revels which may have concluded the masque. However, Milton makes no mention of revels either in the Trinity manuscript or the printed text, even though they were standard in court masques. He was certainly familiar with the convention of the revels; he alludes to them in *L'Allegro* when he requests that Hymen appear "with taper clear / And pomp, and feast, and revelry, / With masque and antique pageantry" (126–28).

William R. Parker argues that immediately following the fifth song ("Noble Lord and Lady bright"), in which the Attendant Spirit shows the children to their parents, "the Earl and his lady arose from their seats of state . . . and then led their guests in appropriate dances." Similarly, Barbara Lewalski attempts to account for the lack of allusions to revels by stating that "Milton could hardly take it upon himself to dictate on this point, but his text invites and makes place for Revels between the masque dances and the Spirit's epilogue."[11] However, given that the staging area at Ludlow Castle was quite small — it measured just 30 by 60 feet, almost half the size of Whitehall at 114 feet — and the fact that the hall seems to have been crowded (line 949 alludes to "many a friend" who have come to the performance to congratulate the Earl), it may be that there simply was not enough room for revels. And such a small area also may have constricted what few dances there were.[12]

Another feature deemed essential to masque, spectacle, was also downplayed in *Comus*, whose effects were far less lavish than court masques. The simplicity of its spectacle could be explained not only by the small staging area in Ludlow Castle, but also by the difficulty of obtaining cloud machines and other devices in a remote area such as Wales. Editors frequently note the contingency of Milton's opening stage direction, which reads, "The Attendant Spirit descends or enters," and of the Spirit's similarly open-ended claim in the epilogue that he can fly or run back to heaven (1013). Such lines indicate that Milton did not know if machinery would be available to lower and raise the Attendant Spirit, and thus gave the actor playing him (Henry Lawes) the opportunity to mimic flight while describing his descent and ascent to the audience. Other effects may also have been narrated rather than staged, including the Lady's vision of the figures of Conscience, Faith, Hope and Chastity (213 et passim) and her registering of the silver lining gleaming from the sable cloud (221–24). Even Sabrina's chariot could have been evoked rather than shown through the dialogue's implicit stage directions. The single direction for her entrance — "Sabrina rises, attended by Water-nymphs, and sings" — would not have required any machinery. Just so, her song, which describes the "sliding chariot . . ./ Thick set with agate" (892–93), may intimate that the chariot did not actually appear to the audience but was instead left behind — off-stage, so to speak — while she stepped out of the water:

> By the rushy-fringèd bank,
> Where grows the willow and the osier dank,
>   My sliding Chariot *stays* . . .
> Whilst from off the waters fleet
> Thus I set my printless feet.   (890–92, 896–97; my emphasis)

Because song, dance, and spectacle are reduced in *Comus*, dramatic components such as plot become more prominent. The mere fact that Milton's masque is plotted is not unusual, for court masques were required to supply some sort of allegorical device or hinge on which to hang their compliments. His plot is distinguished, however, by its comparative intensity, which results, I believe, from his decision to depict masquers and antimasquers clashing both verbally and physically. In court masques, main masquers did not speak at all, nor did they interact in any way with the antimasquers. In his preface to the *Masque of Queens*, Ben Jonson explains what led to the creation of the antimasque. The leading performer, Queen Anne, "had commanded me to think on some dance, or show that might precede hers, and have the place of a foil or false-masque." In this case, the antimasque — twelve women "in the habit of Hags, or Witches" — ran off stage when the music sounded, and moments later the deities (played by the Queen and her ladies) descended on cloud machines.[13]

The segregation of the masquers and antimasquers seems to have been, in large part, a class-based phenomenon. At the end of the published version of Samuel Daniel's court masque, *Tethys' Festival*, he assures the reader — presumably a member of the aristocracy — that the masque's performance involved "no mixing of inferior sort . . . amongst these great personages of state and honor . . . even the tritons were gentlemen of high estate."[14] There were some exceptions to this segregation. Stephen Orgel points out that in Jonson's masque *Oberon*, performed in 1611, the head Satyr, Silenus, though an antimasquer, nonetheless enumerates for his fellow satyrs the virtues of their new ruler, Oberon, who was played by James's eldest son, Henry.[15] I would add that in *Tempe Restored* Circe and the goddess Minerva exchange sharp words near the end of the masque. Only in Milton's masque, however, are interactions between antimasquers and masquers portrayed at length and to considerable effect. Such commerce provided Milton with various opportunities for conflict, suspense, and surprise, and he exploited such features in the work's most dramatic scene, namely, the debate between Comus and the Lady. In it, the two spar verbally; then, just as the magus is on the verge of forcing the Lady to drink from the cup, in what amounts to a nascent oral rape, her brothers rush in and drive off Comus and his rout.

The scene's dramatic interest stems not only from its action, but also from its characterization, particularly Comus's. The magician's disposition is revealed in one item in the Ludlow masque that is more common to plays than masques, to wit, its asides. The first one, spoken just after hearing the Lady's song, constitutes a moment of stupefied goodness on his part, for Comus is completely taken with the Lady and her song, wondering "Can any mortal mixture of earth's mold / Breathe such divine enchanting ravishment?"

(244–45). Comus also seems to confide in the audience by telling them "I'll speak to her / And she shall be my queen" (264–65). More revealing is the aside spoken just after the Lady's denunciation of her captor, a speech that ends with a threat that, were she to try, she could bring down all his "magic structures" on his head (756–99). Here it is evident that the Lady has frightened Comus, for her words act as a "cold shuddering dew" that effectively drenches him (802–03). He then discloses his new strategy to the audience: "I must dissemble / And try her yet more strongly" (805–06). However, it is not only the asides that expose Comus's true personality; Milton also reveals it by the way the magus deploys his glass cup and wand. Milton did not invent the character of Comus, but he did fabricate the story of his birth from Bacchus (his father) and Circe. Milton's Comus apparently carries the cup and wand with him at all times, ready to offer the former to any lost traveler foolish or desperate enough to drink from it. Because Comus's glass is transparent, its contents are easily seen, and indeed its attractiveness helps explain why most travelers accept the cup when it is offered. In fact, he deploys this strategy with the Lady during their debate when he enjoins her to "behold this cordial julep here / That flames, and dances in his crystal bounds / With spirits of balm, and fragrant syrups mixed" (672–74).

The cup and its contents also serve to transform Comus's victims into beasts, while his wand can only affect their bodies, either with what the Attendant Spirit calls a "clasping charm," that is, a sort of magic set of manacles, or a "numbing spell" (853), which paralyzes them. The Attendant Spirit twice mentions that the cup alone has the power to change its victims: first, when describing Comus's background and power to the audience ("Off'ring to every weary traveler / His orient liquor in a crystal glass, / . . . which as they taste /. . . Soon as the potion works, their human count'nance /. . . is changed" [64–66, 68–69]), and then when reiterating the same information to the brothers (520 et passim). Milton also revises the traditional Circean account so that, according to the Attendant Spirit, she too uses only a charmed cup to brutalize her victims (50–53).

Milton thus departs from all classical and early modern accounts of Circe, each of which depicts her wand as the principal means of enchantment, with the cup serving only to drug her victims as a prelude to enchantment.

One purpose of Milton's redaction is to ensure that Comus's victims drink freely from the cup and thus participate in their own bestialization, for having them transformed by mere whisks of a wand would violate their free will. Hence, Comus needs to be a richer character than he might be otherwise, more winsome and persuasive than a cardboard villain who can simply force his victims to change. According to the Attendant Spirit, most travelers in the wood opt to drink because of their "fond intemperate thirst" (67). In the Trinity manuscript, Milton originally wrote "weak" instead of "fond," and Roy Flannagan is probably correct when he surmises that the author "considered the two words nearly synonymous."[16] It would seem, then, that their moral impurity precedes and enables their physical transformation; that is, intemperance leads them to drink, at which point both their faces and their minds are transformed and debased. The Attendant Spirit points out that Comus's victims have no idea that they have been debased, and, in fact, regard themselves as more attractive than ever after their change (74–76). This also constitutes a departure from the Circean sources, which depict her victims as retaining their reason even under enchantment; in *Tempe Restored*, for example, Circe's paramour claims that even while he was charmed, a "Promethean fire" burned within him that fueled his desire to become human again.[17] Although the Attendant Spirit never specifies how Comus "Excels his mother at her mighty art" (63), the insidious mode of Comus's temptation may be one of the ways in which he does so. Milton's instructions for the rout's costuming underscore the fact that their minds are transformed, for according to the stage directions, their heads are altered while their bodies remain human: in the Trinity manuscript, he writes, "Comus enters with his rout all headed like some wild beasts thire garments some like mens & some like womens," and in the 1645 text, he indicates that "Comus enters . . . with him a rout of monsters headed like sundry sorts of wild beasts, but otherwise like men and women, their apparel glistering."

The Lady, of course, claims that her mind is free even if Comus paralyzes her (663–64). That claim, along with Milton's revision of the Circe myth, heightens the tension of the debate scene in several ways. First, in marked contrast to Circe and her victims, there is no hint that Comus has already slept with the Lady and is now attempting to punish her by transmogrifying her; rather, he plies her precisely because she is a virgin. Second, by conflating the two phases of the Circean pattern (drugging, followed by transmogrification), Milton provides the necessary conditions for a sustained debate between Comus and the Lady, for the length and intensity of their argument are based, in part, on the fact that Comus is trying to persuade her to act with her own assent. Third, it is possible that although Comus cannot touch the freedom of the Lady's mind as long as she refuses to drink, he may be able to compel her to partake of the liquor. In fact, he may be attempting precisely that when her brothers rush in, for just before their entrance, he abandons persuasion and resorts to direct command, telling her "Be wise, and taste" (813). At this point her arms and legs are magically fettered, although she does not seem to be fully paralyzed yet. (Precisely when the Lady is frozen is not clear. Perhaps Comus brings this condition about by waving his wand as he flees the scene. Line 817, which refers to his "backward mutters of dissevering power," may hint at such a parting shot.) Hence, even if she were willing to hold the cup, she would not be able to; hence, Comus seems to be trying to make her drink, in a kind of attempted oral rape. The brothers' rescue, then, comes at the last possible moment, and saves her from what would have been a doubly horrible outcome both for them and the masque audience: the Lady's physical transformation, and, perhaps worse, the corruption of her mind. This barely averted result charges the scene with genuine dramatic tension.

On the other hand, certain problems are created by the revisions. The magus's motive for wanting her to drink remains unclear. From the moment he hears her sing he is smitten with the Lady's beauty: he refers to her as a "fair virgin" (689), praises her with Petrarchan blandishments, and clearly savors her "vermeil-tinctured" lips, "love-darting eyes," and "tresses like the morn" (752–53). Why, then, does he urge her to imbibe the potion if doing so would instantly erase that beauty? The Attendant Spirit emphasizes that whoever drinks from his cup is immediately transformed (68–70), so there is no question of Comus's deflowering her, then casting her aside *after* her face changes. Moreover, early in the masque, he declares — significantly, when alone — that he wants her to be his queen (265). Therefore, it seems that Comus wishes both to possess her beauty *and* to destroy it.

One possible explanation for his contradictory desire is that Comus simply does not realize that the potion disfigures those who drink it. Certain lines suggest that he still regards the "women" in his rout as comely, for when he initially enters with them and the rest of the rout he tells them, despite their animal heads, to "Braid your locks with rosy twine" (105), and when the Lady starts to approach the scene, he commands them to hide, since "Our number may affright [her]" (148), without mentioning the more obvious reason, namely, their horrific appearances. Perhaps Comus the sorcerer is merely perpetuating their delusion that they are lovelier than ever, having drunk from his glass. His speech at the beginning of the debate scene, however, indicates that he does not in fact regard them as homely. Just after the Lady has been brought to Comus's palace and seated in the enchanted chair, she attempts to get up and leave, when he beckons her to look around:

> Why are you vexed Lady? why do you frown?
> Here dwell no frowns, nor anger, from these gates
> Sorrow flies far: see here be all pleasures
> That fancy can beget on youthful thoughts.   (666–69)

Among the sights he points out, apparently, are the rout, who have accompanied him to the castle. Not surprisingly, the Lady responds by crying out, "What grim aspects are these, / These ugly-headed monsters? Mercy guard me!" (694–95).

Comus's action here, while appearing to be an astonishing lapse of judgment, is perhaps logical from his perspective. By representing the tempter as proudly showing off the sights of his palace to the Lady, Milton may have intended to convey the extent of Comus's depravity. That is, from Comus's point of view, the discovery of the rout may constitute the *pièce de résistance* in his campaign of seduction. Along with the ambience that he has created with dainties and soft music, Comus may hope that the Lady will see, not objects of horror, but rather, attractive young people enjoying themselves. The fact that he cannot or will not see their actual appearance evidences the extent of his degeneracy. Such complexity makes his character memorable, more like an antagonist in a full-fledged drama than a crude antimasque figure. Thus, Comus exemplifies Milton's experimental joining of drama and masque—a literary achievement that is virtually without precedent.

III. Comus *and Prospero's Entertainment*

What if Milton had continued in the vein of *Arcades* and imagined the Ludlow affair as a "pure" masque? We cannot know for certain, of course, yet some clues may be gleaned from another masque of chastity, namely, Prospero's betrothal entertainment for Miranda and Ferdinand in *The Tempest*. This play is frequently compared with *Comus*, although such comparisons seldom focus on *The Tempest*'s inset masque. To juxtapose the two masques is enlightening, for Prospero's entertainment may have influenced Milton in certain respects, including the choice of chastity as its main theme. At the same time, Prospero's masque hints at what Milton's might have been like had it been composed as a traditional masque.

While both works constitute masques of chastity, each figures the virtue differently. Milton celebrates the Lady's purity by showing her rejecting Comus's blandishments. Prospero, by contrast, presents his entertainment to Miranda, his 14-year-old daughter, who is betrothed to Ferdinand, to reveal the blessings they will obtain if they refrain from premarital intercourse. Prospero's entertainment is minimally plotted: Iris, Juno's messenger, enters and summons Ceres, and Juno herself descends as Iris speaks the summons. Ceres then enters, greets Iris, and asks why Juno has called for her. When she learns the reason — to celebrate a betrothal — she also finds out, from Iris, that Venus and Cupid considered tempting the young couple to unchastity with "some wanton charm upon [them]," but decided against it, put off, presumably, by the young people's fervent vows to forego lovemaking until their marriage (4.1.87 ff).[18] Juno and Ceres proceed to sing a blessing for the two young people, then send Iris to invoke nymphs to come up from their stream to help celebrate the engagement. The nymphs arise and dance with farmers called away from the fields, and the masque ends abruptly when Prospero, recalling the conspiracy hatched against him by Caliban and his confederates, suddenly commands the spirit-actors to cease playing.

While the emphasis on chastity constitutes the most important similarity between the two masques, other salient parallels are also evident. Each begins when a messenger sent from either Juno (Iris) or Jove (the Attendant Spirit) enters, dressed in a rainbow-colored garb; in fact, the Attendant Spirit refers to his costume as "Iris's woof" (83). Both feature young, virginal women who are nearly the same age (Lady Alice was fifteen, Miranda about fourteen and a half), and both present spirit-actors: Ariel and his "rabble," and the Attendant Spirit (Thyrsis). The villains in each masque threaten to seduce their targets with charms: Iris tells Ceres that Venus and Cupid "thought . . . to have done / Some wanton charm upon this man and maid" (4.1.94–95), and of course Comus wields his charming-rod. Both masques feature a primary audience of just two members (Miranda and Ferdinand; the Lord and Lady Bridgewater); both climax with the summoning of water nymphs, who, in each work, are praised for their temperance. And each presents, at or near the end, dances by rustics.

On the other hand, the Ludlow masque is set in an actual place, namely, the forests of Ludlow, while Prospero's is acted before his cave, on a nameless, fictional isle. Also, while Miranda and Ferdinand are the principal spectators for Prospero's entertainment, the

Egerton children are actually *in* the Ludlow masque. Chastity is also treated differently in each masque, as we have seen. Perhaps the most important structural difference between them is that conflict is presented in *Comus* and avoided in Prospero's celebration. The only possible confrontation in Prospero's masque might have occurred if Venus and Cupid attempted to corrupt Miranda and Ferdinand, yet we are told that the two would-be seducers abandon their idea and thus never even appear.

Prospero's masque suggests ways in which Milton's could have been structured more conventionally. The Attendant Spirit still might have entered at the beginning, but the episodes of the brothers and the Lady's journey would not have been necessary. Instead, the antics of Comus and his victims could have been narrated rather than represented, including the villain's decision not to attempt a seduction once word of the Lady's determination to resist was disclosed to him. Sabrina and her attendant nymphs still could have been invoked, but only to help celebrate the Lady's temperance. And finally, rustics still might have danced to intensify the festivities. However, rather than the Attendant Spirit presenting the children to their parents as those who have overcome "hard assays" of thirst, hunger, bewilderment, and Comus's temptations, the children would have been complimented in a simpler fashion. Such a pure masque no doubt would have been shorter and less complicated, albeit less satisfying for the Ludlow audience as they would not have witnessed the testing of the children's virtues, nor would the sincerity of the concluding compliment appear more than mere flattery.

Still, as previously mentioned, Samuel Johnson attacked *Comus* precisely because of its dramatic qualities, and his judgment was often echoed in nineteenth and twentieth century accounts of the masque. In fact, the critique of *Comus* as failed drama accounts for the tendency of twentieth century scholarship to focus primarily on the work's intellectual content.[19] Yet I contend that Johnson's assessment is unfair, for it judges Milton by very high, Shakespearean standards. In fact *Comus* should be regarded as an apprentice work, one whose excellence as drama is readily apparent when compared with *Arcades*. Both employ a basic progressional structure that in *Arcades* develops as the nymphs and shepherds make their way to the Arcadian queen, while in *Comus* the progression follows the children as they wend their way home. Yet *Comus* is a far richer work in virtue of its pronounced plot and characterization, as well as its featuring of direct engagement between masquers and antimasquers. To be sure, the addition of dramatic elements does not always succeed in the Ludlow masque: not only are some speeches long-winded, at times characters repeat information that the audience has already learned, such as the reiteration of Comus's genealogy by the Attendant Spirit (46–77, 520–39). Nevertheless, these elements are effective enough to show that in the year or two following the composition of *Arcades*, Milton had grown considerably as a dramatic artist.

IV. *Milton's Revisions of* Comus — *Toward Poetry or Drama?*

The consensus among Miltonists is that his post–1634 revisions of the Ludlow masque indicate a move away from drama toward poetry. If that assessment is correct, it might appear that Milton was not entirely pleased with his initial attempt to combine drama and masque. On the contrary, I claim that the revisions, in fact, evince Milton's evolving skills as a dramatist as well as a poet. In order to understand the post-performance changes, a brief review of the masque's textual history is in order. Five versions of the Ludlow masque are extant: (1) the one contained in the Trinity manuscript, in Milton's hand; (2) that in the so-called Bridgewater manuscript, which constitutes the closest thing we have to a performance text;[20] (3) the masque's first printed version, published in 1637 by Henry Lawes, apparently in consultation with Milton; (4) the print version of 1645, entitled *Poems of Mr. John Milton*, which, incidentally, constitutes the basis for several editions of the masque, including Roy Flannagan's, John Shawcross's, and Orgel and Goldberg's; and (5) the 1673 print version, *Poems, &c upon Several*

Occasions. The critical reception of the revisions is evident in remarks such as those of William B. Hunter, who claims that the 1645 edition was "offered . . . as poetry to its readers rather than as drama." In like manner, C. S. Lewis argues that certain lines and phrases in the earlier versions are subsequently replaced by more poetic phrases when Milton was preparing the manuscript for publication.[21] And Flannagan asserts that "the movement from the two manuscript versions through the first two printed versions . . . is from . . . the masque as an occasional dramatic piece [to] the masque as a poetic achievement on its own."[22]

I agree with all three critics to some extent: clearly, Milton was thinking of *A Masque* in terms of poetry when he published it, for the titles of both the 1645 and 1673 volumes of his collected works contain the word "poems" in them. If we consider all the changes from the manuscripts to the published versions, however, especially the revisions in the stage directions, I believe a larger pattern emerges, namely, an attempt to provide increased *dramatic* clarity as well as more compelling poetry. In order to demonstrate this point, I begin with the rout's description, quoted from the Trinity manuscript (bracketed words are those Milton later struck out): "Comus enters wth a charming rod & [glass of] liquor, with his rout all headed like some wild beasts thire garments some like mens & some like womens they [begin] come on in a wild & [humorous] antick fashion."[23] In the Bridgewater manuscript, Milton or Lawes expanded this direction by adding certain details, such as the fact that upon entering, the rout is wearing "glistering" apparel, carrying torches, and emitting a riotous and unruly noise.[24] These additions are retained in the 1637, 1645, and 1673 editions, implying that Milton wished to convey a sense of what the rout actually looked and sounded like in performance. If he had been revising away from drama, he easily could have shortened or eliminated such directions.

The Bridgewater edition also clarifies the action at the beginning of the debate between the Lady and Comus. While Milton originally wrote that the Lady was "set in an inchanted chaire She offers to rise," he or Lawes rewrote them as follows: "the lady set in an inchaunted chayre, *to whom he offers his glasse* which she puts by."[25] This addition helps explain why she attempts to get up and leave, and the fact that Milton decided to retain it in all three printed versions indicates that he wanted to clarify this bit of business, even if it were only for readers instead of spectators. The 1637 edition also adds the detail, incorporated into subsequent editions, that "soft music" accompanies Comus and his rout as they feast, just before his debate with the Lady. This also appears as a dramatic item, for it helps to evoke the atmosphere of luxury at the sorcerer's palace.

Nonverbal stage cues are also retained in the printed versions. There is in the Trinity manuscript a long dash after line 212 just before the Lady sees the tableau of Faith, Hope, and Chastity. While this vision was eliminated in performance, perhaps to shorten the masque, Milton alludes to it by including the dash in the 1645 and 1673 editions. Also, just after line 330, in which the Lady and Comus (disguised as a rustic) exit, the Trinity manuscript has the word "Exeunt," which term is eliminated in all four subsequent versions. However, the printed versions include a dash here to signal their exit. Yet these additions, while important, are relatively small compared with the creation of lines 779–806. Milton added these lines in the 1637 edition, and they also appear in the 1645 and 1673 texts. Lewis regards this passage as the single most important post-performance change, describing it as "an alteration not in the dramatic, but in the gnomic and ethical direction," presumably because it is here that the Lady first broaches the doctrine of virginity.[26] One might add that expanding by 27 lines an already sizable (originally 23-line) speech also seems a clear step away from drama. Nevertheless, I contend that the addition serves to render the scene more dramatically effective. In both the Trinity and Bridgewater manuscripts the Lady's reply to Comus ends at line 779 when she asks, rhetorically, "Shall I go on?" and is effectively answered by the magician, who begins his response as follows: "This is mere moral babble, and direct / Against the canon laws of our foundation" (807–08). In the 1637 text, however, the Lady *does* go on, stating, in effect, that she could recount the "sage and serious doctrine of virginity," but to do so would be pointless when dealing with a hardened cynic like Comus. Were she to try, however, she claims that

> the uncontrollèd worth
> Of this pure cause would kindle my rapt spirits
> To such a flame of sacred vehemence
> That dumb things would be moved to sympathize
> And the brute earth would lend her nerves, and shake,
> Till all thy magic structures reared so high
> Were shattered into heaps o'er thy false head.   (793–99)

The most explicated portion of her speech is her reference to the doctrine of virginity, but what has not been noticed is the speech's dramatic function, for it constitutes a direct threat to Comus: She tells him that she can bring down the roof if she so desires, and the magus clearly registers that threat, for in the published versions, he first voices a panicky aside, already mentioned: "She fables not, I feel that I do fear / Her words set off by some superior power" (800–801). He then rallies, determined to "dissemble" (805), to cover up his fear and "try her yet more strongly" (806). The aside thus sheds crucial light on his character, and makes his subsequent action — forcing the cup on her — more plausible, dramatically: he has been deeply shaken by her words, and feels he must do something before she decides to act on her threat.

This is not to say that Milton approved of all the changes made for the performance. For instance, I have already mentioned that Lawes converted the original epilogue, which was meant to be spoken, into a sung prologue, perhaps to help the masque seem more traditional. And most critics agree that Lawes was probably responsible for dividing up the Attendant Spirit's invocation of Sabrina (859–89) and redistributing the lines between the two brothers in an effort to give them more lines to speak. If Lawes consulted Milton as he was preparing the 1637 text for printing, it would appear that Milton was responsible for replacing the epilogue in its original position and having the Attendant Spirit summon Sabrina without the brother's assistance. The 1645 and 1673 editions, I would add, retain Milton's structure. Hence, the changes that were made in performance and allowed to stand in subsequent print editions, such as the ones I have discussed, seem to be authoritative.

Incidentally, the fact that in performance Lawes had the two boys help the Attendant Spirit summon Sabrina might seem like a move toward drama, since having them speak here would appear to flesh out their characterization. However, Milton's subsequent restoration in the print versions of the Attendant Spirit's role as sole summoner of the nymph makes good dramatic sense. Allowing the two boys to assist in the operation would probably gratify the audience, yet would be radically out of character for both young men, who until now have shown themselves to be comparatively, albeit charmingly, ignorant pupils of Thyrsis, who is deeply schooled in the local mythology. Hence, it would be peculiar for them to be suddenly capable of taking part in the Attendant Spirit's complex, learned invocation of Sabrina. Also, just before he begins his invocation, he notes that Sabrina will help them "if she be right invoked in warbled song" (854), and then goes on to say, "This will I try / And add the power of some adjuring verse" (857–58). His song, "Sabrina fair listen where thou art sitting" (859–60), clearly corresponds to the first part of his declaration, while the invocation, which begins at line 867, constitutes the "adjuring verse."

V. Arcades *as Source for Satan's Self-Discovery*

Although it would be nearly four decades before he published *Samson Agonistes* (in 1671), the experience of composing *Arcades* and *Comus* in the 1630s prepared Milton for his later achievement in both epic and drama in important respects. However, instead of proceeding chronologically from the Ludlow masque to document the progression of Milton's artistic development, I wish to return to *Arcades* and elucidate its salient influence on two later compositions, Satan's entrance into Pandaemonium in *Paradise Lost*, book 10, and on *Samson Agonistes*. Moreover, privileging *Arcades* in this fashion elevates the work from its current status in the Miltonic canon as a light and relatively unimportant piece. It is no surprise, then, that the influence on book 10 of *Paradise Lost* has gone unnoticed by editors, perhaps because they tend to focus almost exclusively on the episode's epic sources. First, however, a brief review of the scene is in order. Following his successful temptation of Adam and Eve, Satan returns to the underworld. In order to reach the door of Pandaemonium, which is effectively blocked by devils waiting for their chief to come back, Satan disguises himself as a rank-and-file soldier to make it through the crush. Upon entering the hall, he becomes invisible in order to ascend the throne undetected: "he through the midst unmarked, / In show plebeian angel militant / Of lowest order, passed; and from the door / Of that Plutonian hall, invisible / Ascended his high throne" (10.441–45). After sitting in silence for some time and surveying the audience, he manifests himself: "At last as from a cloud his fulgent head / And shape star-bright appeared, or brighter, clad / With what permissive glory since his Fall / Was left him, or false glitter" (449–52). He proceeds to address his followers with a sneering, self-congratulatory account of the temptation of Eve and Adam, and then turns into a serpent along with the other angels.

As Roy Flannagan notes, Dennis Burden's 1967 monograph *The Logical Epic: A Study of the Argument of "Paradise Lost"* was apparently the first discussion to characterize the arch-fiend's speech and transmogrification in epic terms, and other critics, including Neil Harris, Barbara Lewalski, and Alastair Fowler, have followed Burden's lead.[27] Perhaps because of this focus on epic, editors also seem to regard Satan's entrance and revelation in strictly epic terms. John Leonard, for example, adduces three sources for the scene: the appearance of Sultan Solimano in Tasso's *Gerusalamme Liberata*; Ulysses' self-revelation in the house of Alkinoös (*Odyssey* 7); and the discovery of Aeneas and his companion Achates in book 1 of *The Aeneid*.[28] In Tasso, the Sultan is led by a sorcerer, Ismen, into Jerusalem, on a magic chariot that is concealed in a cloud (10.16). Ismen takes the Sultan to a council of war that is being conducted by Aladine, Prince of Judaea, who is planning his next move against the Christian crusaders. In stanza 49, the Sultan reveals himself; the cloud is rent, and the entire council is dazzled by his radiance. The link with Tasso is strengthened by the fact that when the devils approach Satan they are, in the narrator's words, "raised from their dark Divan," a term referring to a Turkish council of state.[29] Similarly, in book 7 of *The Odyssey*, as Odysseus enters Alkinoös's city, Athena veils him in a fog so that he will be able to proceed unchallenged. Athena, disguised as a young girl, leads him toward Alkinoös's mansion. He gazes at the palace, then enters, still concealed by Athena's cloud. When he reaches Queen Arete and Alkinoös, who are dining, he clasps Arete's knees (7.151), and the mist disappears. Odysseus then pleads for her mercy. In like manner, in *The Aeneid*'s opening book, Aeneas and his companion Achates are hidden in a cloud by Venus as they enter Paphos (Carthage) and proceed to look around. When Dido addresses her people, speaking of Aeneas, he cannot stay hidden, and the cloud disappears (1.798).

Given that Satan is often compared elsewhere in *Paradise Lost* to epic figures such as Ulysses and others, it seems quite reasonable for critics to follow suit when interpreting this scene. Yet the sources adduced by Leonard do not account for all aspects of the devil's unveiling. In none of the epics, for instance, is the discovered person seated; rather, in each case he is on foot. Also, the mist or cloud is actual in the epic texts, while in *Paradise Lost*, by contrast, Satan is enthroned and appears "*as* from a cloud" (10.449; my emphasis). Hence, we need to consider masque conventions as another possible influence on this episode. In particular, the masque-like *Arcades* provides a likely source for the devil's stunning *coup de théâtre*, as well as for his elaborate throne; it also furnishes certain words and phrases that Milton, consciously or not, uses in Satan's unveiling.

As noted, we do not know if Milton was present at the performance of *Arcades*, although I argued that there is good reason to believe he might have been. Yet even if Milton did not see the show he easily could have imagined it, based on his general familiarity with masque conventions, which he could have absorbed by reading Jonson's published works. It is worth noting that both Jonson's *Masque of Blackness* (1605) and its sequel, the *Masque of Beauty* (1608), featured elaborate, silver-colored thrones — and indeed it is possible that such effects were described to him by the Countess herself, who as a young woman acted in these very productions.

Whether witnessed or imagined, the performance of *Arcades* evidently lodged in Milton's psyche, for several phrases from it are echoed in Satan's manifestation. As we saw, what received particular emphasis at the beginning of the entertainment was the immediacy of the Queen's illumination, which shot forth as a "sudden blaze" (2). That phrase is repeated in the Pandaemonium episode: "At that so sudden blaze the Stygian throng / Bent their aspect, and whom they wished beheld, / Their mighty chief returned" (10.453–55). Also, the thrones in each work are referred to as "states," and both seats featured ornate awnings — Satan is described as sitting "under state / Of richest texture spread" (10.445–46). Moreover, both works have the terms "state" and "spread" in close proximity, and in the same order — in line 14 of *Arcades*, one shepherd urges the others to "Mark what radiant state she spreads." Furthermore, the Genius's claim that the Dowager's "*luster* leads us" (76) may be echoed in the description of Satan's throne being "placed in regal *luster*" (10.447; my emphases). What is more, the Arcades "bend" their wishes and vows toward the sun-queen (6), while the devils "bent their aspect" (10.454), that is, turned their faces, towards their own leader. In sum, the repetition of "sudden blaze," "state," "bend/bent," and the close proximity of "state" and "spread" in each work reinforces the impression that *Arcades* influenced, at some level, Milton's composition of Satan's discovery.

Furthermore, if the connection with *Arcades* is accurate, especially its masquelike discovery, Satan's diminishment after the War in Heaven would seem to be emphasized here. As noted earlier, the narrator's description of Satan's radiance poses the question of how much of that brightness is his own — that is, "permissive glory" left over from before his fall (10.451) — or merely "false glitter" (10.452). Prior to book 10, whenever the narrator refers to the arch-fiend's brightness, he suggests that Satan does, in some manner, still possess it.[30] By this point, however, Lucifer, the bearer of light, has been largely supplanted by Satan, and any remaining radiance is in fact as false and fleeting as a masque costume. Such ephemerality is especially acute when considered in relation to actual performance, since few masques were ever put on more than once. Regarding *Arcades* as the inspiration for the Pandaemonium episode in *Paradise Lost* also demonstrates that Milton's turn from stage to epic is not a total abandonment of drama. He clearly kept drama in mind while crafting the diffuse epic, and not just literary drama but staged production. Such awareness instills this episode with genuinely theatrical energy.

THREE

Problem-Solving in Milton's Biblical Drama Sketches

Throughout his early adulthood, Milton kept a private notebook containing both rough drafts and fair copies of several of his early works, including *Lycidas, Arcades, Comus,* and various sonnets. Seven pages of the notebook are also filled with titles, subjects, speech outlines, character lists, and plot summaries for projected tragedies based on biblical and medieval British narratives. Because the document was eventually donated to Trinity College, Cambridge, after the poet's death and remains there to this day, it is called the Trinity manuscript (TMS hereafter). He probably began jotting down the material on tragedies in TMS in the late 1630s, not long after his tour of the Continent (1638–39), and might have continued doing so until as late as 1652, before the onset of total blindness. It is even possible that he had various amanuenses read the plans to him when he began composing *Samson Agonistes,* most likely in the late 1660s.[1] The plans are invaluable because they constitute, in J. Milton French's apt phrase, "chips from the poet's workshop." In them we see a playwright at work, selecting subjects, experimenting with titles, writing down personae lists, outlining plots, and confronting problems of physical staging and characterization. Moreover, while Milton's two dramas were composed nearly forty years apart, the plans evidence his ongoing commitment to drama during a significant portion of that time. With certain exceptions, scholarship has focused on the ways this material forecasts Milton's achievement in the epic, especially since the most developed of the plans constitute multiple drafts for a play about the Fall.[2] However, because the plans also offer a wealth of information on Milton's thinking about drama, as well as insight into his process of composition and revision, they also deserve to be studied in relation to his growth as a dramatist.

I. *Challenges in Dramatizing the Fall*

While the total number of subjects listed for play topics is approximately 100, it is impossible to arrive at an exact count because certain listings may constitute alternate titles rather than separate anticipated dramas. Roughly 61 are biblical in origin, and the rest are taken from medieval British history. Some entries consist of little more than a title (e.g., "The Deluge," based on the Genesis flood), others provide brief plot summaries (e.g., "Wulfer slaying his two sons for being Christians"), and still others are considerably developed, furnishing personae lists, plot outlines, speeches, and staging cues. Four TMS entries are longer and more detailed than any others; these include the Fall and Sodom sketches as well as one on Abraham's near-sacrifice of Isaac and one entitled "Baptistes," on the death of John the Baptist.

It is probable that Milton regarded these entries as potential tragedies as opposed to epics or other types of plays, for two reasons: first, on the opening page of the dramatic plans (TMS, 35), between the two opening Fall drafts, each of which lists the personae in order of appearance, he wrote "other tragedies," and then, underneath this phrase, listed three titles: "Adam in Banishment," "The Flood," and "Abraham in Egypt." Second, the third page of the plans (37) is entitled "British Trag.," which most editors agree is an abbreviation for "British Tragedies." Such a denomination makes sense, for it contrasts with the first two pages of play material (35–36) on biblical tragedies. Furthermore, the projected Abraham drama describes the patriarch in terms that seem to allude to Aristotle's discussion of the ideal tragic hero, set forth in *Poetics* 13, which argues that the tragic hero is a person of high stature, but not faultless, who experiences misfortune. Thus, in Milton's sketches, the chorus laments the supposed "fate of so noble a man [Abraham] fallen from his reputation."

The entries are mostly chronological, following the order of the books of the Old Testament, as if Milton read it through searching for potential tragedies. What was he seeking? One clue is provided by *"The Reason of Church-Government,"* published in 1642, about the same time he was setting down play ideas. As I discussed in chapter 1, this pamphlet furnishes a substantial autobiographical digression that delineates Milton's plans for future literary projects and contemplates the benefits and drawbacks of epic, tragedy, ode, and lyric. In the digression, he voices his hope of ascertaining which genre might prove the most "doctrinal and exemplary to a nation," and adduces the works of Euripides and Sophocles as good examples of how literature can be morally educative to large, public audiences. While he does not specify what kind of subject matter these plays would offer, he states that they would celebrate "the victorious agonies of Martyrs and Saints [and] the deeds and triumphs of just and pious Nations doing valiantly through faith against the enemies of Christ, to deplore the general relapses of Kingdoms and States from justice and Gods true worship." He proposes that the government sponsor "paneguries," that is, large, pseudo-religious assemblies at which such plays could be shown. Milton evidently wished (unsuccessfully, it turned out) to convince the Commonwealth leaders that the theaters did not need to be closed, but instead could be reformed (YP 1:820, 817).

Many of the TMS sketches seem to reflect the vision articulated in the tract, particularly its emphasis on the triumphs of just kingdoms and the fall of corrupt ones. In fact, nearly half (26 of 61) of the biblical plots would have culminated in large-scale disasters, ones that often befall entire cities. In addition to the already mentioned Deluge and Sodom, there is also the rape of Dinah (Gen. 34), including her brothers' ambush of scores of Canaanite men who had recently agreed to be circumcised; the massacre of 3000 unfaithful Jews who had bowed down to the golden calf (Exod. 32); the rebellion of Korah (Num. 16), in which 14,000 died in a plague; the razing of the entire city of Ai by the Jews (Josh. 8); and finally, the slaughter of 3,000 men by Samson with a jawbone (Judg. 15). If produced, such large-scale calamities would have needed to be kept off-stage, and accordingly, "Dinah" lists a "nuncio" in the dramatis personae. And yet, Milton seems to have desired that at least one disaster be partially staged — the destruction of Sodom. He may have felt that such a catastrophe would provide a much more impressive educational device than a narrated one. At the end of the Sodom sketch, the angel who brings down fire and brimstone on the audience would have done so "with some short warning to all other nations to take heed" (39).

Even if the destruction of Sodom were narrated, however, the fact that it and the others projected in TMS were such large-scale affairs would have violated the spirit of Greek drama, a genre to which Milton, I believe, was essentially committed in the 1640s. While the extent of that influence is debated by scholars, the evidence tends to favor his preference for tragedy by the late 1630s.[3] For one thing, by the time he started the plans, the poet had already begun editing his copy of Euripides' plays, which he had purchased in 1634. Also, Matthew Steggle has recently made a compelling case that *Comus* was influenced in part by Greek drama, and contains at least five Greek features: a prologue, stichomythia, an agon, a *deus ex machina*, and an epilogue.[4] Furthermore, not only does *The Reason of Church-Government* (*RCG* hereafter) adduce Euripides and Sophocles as exemplary public authors, one TMS sketch, "Abias Thersaeus," alters its biblical source (1 Kings 14), with the result that the projected play would have contained a plot twist somewhat reminiscent of *Oedipus the King*.[5] Moreover, in the plans for tragedies, Milton employs Greek phrases such as "epitasis," which refers to the part of the play that develops the main action and leads to the catastrophe, and "prologizei," which denominates the first speaker of a play. He also considered, as possible titles for his Samson play, "Samson Hybristes." Parker points out, " 'Hybristes' means one who is violent through the pride of strength or passion.' The specific reference is vague, but the title shows a definite sympathy with Greek tragedy."[6]

To be sure, although Milton wanted to emulate classical dramaturgy he was also willing to modify its strictures for his own purposes. In his remarks in *RCG* on epic conventions Milton wonders "whether the rules of Aristotle [regarding epic] are strictly to be kept, or nature [that is, the poet's genius] to be followed, which in them that know art and use judgment is no transgression, but an enriching of art."[7] Milton cites examples of "pure" classical epics, including works composed by Homer, Virgil, and Tasso, as well as the book of Job. Thus, the fact that Milton was wavering between writing an orthodox Aristotelian epic and one that departed from classical rules raises the possibility that he was approaching tragedy with a similar frame of mind. He may have intended to follow classical rules for tragedians, while being ready to ignore and transcend them whenever his eye for innovation was so compelled. Even so, it is worth noting that just two years after *RCG* was published, *Of Education* appeared, in 1644; it cites *The Poetics* as the best guide to composition of true tragedy. And of course *The Poetics* is central to the prefatory epistle for *Samson Agonistes*. Hence, Aristotle's authority for Milton seems to have increased the longer he lived.

However, such respect for *The Poetics* apparently created a problem for Milton. On the one hand, his loyalty to Aristotle and the Greek playwrights compelled him to make a serious effort to follow the unities, a commitment that many of the plans evidence. On the other hand, his desire for a large-scale, impressive disaster would have been unclassical since Greek drama contains little on-stage violence, and is almost completely lacking in big catastrophes. Furthermore, many of the biblical calamities in TMS take place in more than one location, and frequently occur over long periods of time. The Deluge is an obvious example, involving 40 days of rain, but many of the other Old Testament plots, though occurring in less than 24 hours, and thus technically unified in terms of time, would nonetheless involve protracted catastrophes. Such extenuated climaxes would be much less effective than the tight, focused fourth acts characteristic of Greek drama. Moreover, it would be difficult to incorporate an effective peripety into such a plot, even though for Aristotle the best plots are complex, involving stunning reversals. Milton may have begun to solve this problem while writing and reworking the TMS plot outlines, and possibly achieved the final solution when he settled on the Samson narrative. I shall take up this matter below when I discuss the Sodom plans. First, however, it is necessary to provide an idea of how the TMS plans function as a site of experimentation, one in which the poet first set down ideas, and then subsequently turned to practical staging matters. The Fall sketches and the speech(es) for a tragedy on the Fall provide the best example of this process. The sketches consist of two tables of characters (TMS 35), a five-act outline entitled "Paradise Lost" (TMS 35), and a prose synopsis initially entitled "Adam's Banishment," then scratched out and replaced with "Adam Unparadised" (40). The tables appear in the manuscript as follows:

Michael. Heavenly Love	Moses or Divine Wisdom
	Michael [or?] Justice. Mercy
Chorus of Angels	Heavenly Love
Lucifer	The Evening Star Hesperus
Adam	Chorus of Angels
with the serpent	Lucifer
Eve	Adam
Conscience	Eve
Death	Conscience
	Death
Labor	Labor
Sickness	Sickness
Discontent mutes	Discontent mutes
Ignorance	Ignorance

with others	Fear
Faith	Death
Hope	Faith
Charity	Hope
	Charity

Milton drew a line in the left column extending from Labor to "with others." Each figure enclosed by this line he classified as a mute. Similarly, the right column has a line extending from Labor to Death (that is, the Death that is listed most closely to the bottom of the page) that groups the mute characters. Both tables are crossed out in the manuscript. The words Michael, Divine, and the first listing of Death are also struck out in the right table.

While it is possible that the right column was written before the left one, in all probability Milton entered it later, for Fear and Death appear in the list of mutes in the right column, thus apparently fulfilling the promise in the first table that "other [mutes]" would be offered. The right list also includes "The Evening Star Hesperus," which does not appear in the left one. Moreover, in the left list, Heavenly Love was almost certainly an afterthought, for it is wedged in between Michael and the chorus of angels. In the right list, however, it is part of the main column. The tables list the persons and indicate the order in which each would enter. The order of appearance is more evident in the third sketch, "Paradise Lost."[8]

That the order of entrances in *Paradise Lost* was uppermost in Milton's mind while composing this draft is evident not only from its act divisions, but also by the outline he provides for Moses' prologue speech. The patriarch claims that because he was on Mt. Sinai with God, his body did not suffer corruption like all other human bodies, save those of Enoch and Elijah, who also may have visited with or at least beheld Yahweh. While on Sinai, Moses was able to see "with the sight of God," which enabled him to witness Adam and Eve in their naked, prelapsarian state. The speech thus explains how he could have written about events that predated his earthly existence, and also informs audiences that they cannot see Adam and Eve "in the state of innocence" because of "their [the audience's] sin," which clouds their spiritual perception.

At first, Milton seems to have envisioned Adam and Eve entering fairly early in the drama since in the original table, they constitute the fourth and fifth persons, respectively; likewise, the fact that they appear "with the serpent" suggests that they enter just before the Fall. It would seem, then, that at this point Milton imagined the Temptation as an on-stage event. The serpent is omitted from the second table, however, and Adam and Eve arrive somewhat later, perhaps after they have eaten the apple. In "Paradise Lost," they first arrive in act 4, and, according to the sketch, somehow appear "fallen." As he deferred the protagonists' entrances more and more with each successive draft, Milton projected various non-dramatic effects to fill up the time until they arrived. Thus, in *Paradise Lost* the angel chorus sings a "hymn of the creation" as well as the "marriage song" to celebrate Adam and Eve's offstage nuptials; they also describe Paradise — it too would be inaccessible to fallen spectators — and "[relate] Lucifer's rebellion and fall." The fourth draft, "Adam Unparadised," offers more narrative. It consists of a prose conspectus, with no explicit act divisions, although it does contain five long sentences, as well as specific stage directions.

Following the pattern of the prior Fall material, Adam and Eve's entrance in "Adam Unparadised" is put off until what may be the fourth act, occurring in the conspectus's fourth sentence out of five. Upon entering, their postlapsarian status is stressed: "man next and Eve having by this time been seduced by the serpent." A stage direction notes that they arrive "confusedly covered with leaves"; clearly, this action constitutes a hasty attempt to conceal their newly discovered nakedness. Before their arrival, a considerable amount of material is related by the angel chorus and by Gabriel, who is the chief angelic guard of Paradise and the audience's sole source for information on the physical layout of Eden, on Lucifer's rebellion and battle against the forces of heaven, on the creation of Eve, and on the marriage of Adam and Eve. When Gabriel first arrives in Eden, he "traces" it, either by walking around it or flying over it. The archangel then returns to the gate where the angel chorus is stationed. Because they have to remain at their post, and thus cannot enter the Garden, the other angels ask Gabriel to tell them "what he knew of man as the creation of Eve with their love, and marriage." Thus, the chorus functions as a surrogate for the off-stage audience, who are also unable to see into the Garden.

The blocking in this draft is problematic for at least two reasons. First, because the projected play would be set at Eden's gate, the couple's post-Fall entrance would be quite brief, lasting just long enough for the audience to witness them in their guilty state as they leave the Garden momentarily. They would then have to exit hastily in order to go back to meet with Jehovah, who has called to them from the Garden. Meanwhile, the chorus "entertains the stage," a phrase that suggests a kind of perfunctory diversion, in contrast to the unseen action taking place behind the scenes. Also, the only suspense offered in such a play would be the near-fight between Lucifer and the chorus of angels, a conflict that is averted when Lucifer, for some unspecified reason, exits.

The biggest problem raised by this draft is the deferral of Adam and Eve's entrance. Why did Milton delay their appearance if his models were the Greeks, who usually present the protagonists early? Anthony Low suggests that he did so because of the "impossibility in a staged tragedy . . . of bringing in [the principals] before the Fall since they are naked."[9] Milton seems to have recognized and dealt with the difficulty by the third draft. In the first sketch, and possibly in the second as well, they clearly enter prior to the Fall; in fact, as we saw, the first one may have included a scene of the actual Temptation, since Adam, or Eve, or perhaps both, enter "with the serpent." In the third sketch, however, the two arrive "fallen," possibly wearing fig leaves, and in the fourth, they come on stage "confusedly covered with leaves."

Low suggests that Milton was initially preoccupied with plot and characterization, and only later considered matters of staging in the second two drafts. John Leonard, however, contends that the poet had staging in mind from the start, and argues that Milton probably planned to have the actors wear "flesh-coloured robes when he prepared his first outline for a Fall tragedy." As noted, the poet may have attended puppet shows as a child; their plots were derived from mystery plays. This experience could also have provided him with some hints about the staging of medieval plays, including the body-stockings common in such productions. By the time he composed the later drafts, according to Leonard, the poet had "escape[d] the absurdity of [such robes]."[10] It may be that Milton grew disenchanted with such costumes because of their artificiality. In a well-known remark from *Areopagitica,* composed in 1644, perhaps about the time when he was rethinking the early drafts for the Fall tragedy, Milton castigates those who criticize God for bestowing freedom of choice on Adam: "Many there be that complain of divine Providence for suffering Adam to transgress. Foolish tongues! when God gave him reason, he gave him freedom to choose, for reason is but choosing; he had been else a mere artificial Adam, such an Adam as he is in the motions [puppet shows]" (YP 2:527).

Might he have developed a similar contempt for body-suits? Such costuming perhaps struck him as too constrictive, literally and figuratively, to convey the psychological depth he hoped to instill in the protagonists. For one of the most remarkable qualities of the Fall sketches, especially *Paradise Lost* and "Adam Unparadised," is that they flesh out the skeletal narrative of Genesis 3 by showing our grand parents grappling with conflicting emotions as they seek to understand the effects of the Fall. By contrast, there is no suggestion of such a protracted repentance in Genesis; indeed, the reader is not even given a hint of Adam or Eve's state of mind after the curses are spoken. God questions them, declares them guilty, states the curses, then banishes them from the Garden. In the parallel scene in "Adam Unparadised" the two remain unrepentant even after that encounter. They then begin accusing one another, with Adam "especially laying the blame to his wife." At this point,

Justice and Reason appear to Adam, and while they manage to get him to confess, his contrition is not heartfelt. Hence, the chorus follows up in order to "admonish Adam, and bid him beware by Lucifer's example of impenitence." Even that is not enough, however, for the (unnamed) angel who is sent to banish Adam "causes to pass before his eyes a masque of all the evils of this life and world." After seeing it, Adam "is humbled [and] relents," then lapses into the sinful state of despair. Only when Mercy appears, comforts him, promises the Messiah, and calls in Faith, Hope and Charity, does Adam truly repent.

Perhaps Milton felt that such a welter of emotions would have been conveyed more effectively with realistic costuming than with mere robes. The stage direction of the fourth draft, in which Adam and Eve enter "confusedly covered with leaves," suggests a move towards such naturalism. Similarly, it is possible that the poet omitted the serpent after the first draft because rudimentary animal costumes, such as the type used in the 1634 *Comus* production, would not have been able to convey the subtleties of a snake possessed by superhuman intelligence. Alternatively, the serpent's omission may have resulted from Milton's decision to delay the humans' entrance until after the Temptation.

In any event, the problem of nudity was solved when he turned to epic, thereby allowing himself the freedom to represent his subjects in relatively precise, lavish detail. In *Paradise Lost*, Adam and Eve appear in their naked, pre-Fall glory, though not immodestly. Indeed, Charles Lamb praised the poet's tact in depicting that nakedness indirectly. And the serpent's representation is, of course, one of the work's most compelling features. The variety, force, and precision of Milton's epic descriptions have been justly celebrated by critics and artists alike, and may be due, in part, to the elation he felt when he escaped from the confines of the stage for the greater scope afforded by the epic, a genre bounded only by his powers of description and the reader's imagination.

Still, it took time for him to come to grips with the problems of staging, and not all obstacles were confronted in the course of the revisions of the TMS outlines. Some appear to have been worked out in a speech he composed in the 1640s, after the TMS plans. This speech is a soliloquy for Satan, and would have been the first one in a tragedy based on the Fall. This speech is clearly related to the manuscript's projected dramas on the Fall, yet its finished quality contrasts with the roughness that characterizes the plans. According to the antiquarian John Aubrey (1626–97), "In the [4th] book of Paradise Lost there are about 6 verses of Satan's exclamation to the sun, which Mr. E. Phillips remembers about 15 or 16 years before ever his Poem was thought of; which verses were intended for the beginning of a tragedy, which he had designed, but was diverted from by other business." Similarly, Edward Phillips's 1694 biography of his uncle states that

> the height of his noble fancy and invention began now to be seriously and mainly employed in a subject worthy of such a Muse, viz., a heroic poem, entitled *Paradise Lost*. . . . This subject was first designed a tragedy, and in the fourth book of the poem there are six verses, which several years before the poem was begun, were shown to me and some others, as designed for the very beginning of the said tragedy. The verses are these:
>
> > O thou that with surpassing glory crown'd!
> > Look'st from thy sole dominion, like the god
> > Of this new world; at whose sight all the stars
> > Hide their diminish'd heads; to thee I call,
> > But with no friendly voice; and add thy name,
> > O Sun! to tell thee how I hate thy beams
> > That bring to my remembrance, from what state
> > I fell, how glorious once above thy sphere;
> > Till pride and worse ambition threw me down,
> > Warring in Heaven, against Heaven's glorious king.

Most Milton scholars believe that the speech was probably written around 1642 or 1643, likely dates given Aubrey's remark that it was composed "15 or 16 years" before Milton began work in earnest on *Paradise Lost* about 1658. It is ten lines long, set in blank verse, and was eventually incorporated wholesale into *Paradise Lost* 4.32–41.[11] Internal evidence confirms that the speech was written after the Fall outlines: for instance, it differs from them in that the speech would open the projected tragedy, whereas in the TMS entries Satan does not appear until the third act (or its equivalent moment in the fourth draft); also, in TMS the devil is always referred to as Lucifer, never as Satan.

Certain difficulties raised by the devil's characterization in the Fall sketches are solved by the speech. For one thing, it is not evident in "Adam Unparadised" where the fiend would stand in order to "[bemoan] himself and [seek] revenge on man." It is likely that the bemoaning would have been intended to reveal his true thoughts, for according to the draft he would voice his outrage after being thrown down from heaven. Yet unless Milton envisioned him alighting in a locale other than just outside of Eden, Satan would be too close to the angel chorus, and perhaps Gabriel as well, for that speech to constitute a genuine, or for that matter, a plausible, honest, soliloquy. In the address to the Sun, however, Milton makes it clear that the devil is completely alone: he would be the first character on stage and would speak his lines before any other personage arrives. Also, the speech emphasizes the devil's former state, when he was still known as Lucifer, or light-bearer, and contrasts that condition with his current one. As noted earlier, throughout the Fall sketches the devil is referred to only as Lucifer. In the process of composing the speech, it is plausible that Milton looked over or remembered the Fall drafts, realized the incongruity of referring to a fallen, diminished angel as a "light-bearer," and changed it in the epic. In addition to this one, several other passages in *Paradise Lost* hint at such a revaluation: in book 5 the narrator refers to "Satan, so call him now, [for] his former name / Is heard no more in Heav'n" (5.658–59); later, the narrator mentions Pandaemonium, that "city and proud seat / Of Lucifer, so by allusion called, / Of that bright star to Satan paragoned" (10.424–26). And in book 7, when Raphael is telling Adam about the devil, he at one point calls him "Lucifer," remarking to Adam that he does so because the fallen angel was "brighter once amidst the host / Of angels, than that star the stars among" (132–33).

Does Satan's speech constitute the extent of Milton's work on a Fall play apart from the TMS outlines? Both Phillips's and Aubrey's use of the term "designed" to explain what the poet intended is ambiguous and could refer to nothing other than the TMS plans and the speech. Francis Peck, however, suspected that the poet composed additional material. In 1740 he wrote, "I cannot help thinking that, beside the bare plans, he also wrote a good deal of the Drama itself (perhaps all)." Voltaire, in a 1732 essay, claimed that the poet had seen Giovanni Andreini's comic play *L'Adamo* in either Florence or Milan, and added that in 1638 Milton "conceived the design of making a tragedy of Andreini's farce; he even composed one act and a half. I was assured of this fact by some men of letters who had it from his daughter." And in 1966, Allan Gilbert noted, "Considering Milton's interest in the [Fall] over many years, it is hard to believe that he had not produced a good deal of manuscript. Is it not likely that in the 'several years' between Phillips's sight of the ten lines and Milton's first work on the epic, much of the tragedy, or even all of it, was written according to the fifth plan? But we can only infer."[12] If a separate manuscript for such a play is extant, we have yet to discover it.

Another intriguing possibility is that this play is not lost, at least not entirely, but incorporated into *Paradise Lost*. Gilbert cites two passages from the epic, originally noted by C. S. Lewis, that seem to have been written for the stage. The first is Satan's remark at 4.36–37: "and add thy name / O sun." The phrase is somewhat redundant in the epic, since the narrator's prior remark, "his grieved looks he fixes sad, /. . . towards heav'n and the full-blazing sun" (28–29), makes it clear who is being addressed. Lewis also mentions Satan's speech at the beginning of book 9, where the fiend notes that he is hiding from the angels guarding Eden:

> Of these [angels guarding Eden] the vigilance
> I dread, and to elude, thus wrapped in mist
> Of midnight vapor glide obscure, and pry
> In every bush and brake, where hap may find
> The serpent sleeping.   (157–61)

These lines seem to constitute, among other things, a hint about Satan's costume, particularly the reference to the mist. They function as embedded stage directions, telling us not only what the fiend wears, but also how he moves and what he does as he glides through the garden. However, such information repeats what the narrator had already told us, both in the Argument ("Satan . . . returns as a mist by night into Paradise") and at 9.75 (Satan is described as "involved in rising mist"), suggesting that the phrase "thus wrapped in mist" could be a vestige from the stage.

A third passage, also from book 9, is cited by Lewis but not by Gilbert. It is not clear if Gilbert omitted it because he found it less compelling than the other two or simply overlooked it. In it, Satan, now having entered the serpent, spies Eve from afar and then exults: "behold alone / The woman, opportune to all attempts, / Her husband, for I view far round, not nigh, / Whose higher intellectual more I shun" (480–83). For Lewis, the phrase "I view far round," suggests the stage.[13] He does not say why, but perhaps he means that the phrase would have forestalled any potentially awkward business involved with a snake costume, such as the rotation of its head or eyes when peering around. Instead of risking an inadvertently comic effect, an actor playing the snake would simply tell the audience what he was doing. However, the epic narrator's long prefatory description to Satan's soliloquy notes, among other things, that the fiend

> sought them [Adam and Eve] both, but wished his hap might find
> Eve separate; he wished, but not with hope
> Of what so seldom chanced, when to his wish,
> Beyond his hope, Eve separate he spies,
> Veiled in a cloud of fragrance. (421–25)

The narrator also notes that the serpent took pleasure in viewing "This flow'ry plat, the sweet recess of Eve / Thus early, thus alone" (456–57). In other words, Satan has already ascertained that Adam is not on the premises, so his remark that he "view[s] far round" feels redundant. Like "wrapped in mist," it too may be left over from a stage version.

Given Phillips's and Aubrey's statements about the speech at 4.32–42, Lewis is obviously correct in identifying a stage origin for the address to the sun. The book 9 passages, however, are harder to assess. The fact that Milton was willing to transplant wholesale the book 4 speech from tragedy to epic raises the possibility that he did so with others as well. If so, it would appear that he composed lines not just for the tragedy's opening scene, but for two others as well: the action leading up to Satan's possession of the snake, and the Temptation. Regarding the latter, we noted earlier that the first draft of the projected Fall tragedy seems to indicate that Milton was initially planning on staging the Temptation. Perhaps he composed lines for the scene. If he did so for either that episode or for Satan's possession of the snake, then the conjectures voiced by Peck, Voltaire, and Gilbert about Milton completing all or part of a Fall tragedy, would seem more plausible, and would help to account for the common reaction that *Paradise Lost* often feels like a drama. That is, this impression might stem not only from the fact that it was first conceived of as a play, but also because Milton composed a Fall drama and put some of its lines, essentially unchanged, into the epic. Grant McColley refers to the completed drama as the poet's "lost tragedy," but it may not be completely lost, since we may read entire lines from it every time we peruse books 4 and 9.[14]

In addition, it might be significant that Satan's possession of the serpent in *Paradise Lost* seems indebted to stage costuming. For instance, just prior to the Temptation, the narrator notes that the fiend "with serpent tongue / Organic or impulse of vocal air / His fraudulent temptation thus began" (9.529–31). Commenting on these lines, Gordon Teskey notes, "Satan emits sound through the serpent either by using the serpent's tongue or by emitting pulses of air, which make sound by vibrating in the elongated tube of the serpent's body."[15] As previously noted, Milton probably had no first-hand experience with any of the mystery plays, yet he could have witnessed the performance of *Comus,* which did feature animal costumes, some of which might have been similarly operated by the actors whenever they wished to make vocal sounds. Such exposure could have influenced him as he composed lines for the Temptation scene.

If Milton composed all or part of a Fall tragedy, this fact would go a long way towards explaining one of the central debates in Milton studies, namely, the question as to why Satan feels like the hero of the diffuse epic. This impression might have come about if Milton, so to speak, promoted Satan from chief villain, as he is in the TMS plans, to tragic protagonist of a play. As we noted, in "Adam Unparadised," Lucifer appears only twice, first when he enters and "bemoans himself, [and] seeks revenge on man," and again, boasting about his ruin of mankind. What is more, the second entrance is provisional: "here again *may* appear Lucifer." By contrast, in the (projected) tragedy, he is no longer Lucifer, but Satan, and he is the first to enter and speak. His speech, which alludes to his fall from a glorious state, accords with Aristotle's definition of a tragic hero. And judging from this opening speech, Satan seems poised to play a prominent, even central, role in the tragedy.

Such a prior promotion, before Milton turned to epic, could help account for Satan's tremendous appeal and charisma in *Paradise Lost*. The effect could have been comparable to transplanting a figure as compelling as Shakespeare's Macbeth or Richard III from tragedy to epic, then trying vainly to contain or offset their energy and charisma with narrative comments, and/or by fashioning good characters to counter them, characters who would inevitably fail to do so convincingly because, unlike Satan, they themselves would not have first been fully conceived and fleshed out for a tragedy.[16]

On the other hand, if in TMS Milton had already worked to overcome the problems inherent in nude protagonists and a potentially comic snake, why would he reintroduce such difficulties in a post-TMS composition? It may be that he intended to show only the devil's possession of the serpent, with the Temptation kept off-stage, though as Gilbert points out, "to write a dramatic [version of the Fall] without showing the taking of the fruit seems like playing all around the main action without actually touching it."[17] Perhaps Milton first needed to compose a significant portion of the tragedy before realizing that the snake would have presented staging obstacles; in fact, this problem may have dawned on him precisely when he composed the line about the serpent "viewing far around." Perhaps, too, it was only then that he fully recognized the problem of having the main action off-stage, a realization that could have prevented him from completing the projected tragedy.

II. *The Search for an Impressive Catastrophe: The Sodom Sketches*

Like the Fall plans and Satan's speech, the Sodom material evinces Milton's progress as a dramatist. For one thing, it amplifies both the theme and imagery of the Ludlow masque. According to J. M. French, the sketch's allusions to Venus, Urania, Peor, Ganymede, and lust in general "relate [it] closely to that of *Comus*," and Michael Lieb declares that "In many respects, [the projected Sodom play] is first enacted in *Comus*, after which its themes find even greater elaboration as Milton develops the distinctions between love and lust elsewhere in his work."[18] The Sodom sketch also demonstrates his growing awareness of what would and would not work on stage. As with "Adam Unparadised," the Sodom play would have been impeded by a staging obstacle; in this case, it was the tragedy's projected catastrophe. Despite Milton's attempts to solve this problem, his eventual decision to dramatize the Samson narrative, rather than Sodom, may have been due in part to the fact that the destruction of Dagon's temple was, dramatically, a far more effective catastrophe.

Judging from the way he titles the Sodom sketch in TMS, it appears that the city's obliteration was uppermost in Milton's mind:

Sodom. The scene before Lot's gate.
The title: Cupid's Funeral Pile. Sodom Burning.

In Hebrew "Sodom" means "burnt," which implies that the city's destruction was so complete that the very memory of its original name was obliterated in fire and brimstone. Hence, by subtitling the sketch "Sodom Burning," Milton alludes to the etymology of the city's name. The title also functions as a double entendre, of course, referring at once to the citizens' lust and the literal conflagration at the end of the play.

This tragedy would have observed unity of time, for it opens in the evening with Lot's shepherds waiting for him to return from his walk "towards the city gates" and would end, apparently, the next day after he and his family exit. Unity of place is indicated by the stage direction "the scene before Lot's gate." Genesis 19:1–3 suggests that Lot's house was right next to the city gates, for he is sitting "in the gateways of Sodom" when he first sees the angels approach, at which point he invites them to "turn aside" and spend the night at his house. By contrast, Milton calls for two separate gates, with Lot's as the on-stage location and the city gates as off-stage. Various lines indicate this intention: for instance, at the start of the projected play, the shepherds would have waited for Lot to return home, which he does, accompanied by the angels. And the first chorus narrates the "course of the city each evening," with the citizenry serenading one another, picnicking, or boating on the Jordan. Furthermore, Lot has to exit the scene to go and warn his friends and sons-in-law about the city's imminent destruction.

At the same time, it is difficult to determine whether unity of action is maintained in the sketch. William R. Parker argues that "[it] gives . . . no indication of that fine concentration, that strict unity of action, which is characteristic of the best Attic dramas and which Milton imitated successfully in *Samson Agonistes*." Anthony Low, however, contends that "Milton's concern for the most important unity — the action — is confirmed by the tight structure of the fuller plot summaries [in TMS]."[19] Parker bases his contention partly on the fact that the projected drama would have had many characters on stage, including Lot, his shepherds and the rest of his "serviture," as well as the "whole assembly" of Sodomites returning from the temple. Yet Milton would have grouped at least some of the personae into two, perhaps even three, choruses: the shepherds constitute the "first chorus" and the angels a second. The

citizenry may be united chorically as well, for they "pass by in pro-
cession with music and song" on their way to the temple. Multiple
choruses, though rare in Greek drama, are not unheard of: Euripides'
Hippolytus calls for a chorus of huntsmen in addition to the main
chorus, while Aristophanes' *Frogs* uses a secondary chorus.[20] Hence,
it may be that in the sketch Milton wanted to justify the large groups
of people in terms of classical staging, although the "assembly" who
threaten to attack Lot's house comprises the entirety of the city's
population and are not grouped in any apparent way.

While no directions for the shepherds' costumes are provided,
they most likely would have looked ordinary so as not to upstage
the entrance of Lot and his two visitors, who appear young and "of
noble form." Milton expands on Genesis by figuring the visitors
as both youthful and comely. He also would have depicted at least
some of the Sodomites as handsome, which is exemplified by the
emissary sent to the angels that is composed of "2 of their choic-
est youth." Clearly the citizens hope that the beauty of these
young men will entice the visitors to attend the festival. The strategy does not work, of course, yet the angels pity the youths for their
"beauty" and debate with them of "love and how it differs from
lust," seeking to "win them," not carnally, but by persuading them
to righteous conduct.

Milton attempted two versions of the catastrophe, suggesting
that he was uncertain whether to narrate or depict it. In the first,
he simply notes that "the angels do the deed with all dreadful execution," adding that the King of Sodom and his nobles "come
forth" from the (off-stage) city square and "set out the terror" of
the city's destruction. This version concludes with a chorus of angels
who relate "the events of Lot's journey, and of his wife" — the latter, of course, is turned to salt when she turns around for a final
look at the city. A second account, contained in a ten-line description, was added later to the original sketch. In it, as "fiery
thunders" begin "aloft" — perhaps as a sound effect — a single
angel enters "all girt with flames" in a costume reminiscent of Inigo
Jones's spirit masquers. The angel explains that he is wearing "the

true flames of love." Here too the scene takes place at the city's edge, and again, the King enters to describe what is happening off-stage. Yet Milton now emphasizes the monarch's dread, indicating in a stage direction that he "falls down with terror." He also adds one, or perhaps two other figures, sons-in-law to Lot, who also come on stage shrinking in horror. After upbraiding these men for not listening to Lot's warnings, the angel calls to the thunder, lightning and fire to come and "destroy a godless nation," and then "brings [the elements] down," perhaps by gesturing to the (stage) heavens. Or, if the angel himself initially appears in the heavens on a cloud-machine, he might "bring down" the lightning and fire himself, somewhat like Jupiter's descent in *Cymbeline*'s inset masque, which is characterized by the god hurling bolts of lightning.

This second version constitutes a partially symbolic depiction of the catastrophe, particularly in the angel's costume, whose blazing appearance seems at once to anticipate the approaching holocaust and to personify it. In like manner, the cringing men may represent the entirety of the Sodom population. Milton might have chosen this symbolic mode of presentation because a full scale, realistic staging of the disaster would have been too expensive and difficult, while a narrated catastrophe, strictly speaking, would have been impossible. After all, Milton could not even invent an effective nuntius eyewitness, as employed in *Samson Agonistes*, for anyone who looked directly at the blazing city would suffer the same fate Lot's wife did. An angelic eyewitness of the destruction might be possible, yet an angel would not experience the terror of the catastrophe as a human would, and thus would not serve as a fully sympathetic messenger.

Having stage fire and lightning "fall" on a few trembling figures seems to be a compromise, yet such a scene would come off as rather incongruous, even anticlimactic, compared to the vivid pageantry and energy that characterize the tragedy's earlier action. Furthermore, such an ending would potentially be comic, especially if the avenging angel was himself engulfed in the flames. Milton notes that the angel's warning to his off-stage audience to heed the lesson of Sodom is a "short" one, suggesting that the angel has just a few seconds to blurt it out before the brimstone rains down.

As I noted earlier, the Sodom sketch is one of 26 (out of 61) TMS plots that end with a large-scale disaster. Others include "The Taking of Jerusalem," which would have shown the torching of the holy city at the hands of one "Nabuzaradan"; "The Massacre in Horeb," which would have depicted God destroying the disobedient faction of Israelites; "The Murmurers," which would have ended similarly; and "Corah Dathan &c," which would have shown Korah and the other schismatics being swallowed by the earth. Again, however, big disaster scenes were unknown in classical theater. Parker observes that "in thirteen different Greek tragedies . . . a corpse is exhibited on the stage," yet none of the ancient tragedies represents the obliteration of an entire city or population.[21] A large-scale catastrophe would require too many on-stage personages and would constitute a flagrant violation of the convention of keeping violence offstage. Furthermore, such an effect would be far too difficult and costly to stage. Nonetheless, as noted previously, Milton was apparently attracted to cataclysmic endings because he was determined to provide impressive object lessons for the English nation. Some version of the angel's warning at the end of the Sodom tragedy — the sketch concludes as "he [the angel] brings them [i.e., fire and brimstone] down with some short warning to all other nations to take heed" — would doubtlessly have been spoken at the end of many of the plays sketched out in TMS. It is important to remember, first, that the poet wanted to reach not just individual theatergoers but a national audience; and second, that he wished to teach them virtue. Plots that portrayed the demise of a considerably large group of people would most effectively mirror the sins and potential doom of an entire nation. It was not enough, moreover, to have a large on-stage cast to reflect the sizeable off-stage audiences Milton hoped for. Because he intended for his Sodom tragedy to serve as an object lesson, he needed to find a way to render the grim, remote narrative of Genesis 19 somewhat recognizable, even superficially appealing. He seems to have done so in one of the Sodom sketches' most striking features, to wit, its updating and familiarizing of the city, which was transformed into one that suggests early modern Florence or Milan. While Genesis figures the citizenry (excepting Lot) as a lust-crazed mob, the Sodom tragedy would have represented them as beautiful gallants who sing and strum guitars. Also, the fact that not all the citizens in Milton's Sodom are pederasts — some consort with mistresses rather than boys — might have softened the picture of Sodom to its anticipated audience. So, too, would the depiction of them as being at least superficially hospitable to strangers. For instance, in Genesis 19:4 the entire city shows up to demand sex from the two strangers, while in Milton's sketch the emissaries from Sodom "invite them to their city solemnities."

Yet the difficulties of bringing off the catastrophe may have finally prevented Milton from further development of the Sodom tragedy. These challenges may also help to explain, in part, why he eventually chose the Samson narrative. The usual reasons adduced for that selection — the author's blindness, marital troubles, and general interest in the Samson tale in his prose — have been explored at length by scholars. And yet, to my knowledge, no one has yet advanced the argument that the Samson narrative also appealed to him from a formal standpoint, by providing the basis for a swift, compact catastrophe.

Four of the TMS titles are in fact based on the Samson narrative. Milton probably jotted down "Samson in Ramath Lechi" first in the manuscript's right-hand column, then "Dagonalia" below it. He then seems to have added, in the manuscript's left hand column, "Samson pursophorus or Hybristes," and then, above the title "Samson in Ramath Lechi," the alternate title, "[Samson] marriing" (TMS 36). These titles refer to at least four distinct episodes from the Samson narrative, including his victory over the Philistines, recounted in Judges 15:14–17, in which he slays one thousand men with a donkey's jawbone; his wedding feast, described in 14:15–20; the festival of the Philistines in honor of Dagon, set forth in 16:23–31; and Samson's burning of the Philistines' crops by tying torches to the tails of 300 foxes, then letting them into the grain fields (15:1–8).

In *Samson Agonistes*, the foxfire episode is omitted. Parker rightly points out that "the whole grotesque affair of the foxes (as Milton later must have realized) is unworthy of a true hero of tragedy. Milton's Samson had his faults, but they were not subheroic."[22] However, the wedding feast and the jawbone episode are referred to during Samson's agon with Harapha. Most notably, the Dagonalia is incorporated into the play, though as a narrated event rather than a staged one. Still, the catastrophe is aurally, if not visually, present — even though it occurs off-stage, we "hear" the crash of the pillars, the fall of the roof, and the cries of the trapped victims. Milton thus has it both ways: the disaster occurs backstage yet feels at hand. By comparison, the offstage aspects of the conflagration in the projected Sodom play seem vague.

Perhaps the biggest advantage, dramatically, to the Samson tale is that, unlike nearly all the other biblical plots considered in TMS, the entire disaster of the tale occurs in a few moments, both in Judges 16 and in the tragedy, even though it involves the deaths of thousands. As the Hebrew Messenger narrates it, with the possible exception of the moderate lords, the entire city of Gaza is present at the Dagonalia, and all, save the vulgar, are killed almost immediately, "all in a moment overwhelmed and fallen" (1559). This catastrophe is thus unified, and hence far more dramatically impressive, than the traditional firing of a city, which as we saw could take hours, even days, to accomplish. The catastrophe's brevity constitutes the ideal Aristotelian peripety described in the opening sentence of *Poetics* 11: "A Peripety is the change of the kind described from one state of things within the play to its opposite."[23] At the same time, given the large number of those killed, the catastrophe would have provided a terrifying cautionary tale to Milton's hoped-for national audience.

The only other biblical plot listed in TMS that involves a nearly instantaneous catastrophe is Korah's rebellion (Num. 16), in which he and his kin are swallowed up by the earth in a moment (16:32).

Why Milton chose Samson's tale instead of Korah's is unclear. The poet may have felt more personal affinities with Samson than he did with Korah, though it is also possible that Korah's destruction was simply not impressive enough for the kind of tragedy he envisioned. After all, the doom of Korah and his people is prophesied by Moses to the rest of the Jews, giving the innocent ample time to move away from the tents of the schismatics, so the disaster is not much of a surprise. Moreover, the smiting of evildoers by falling roofs is somewhat of a motif for Milton. Just as the Lady's threat to Comus, to bring down his "magic structures reared so high, /. . . into heaps o'er his false head" (798–99), forecasts the destruction of Dagon's temple.

Conversely, the fall of Jericho does not appear in the TMS plans, even though the walls of the city come down the moment the Israelites blow their horns and shout (Josh. 6:20). However, the walls' demolition does not seem to kill everyone within; instead, it exposes the city to the Jewish troops, who rush in and slaughter every person and animal, save Rahab the prostitute and her family. That process seems to have taken some time, perhaps too long to serve as a unified catastrophe.

Finally, it is worth noting that in addition to the Samson titles, some of the other TMS material may have influenced the composition of *Samson Agonistes*. "Gideon pursuing Jud. 8" is echoed when the Chorus answer Samson's complaint about not receiving aid from his countrymen:

> Thy words to my remembrance bring
> How Succoth and the fort of Penuel
> Their great deliverer contemned,
> The matchless *Gideon in pursuit*
> Of Madian and her vanquished kings.   (277–81; my emphasis)

There may also be an indirect influence on Samson's characterization from the very brief New Testament sketch "Christus Patiens": "The Scene in the garden beginning from the coming thither till Judas betrays and the officers lead him away the rest by message and chorus. His agony may receive noble expressions" (411). Several parallels between this sketch and the tragedy are evident, such as that Samson is described by the Chorus as a hero of "patience" (1285–96). Also, the use of "agony" may anticipate "Agonistes," especially since the phrase refers here less to Christ's physical sufferings — which would have been depicted primarily in other dominical play topics considered by Milton, such as "Christ bound" and "Christ Crucifi'd" — and more to his spiritual anguish in Gethsemane. It is also worth noting that Jesus' anguish in the garden is referred to in Luke 22:44 as "an agony" in the Authorized Version, which is based on the Greek *agonia*. Moreover, like Samson, Christ is led away by soldiers, and his suffering and death are related by a messenger, as are Samson's. Another possible link between the sketch and the tragedy occurs in the latter's prefatory epistle; it mentions the tragedy *Christ Suffering*, which is, of course, the English translation of "Christus Patiens." The work was held by Milton and others — mistakenly, it is now believed — to have been written by the church father Gregory Nazianzen, bishop of Constantinople.

   Another striking parallel is Milton's characterization of Lot in the Sodom plan, which may have affected the portrait of Samson in the tragedy. Lot's refusal to attend the city's "solemnities" and the Sodomites' violent response to his abstention anticipate the captive's initial unwillingness to take part in the Dagonalia, as well as the Philistines' anger at his stubbornness. Such echoes of the TMS titles and plans in Milton's tragedy are important because they suggest that he may have consulted the plans as he began work on the play, that is, after his blindness had set in. It is possible that his amanuenses — whose handwriting is evident on various pages of the manuscript — read the plans to him when he began the tragedy, probably in the late 1660s. If so, it would seem that the TMS outlines served a two-fold function in Milton's ripening as a dramatist: first, as a site of experimentation, where he could work through practical problems of plot, characterization, and staging; and second, as a repository of themes and motifs to consult when he set about composing *Samson Agonistes*. Because those themes come from a period during which Milton was still hoping to write a play for public performance, they instill his tragedy with many stage qualities.

FOUR

Theatrical Spectacle in *Samson Agonistes*

IMPLICATIONS FOR THE TERRORISM CONTROVERSY AND OTHER INTERPRETIVE DISPUTES

Commentators have never reached consensus about the meaning of one of Milton's declarations in the prefatory epistle to *Samson Agonistes*, where he notes, "Division into Act and Scene referring chiefly to the Stage (to which this work never was intended) is here omitted." Some scholars feel that by removing these divisions, Milton wished to render the work intrinsically unstageable. Such an intention might seem to be confirmed by the dearth of stichomythia and physical action in the tragedy, and by the lengthiness of its speeches. One problem with this line of argument, however, is the abundance of "stage" cues implicit in the tragedy's dialogue. Others argue that "never intended" applied only to the Restoration stage, not to all theaters. Nonetheless, while Milton certainly would have disapproved of Restoration comedies such as William Wycherly's *Love in a Wood* (1671), Robert Hume has recently pointed out that "the 'libertinism' universally ascribed to 'Restoration comedy' . . . is found only in a minority of the comedies of the time, and more often than not the libertine is punished (or reformed and married off) at the end of the play."[1] Furthermore, Milton's attitude toward the Restoration theater seems not to have been completely negative, for in 1674 he granted John Dryden permission to "tag," that is, to put into rhyming couplets, *Paradise Lost*, for an opera called *The State of Innocence*, registered (though never acted) in 1677.

I wish to offer a third possibility, namely, that the tragedy was "never intended" for the stage, not from any fundamental antipathy on Milton's part toward the theater, but because his exposure to the public stage almost certainly ended in 1642 (the year the theaters closed), nearly thirty years before the 1671 publication of *Samson*. Milton went completely blind in 1652, and after the Act of Oblivion (1660) lived a secluded life. None of his early biographers, including John Aubrey, Cyriak Skinner, Anthony à Wood, or Edward Phillips, records any visits by the poet to the Restoration playhouses, nor does Samuel Pepys mention him in his diaries, which frequently describe Pepys's own theater-going.

True, the poet does evince skepticism about theater production earlier in his career. For instance, in an entry in his commonplace book, probably set down about 1637, Milton commends the power of tragedy to evoke virtue, while adding that this effect is possible only from plays that are "rightly produced" (YP 1:491). And, as we saw, the structure of *Comus* was altered for performance by Henry Lawes, who converted part of the original epilogue to a prologue. Milton restored the lines to their original location when he revised the masque in the 1640s, thus indicating his disapproval of the change. The whole experience might have made him wary of stage production. Nonetheless, that distrust was not absolute, as is evident from his granting of permission to Dryden to mount *Paradise Lost*. Hence, I believe that Milton's unwillingness to put *Samson* on stage stemmed principally from his lack of significant personal contact with the theater of his day, and from the fact that he would have had little control over production details. That he conceived the tragedy in terms of the stage is especially clear from its abundance of implicit stage directions embedded in the dialogue. These directions tell us much about the characters' physical appearances, gestures, movements, facial expressions, setting, and scenery.

Even so, scholars have been divided over the importance of spectacle in *Samson*. A significant number tend to downplay or dismiss it. For instance, Radzinowicz claims that the drama is

> stripped of spectacle. The only visual effects from movement available to the mind's eye lies in the approach of the Chorus, their advance toward Samson, and their accompaniment of the other limited characters a short distance away from him. . . . The impression which the overall disposition of the fable gives [is] of having been devised to draw attention to an intellectual conflict within the mind of the protagonist.

Similarly, F. T. Prince argues that "When Milton wants us to visualize a setting, a character, or a movement, he [provides] just as much indication as we need." Anne Ferry declares that Milton "chose a dramatic form which yet avoids . . . the visual effects that a play performed must inevitably have." In like manner, John Shawcross states that "visual image [in *Samson Agonistes*] is not significant," and John Steadman would seemingly concur, remarking that the play is "psychological and spiritual rather than external and physical." Just so, in a 1998 essay Elizabeth Sauer argues that the work is a closet drama that "denies performability."[2]

By contrast, in his seminal study *Milton's Debt to Greek Tragedy*, first published in 1937, William R. Parker argues that many lines in the drama "indicate that [Milton] pictured both the setting and the characters." Moreover, in his introduction to the play in *The Riverside Milton*, Roy Flannagan claims that "Despite Milton's stated desire to avoid the trappings of the stage, [he] does give us some stage directions that tell us what Samson, Dalila, Manoa, and Harapha should look like or do on stage." David Loewenstein has even remarked that the work is "eminently theatrical," and as I show in chapter 5, the tragedy has been produced dozens of times, with several productions prepared in close consultation with scholars: Nevill Coghill mounted the tragedy three times, Dennis Danielson supervised a 1979 performance, and Flannagan oversaw a 2003 partial staging of the play.[3] So in light of these conflicting impressions, the following investigation into the amount and function of spectacle in *Samson Agonistes* is certainly apt. I shall argue (a) that the tragedy offers an abundance of implicit spectacle, particularly in Samson's representation and in the other persons' entrances and exits; (b) that this spectacle is often overlooked or misconstrued by scholars, who have tended to focus almost exclusively on what is said in the tragedy, rather than how the characters look; (c) that the failure to visualize the work has had far-reaching consequences for the interpretation of the tragedy, particularly the debate over whether Samson is a terrorist, as well as the Dalila controversy and the charges that the play is misogynistic or static; and (d) that greater attention to the drama's spectacle sheds light on these and related controversies.[4]

I. Milton's View of Spectacle

The influence of the *Poetics* on *Samson Agonistes* is evident in the drama's original (1671) title page, which quotes, in Greek, the opening words of the famous definition of tragedy from the sixth chapter of the treatise, and in Latin, the opening and closing words of that same definition. Furthermore, the tragedy's epistolary self-defense, "Of that sort of Dramatic Poem which is called Tragedy," echoes the definition in its opening sentence. Milton obviously would have been familiar with Aristotle's remarks on spectacle (*opsis*), a term mentioned seven times in the *Poetics*. The two longest passages pertaining to *opsis* from Ingram Bywater's translation are as follows:

> As [the actors] act the stories, it follows that in the first place the Spectacle (or stage appearance of the actors) must be some part of the whole. . . . The Spectacle, though an attraction, is the least artistic of all the parts, and has least to do with the art of poetry. The tragic effect is quite possible without a public performance and actors; and besides, the getting up of the Spectacle is more a matter for the costumier [*skeuopoios*] than the poet. (6:4,19)

> The tragic fear and pity may be aroused by the Spectacle; but they may also be aroused by the very structure and incidents of the play — which is the better way and shows the better poet. The Plot in fact should be so framed that, even without seeing the things take place, he who simply hears the account of them shall be filled with horror and pity at the incidents; which is just the effect that the mere recital of the story of Oedipus would have on one. To produce this same effect by the means of the Spectacle is less artistic, and requires extraneous aid. (19:1–8)[5]

These excerpts indicate that for Aristotle spectacle normally constitutes one of the six parts of drama, along with plot, character, thought, diction, and music. It is least integral to the poet's task, however, because another person, the *skeuopoios* — translated variously as costumier, property man, and stage-manager — is responsible for producing the spectacle. While the poet may provide some hints about sets, costumes, and so on, the *skeuopoios* executes them. Moreover, the tragic effect can be elicited without a staged performance of the play through recital of the plot.

With *Samson*, however, poet and *skeuopoios* merge, and the dialogue bodies forth visual effects that register in the mind's eye. Yet Aristotle seems to address this possibility as well. In chapter 36 he notes that "Tragedy may produce its effect even without movement or action *in just the same way as Epic poetry*; for *from the mere reading of a play its quality may be seen* . . . . . [Its] reality of presentation is felt in the play as read, as well as in the play as acted" (36:31–33, 36–38; my emphases). Such a remark could have inspired Milton to include a kind of spectacle that is, though not meant for the stage, nonetheless perceptible by readers. That it did so is suggested both by the tragedy's title page and the opening statement of the prefatory epistle. Not only does the epistle echo the sixth chapter of the *Poetics*, it rearranges it in a very interesting way. Aristotle claims that tragedy is the "imitation of an action that is serious and also, as having magnitude, complete in itself; in language with pleasurable accessories, each kind brought in separately in the parts of the work; *in a dramatic, not in a narrative form*; with incidents arousing fear and pity, wherewith to accomplish its catharsis of such emotions" (4.1–10; my emphasis). However, he does not allude to the reading of tragedies until twenty chapters later. By contrast, in paraphrasing this definition in the prefatory epistle, Milton brings in reading (that is, the "narrative form") and places it on the same level as dramatic representation: "Tragedy . . . [is] said by Aristotle to be of power by raising pity and fear, or terror, to purge the mind of those and such like passions, that is to temper and reduce them to just measure with a kind of delight stirred up *by reading* or seeing those passions well-imitated" (my emphasis).[6] This revision of Aristotle provides the foundation for embedded spectacle in *Samson.*

It is also important to remember that while the *Poetics* furnished Milton with a theoretical framework for the spectacle, the plays of Aeschylus, Sophocles, and Euripides supplied him with models for such effects. As noted, Milton probably never saw a full performance of classical tragedy, but he certainly was an avid, highly imaginative reader of the genre, as evidenced by his annotations of Euripides, his frequent citations of the three tragedians throughout his prose, and his eighth and nineteenth sonnets, as well as the fact that Deborah Milton regularly read to him from Euripides' works after he went blind. Such intense engagement with Greek drama undoubtedly influenced the composition of his own tragedy, and he probably expected his audience to read *Samson* as actively as he himself engaged with such plays as *Alcestis, Electra, Orestes,* and *Hercules Furens.*

II. *Is* Samson Agonistes *a Closet Drama?*

Not only do the work's staging cues help us visualize its action, they also set *Samson* apart from other closet dramas. Indeed, the term "closet drama" does not accurately apply to Milton's play, not even retrospectively. In her 1998 essay on the play, Elizabeth Sauer interprets Milton's tragedy in the context of closet drama composed by writers such as Fulke Greville, Samuel Daniel, William Alexander, George Buchanan, and Elizabeth Cary. She cites formal elements common to such works: "Generic features include the trappings of Italianate Senecanism: the primacy of speech and narrative over action; long rhetorical monologues and philosophical and moral discourses; the casting of women as heroes and villains; and the inclusion of a nuntius and a chorus that speaks from a limited rather than an authoritative position."[7] A number of these items, such as the long speeches, the nuntius, and the chorus, can also be found in *Samson*; however, the tragedy's implied spectacle differentiates it from these closet plays. The difference is especially striking when we consider that in the neo-Senecan works, apart from the fact that the speaker(s) of each scene is listed at the beginning of their scenes, information about place, dress, and body language is virtually non-existent. Much the same can be said for Byron's *Manfred*, Shelley's *Prometheus Unbound*, and other closet dramas by the Romantics.

It is true that Cary's *Mariam, Queen of Jewry* (1613) was performed three times in the 1990s, and that Alison Findlay and Gweno Williams, along with Stephanie J. Hodgson-Wright, who produced a 1994 dramatization of the tragedy, have coauthored an article arguing for its suitability for the stage. The play offers a sword fight (2.3) as well as one property, a poisoned chalice (4.1). There are, as well, brief references to the heroine's tears (1.1), to her clothing (4.4), and to buildings (2.3, 4.1). Yet such items are barely mentioned, whereas in *Samson Agonistes* costumes, gestures, and other aspects of the physical appearances of the personae are limned in considerable detail.

In order to see the differences between these two plays in terms of staging, it is worth contrasting the arguments that introduce each drama. Cary's, which is seven paragraphs long, is pure plot summary, with nothing about how any character looks or dresses other than a note that Mariam is "of singular beauty." Like Cary's, Milton's summarizes the ensuing plot, yet he also mentions that Samson is "captive, blind, and now in the prison at Gaza, there to labor as in a common work-house, on a festival day, in the general cessation of labor, [and] comes forth into the open air, to a place somewhat nigh, somewhat retired there to sit a while and bemoan his condition." These lines give some indication of the prisoner's appearance, as well as his actions. Also, the fact that Milton's argument is in present tense (Cary's is in past tense) causes the description to function, in a sense, as a scenic prelude.

Similarly, Milton's single traditional stage direction — "The scene before the prison in Gaza" — provides specific information that has no equivalent in *Mariam*. Both the singular form of "scene" and the definite article preceding it indicate that Milton intended to observe unity of place, and, with one possible exception, he succeeded. The direction is indebted to Greek drama, which according to Oliver Taplin often had a "stage building . . . whose front outside [stood] for a palace or temple or whatever [was] called for."[8] The prison is described as a "common workhouse" in "The Argument"; Samson calls it "the common Prison" (6) and "the Mill" (41), Dalila "this loathsome prison-house" (922), and Manoa the "calamitous prison" (1480). These allusions keep the setting present to the reader's imagination, something which *Mariam* and the other neo-Senecan closet plays fail to do.

All other directions in Milton's tragedy are implicit, embedded in the play's speeches, and usually deal with costumes, gestures, and body language. Many are related to Samson, and in a sense he remains before us throughout the play, for even though he exits to perform in the Dagonalia, the Hebrew Messenger's vivid account of that scene causes it to metamorphose from an offstage, narrated event to one that effectively occurs before the mind's eye. That is, we tend to replace the scene of the Messenger standing before the Chorus with the one he so precisely describes. It is not just the nuntius's speech that evokes the scene so sharply, for immediacy is characteristic of such speeches; indeed, the nuntius's role is traditionally awarded to the second-strongest actor in a company. What makes the Messenger's account so vivid is that it transforms us from readers into spectators: we see the temple through his perspective, which is that of an audience member arriving at a theater and looking around, then watching a performance. This impression is due, in part, to the fact that Milton departs from Judges 16:27, which refers to the building as a "house," and instead has the nuntius describe it as a "theater" (1605).[9] With him, then, we observe "a spacious theater / Half round on two main pillars vaulted high," the "seats where all the lords and each degree / Of sort, might sit in order to behold," as well as the "banks and scaffolds under sky" where the commoners stand, and we also visualize the "feast and noon [growing] high" (1605–06, 1607–08, 1610, 1612). In addition, we observe Samson being led in by a small army of archers, slingers, spearsmen, and soldiers, and accompanied by musicians playing pipes and tambourines. The theatricality of this play-within-a-play is probably due to the fact that Milton considered staging a version of the Dagonalia, as is clear from the Trinity manuscript plans. And indeed, two productions of the tragedy have had the temple partially on-stage.[10]

At any rate, even in the tragedy's opening lines, spoken by Samson, there are a number of concrete staging clues:

> A little onward lend thy guiding hand
> To these dark steps, a little further on;
> For yonder bank hath choice of sun or shade,
> There I am wont to sit, when any chance
> Relieves me from my task of servile toil,
> Daily in the common prison else enjoined me,
> Where I a prisoner chained, scarce freely draw
> The air imprisoned also, close and damp,
> Unwholesome draught; but here I feel amends,
> The breath of heav'n fresh-blowing, pure and sweet,
> With day-spring born; here leave me to respire.
> This day a solemn feast the people hold
> To Dagon their sea-idol, and forbid
> Laborious works; unwillingly this rest
> Their superstition yields me; hence with leave
> Retiring from the popular noise, I seek
> This unfrequented place to find some ease.   (1–17)

These lines indicate that the blind and chained captive is being led away from the prison by an unnamed guide. Apparently the guide has taken his charge just so far and is now starting to let go of him, when Samson asks to be led somewhat further. "Yonder" (3) and "There" (4) intimate the pair's initial distance from a dirt mound, which offers "choice of sun or shade," presumably because trees or large bushes are growing on or near it, while "here," used both at lines 9 and 11, implies that they have reached it. When they do so, Samson dismisses his helper, although it is not clear if the guide exits or simply moves away from the mound to let the prisoner "respire." One complaint voiced by Samson after he sits on the bank is that he is always "In power of others, never in my own" (78), and it would seem unlikely that the Philistines would leave their prize captive completely unsupervised. No sooner is he seated, however, than Samson delivers an apparent, and uninhibited, soliloquy in which he complains about, among other things, the harsh treatment meted out to him by his captors.

J. Michael Walton points out that "in performance [of Greek plays] nonspeaking actors effectively did not exist *until they were addressed. . . .* Such actors were to all intents and purposes invisible. . . . Thus they were able to function as stagehands, supplying properties [and] moving furniture."[11] The play's opening suggests that Milton intuited this principle, for the guide becomes essentially invisible once Samson ceases to speak to him, although I believe that we are meant to keep his presence in mind. That we are to remember the guide becomes evident in the second entrance of the Public Officer (1390), who arrives to tell Samson (once more) to come to the temple. The Officer promptly lets the prisoner know that he is prepared to drag him to the Dagonalia if necessary. When Samson complies with the herald's demands, just in time, the Officer tells someone to "doff these links" (1410). No editor has mentioned or designated the addressee, whom I take to be Samson's escort. Apparently, ever since his earlier departure, the guide has been standing off to the side. It is logical that he would have the key to the prisoner's fetters. Also, the fact that Milton apparently expects us to remember the attendant, who is dismissed in the opening lines, underscores the play's theatricality. That is, if

we merely read the play, the guide effectively disappears from
thought until he is recalled here, but if we truly envision the drama
in our mind's eye, or better, witness it in performance, the guide
remains present, sidelined but ready to assist when needed.

Meanwhile, the theatrical quality of *Samson*'s opening lines is
reinforced when they are compared with the opening of *Mariam*,
which offers little spectacle. Cary (1585?–1639) most likely attended
the theater, and as noted *Mariam* certainly has dramatic touches,
yet its beginning could not be more different from *Samson*'s. There
is no entrance by the heroine, nor any indication as to where she
is standing, whether indoors or out. Instead, we simply have the
information, "Mariam sola," followed by her speech:

> How oft have I with public voice run on?
> To censure Rome's last hero for deceit;
> Because he wept when Pompey's life was gone,
> Yet when he lived, he thought his name too great.
> But now I do recant, and, Roman lord,
> Excuse too rash a judgment in a woman;
> My sex pleads pardon, pardon then afford,
> Mistaking is with us, but too too common.
> Now do I find by self-experience taught,
> One object yields both grief and joy;
> You wept indeed, when on his worth you thought,
> But joyed that slaughter did your foe destroy.
> So at his death your eyes true drops did rain,
> Whom dead, you did not wish alive again.
> When Herod lived, that now is done to death,
> Oft have I wished that I from him were free;
> Oft have I wished that he might lose his breath;
> Oft have I wished his carcass dead to see.
> Then rage and scorn had put my love to flight,
> That love which once on him was firmly set;
> Hate hid his true affection from my sight,
> And kept my heart from paying him his debt.
> And blame me not, for Herod's jealousy
> Had power even constancy itself to change;
> For he, by barring me from liberty,
> To shun my ranging, taught me first to range.

But yet too chaste a scholar was my heart,
To léarn to love another than my lord;
To leave his love, my lesson's former part,
I quickly learned, the other I abhorred.
But now his death to memory doth call,
The tender love, that he to Mariam bare;
And mine to him, this makes those rivers fall,
Which by another thought unmoistened are.[12]   (1–34)

The entire speech is 78 lines in length, and the only implicit stage directions are the references to her tears ("those rivers" [33]), and her command to "fly back, and hide you in your banks" (75) as she starts to choke up with grief. (Her address to Caesar, starting at line 5, is a poetic apostrophe; he is not present in the scene.)

Act 1.1 of Fulke Greville's *Mustapha* is similarly devoid of any stage directions. It provides just two words in the superscript, "Soliman, Rossa," which refers to the Turkish emperor and his wife, respectively. Again, we have no idea where they are or what they look like as Soliman begins speaking to the queen:

Rossa! Th'eternal wisdom doth not covet
Of man, his strength or reason but his love.
And not in vain: since love, of all the powers,
Is it which governs every thought of ours.
I speak by Mustapha: for as a father,
How often deemed I those light-judging praises
Of multitudes, whom my love taught to flatter,
Truth's oracles, and Mustapha's true stories?
So dearly nature bids our own be loved:
So ill a judge is love of things beloved.
But is contempt the fruit of parents' care?
Doth kindness lessen kings' authority,
Teaching our children pride, our vassals wit,
To subject us, that subject are to it?
This frailty in myself I conquer must,
And stay the false untimely hopes it works,
Threat'ning the father's ruin in the son:
Many with trust, with doubt, few are undone.[13]   (1–18)

Milton's tragedy, on the other hand, furnishes abundant spectacle, not only in its opening but throughout the play. Some of the most striking spectacle items are the protagonist's bodily features, particularly his surprisingly ordinary physique; his extremely long, thick hair; and his intact, if inoperative, eyeballs. Each of these features is remarkable, even miraculous, either in itself or in what it implies, and thus would seem to pose a considerable challenge to the revisionist interpretations of the drama, which often reduce the protagonist to an all-too-human figure who merely asserts divine sanction for his actions. Indeed, I suspect that the neglect of the prisoner's physical features — often by commentators who concentrate almost exclusively on what the characters say, rather than how they look — may have made the terrorist readings more plausible. It is only when we truly register the extraordinary nature of Samson's physical appearance that the force of the terrorist interpretations begins to diminish.

III. *On Samson's Body*

The captive's physique is extraordinary in its very ordinariness — a subtle fact that is all too often disregarded and misunderstood. To achieve an accurate sense of Samson's physical appearance it is necessary to commence with the play's initial description of the captive and of his compatriots during the Chorus's entrance. When they approach, Samson wonders aloud, "But who are these? for with joint pace I hear / The tread of many feet steering this way" (110–11). Although he fears that it is the Philistines who harass him daily, it turns out to be the Chorus of Danites. The typical Greek chorus was composed of about 15 members, yet the precise number of Milton's is not specified; we know only that they are numerous enough that their tread is audible to Samson from some distance away. The fact that they walk in formation, almost in a march, makes his ability to hear them plausible. While the Chorus's physical appearance is not described, the group seems to be entirely male. Manoa's initial response upon first entering the scene is to call them

"Brethren and men of Dan," as "such [they] seem," which presumably means that they look Semitic (332).

Samson's appearance, on the other hand, is depicted by the Chorus. In the first place, before taking up their places near Samson, the Chorus pause, telling one another, "softly awhile, / Let us not break in upon him" (115–16). Apparently they think he is resting or sleeping and do not wish to disturb him with loud speech. Hence, their initial account of the fallen hero is credible and candid since they believe he cannot understand it. As it turns out, they are correct: the prisoner notes to himself that while he hears "the sound of words, their sense the air / Dissolves unjointed ere it reach my ear" (176–77). The Chorus covertly describes the captive:

> See how he lies at random, carelessly diffused,
> With languished head unpropped,
> As one past hope, abandoned,
> And by himself given over;
> In slavish habit, ill-fitted weeds
> O'er-worn and soiled.   (118–23)

The first line may indicate either that Samson has already lain down on the bank after initially sitting on it, before the Danites' arrival, or that he is in the process of doing so as they walk up to him. His eventual posture, in any case, is clear: he lies "at random" without seeming to care about anything. Samson is *not* fully prone, perhaps because this would make him appear like a dead man, a sight that quite possibly would alarm the visitors. Instead, his head is barely propped up, yet drooping, for he is about to give himself up once again to the jeers of what he thinks are his approaching enemies. His badly fitting slaves' garb, filthy and stale, testifies to the Philistines' degrading treatment of their captive. Their contempt for him, incidentally, may be indicated not just by his clothing but by the possibility that they have either had the word "Fool" or a large *F* written on his forehead, as line 496 ("the mark of fool set on [my] front") suggests.[14]

His ill-fitting clothing could suggest that Samson's body is large, too large for any Philistine garb to fit him properly, yet other scenes in the tragedy indicate the opposite. For instance, he is not nearly as tall as the giant Harapha, whom he threatens to "run upon" as if scaling a building, and whom he calls a "bulk without spirit vast," vowing to "lay thy structure low" (1238, 1239). Furthermore, the fact that Harapha needs to survey each of Samson's limbs testifies to the fact that the captive's musculature is not obviously massive. Just so, the efforts of the Philistine leaders and Dalila to discover the source of his strength indicate that his appearance is not physically impressive.

David Berkeley has noted that despite the text's indications of Samson's ordinary physique, a surprising number of eminent Miltonists refer to him, variously, as a giant, giantesque, Paul Bunyan-like, Titanesque, and so on. Moreover, some of these characterizations are accompanied by derogatory descriptions of the prisoner. Robert Adams, for instance, calls him a "burly, truculent, and not-very-clever giant," Virginia Mollenkott deems him a "blind giant . . . the crude muscleman of the Old Testament," Flannagan describes him as a "negative . . . overmuscular, testosterone-filled goon," and William Kerrigan refers to him as a "self-tormenting giant."[15] Again, an important question is to what extent the tendency to erroneously register Samson as a giant — and often, as a bully — has rendered the terrorist readings more plausible. Because unless his average physique is kept steadily in mind, it is perhaps easier to forget that all of Samson's deeds prior to the play have been carried out by divine power, albeit as an amplification of his own exertions. Such an oversight may also make it easier to misinterpret his actions as arising from a bullying instinct when he goes to the temple, imposing himself on his foes rather than being summoned by God to the arena.

In any case, one physical feature that has not escaped critical notice is the protagonist's hair; its presence and fullness are emphasized throughout the play, and are noted by a number of commentators, including Joseph Wittreich and Stanley Fish. Their observations are based on the fact that, when speaking with his father, Samson fears that if he returns home, he will become a "pitied object," with "these redundant locks / Robustious to no purpose clust'ring down / Vain monument of strength" (568–70). "Redundant" intimates that the hair is "plentiful and exuberant" (*OED* 2), and that its accompanying, symbolized strength is useless. "Robustious" also indicates its abundance and reinforces its role as a sign of Samson's vigor; in fact, the term suggests that the hair itself is not merely a sign of his power, but is itself mysteriously alive. Other passages intimate the hair's copiousness and vitality: Harapha refers to "those boist'rous locks" (1164), a term whose primary meaning is "coarse-growing" (*OED* 6), with a secondary sense of exuberance or high-spiritedness. And late in the drama Manoa notes that his son's hair "wav[es] down" on his shoulders and is "Garrison'd round about him like a camp / Of faithful soldiery" (1493, 1497–98).

Such imagery may contrast with the biblical account, which is unclear about the precise length of his hair at the festival. After Samson is shaved, the Judges narrator comments that "the hair of his head *began* to grow again after he was shaven"[16] (16:22; my emphasis), yet it is not evident just how long his hair is when he is brought in to perform for the Philistines. Apparently his full strength has not returned, for just before pulling down the pillars, Samson prays "O Lord God, remember me, I pray thee, and *strengthen* me, I pray thee, *only this once*, O God" (16:28; my emphases). Similarly, the Douay-Rheims edition renders the verse as "O Lord God, remember me, and *restore to me now my former strength*, O my God" (my emphasis). Because he asks for, and receives, a miraculous accession of might here, it seems that Samson's hair has not grown back fully at this point.

The Miltonic Samson, on the other hand, possesses much of his vigor throughout the play, as is indicated by the frequent references to his long hair, and by descriptions of his potency spoken by him and others, such as "this Heav'n-gifted strength" and "glorious strength" (36). Nonetheless, it is possible that when he prays just before his final deed, he asks not for a complete restoration of power, like his biblical counterpart, but rather for a fresh, additional endowment of might. After all, he describes this final deed as a trial of strength "yet greater" than those he has demonstrated up to this point (1644). His "over-tired" condition following his initial exploits (1632) impels him to lean on the two pillars supporting the house, making a request for further empowering plausible. Germane, too, is the fact that one of Milton's probable sources, George Sandys's *A Relation of a Journey* (1615), represents the columns as "marble pillars of an incredible bigness," a phrase that seems to inform the nuntius's depiction of them as "massy pillars" (1648).[17] That Samson proceeds to perform this far more difficult task indicates, I believe, that the prayer has been answered.

Another striking physical feature of Samson's is his eyeballs, which are whole and intact despite being gouged out by the Philistines before the play begins. The Hebrew, Greek, and Latin renderings of Judges 16:21, which according to the Authorized Version reads as "the Philistines took him, and put out his eyes," indicate that Samson is violently blinded by his enemies. The Hebrew (Masoretic) text for the verb "put out" is *nakru*, which denotes a picking or tearing out; the Alexandrine codex of the Septuagint is *execopsan*, and also indicates a cutting out of the eyeballs; and the Vulgate's *eruerent* denotes a tearing out or uprooting. Yet Milton depicts the eyes as whole, most clearly in the Messenger's observation of Samson's appearance just before he pulls down the pillars, when "with head a while inclined / *And eyes fast fixed* . . . [he] stood, as one who prayed" (1636–37; my emphasis). Similarly, Manoa attempts earlier in the drama to encourage his son by remarking that "God [can] . . . / Cause light within thy eyes to spring" (581, 584), and Samson disagrees, claiming that "these dark *orbs* shall no more treat with light" (591; my emphasis). A conversation between the Chorus and Manoa also confirms the eyes' presence: After the Chorus remark that Manoa may soon have to "nurse" his own son back to health (1488), he responds that "it shall be my delight to tend [Samson's] *eyes*" (1490; my emphasis). He then expresses the wish that "since [Samson's] strength with eyesight was not lost, / God will restore him eyesight to his strength" (1502–03), the Chorus responding "Thy hopes are not ill-founded" (1504). And soon after, the Chorus, hearing the sounds of the catastrophe, voice this expectation: "What if [Samson's] eyesight . . . / . . . [is] by miracle restored?" (1527–28). The fact that they refer to the possible return of his eyesight implies that the eyes themselves are whole, merely in need of reactivation.

It also is telling that, with the possible exception of Dalila, none of Samson's visitors say anything about a facial injury when they first encounter the fallen champion. As noted earlier, the Danites' description mentions his rags, filth, and dejected posture, but not his eyes (115–23). By contrast, in *Oedipus at Colonus*, often considered one of the principal sources of Milton's tragedy, the Chorus's first response to Oedipus is "Ah! His face is dreadful!" (141), and then, moments later, "Ah! His eyes are blind" (150); in like manner, Theseus tells him "[your] tortured face / Make[s] plain your identity" (555), while Antigone laments her father's "lost, irrecoverable eyes" (1200).[18] It is true that Dalila has returned, she claims, "to behold / Once more thy face" (741–42), and that she wishes to take him from the prison and bring him home, where she, "with nursing diligence . . . / May ever tend about thee to old age" (924–25). Yet she does not directly allude to facial injury, and the fact that she is still sexually attracted to him strengthens the notion that his face appears normal.

On the other hand, certain lines do seem to suggest that Samson's eyeballs are indeed missing. For instance, Samson laments the fact that as one "separate to God" (31) he nonetheless "must die / Betrayed, captíved, [with] both my eyes put out" (32–33). Less than ten lines later he remarks that those who ask for Israel's great deliverer will "find him / Eyeless in Gaza at the mill with slaves" (40–41). Similarly, in the Harapha episode, the giant tells Samson not to expect any help from God since he has "delivered [thee] up / Into thy enemies' hand, permitted them / To put out both thine eyes" (1158–60). Harapha also refuses to fight the captive, claiming that "both thy eyes [are] put out" (1103). And at the end of the tragedy Manoa predicts that virgins shall "visit [Samson's] tomb with flowers, only bewailing / His lot unfortunate in nuptial choice, / From whence captivity and loss of eyes" (1742–44).

Yet these lines are not unequivocal, and could mean only that Samson's eyesight is extinguished, not that the eyes themselves are ruined. In fact, the phrase "put out" was ambiguous in early modern usage: *OED* 48bb defines it as meaning, "To destroy the sight of, to blind (an eye), either by literally gouging it out, or by burning or other means." The editors cite, among other passages, *Samson Agonistes* line 33, although they do not specify which method — gouging, burning, or something else — is exemplified by the passage. Cauterizing the eyes could destroy their function while leaving them intact. Moreover, *OED* 48eb glosses "put out" as "To extinguish (fire or light, or a burning or luminous body)," with the first usage occurring in 1526. Although this entry does not cite the tragedy, it is plausible that Milton intended "put out" in this sense. For instance, reflecting on his blindness in the opening monologue, Samson asks, "why was the sight / To such a tender ball as th'eye confined? / So obvious and so easy to be *quenched*" (93–95; my emphasis). Incidentally, Milton's own facial appearance remained normal after his sight failed him, and he refers to his blindness as a "loss of my eyes" throughout *Defensio Secunda*. Thus, the final impression we are left with after reading the play is that Samson's eyes are intact, albeit powerless.[19]

There are no precedents for depicting the eyes as devoid of physically apparent damage in scripture, in any of Milton's prose references to Samson, or in other early modern Samson plays. In fact, both Hieronymus Zieglerus's *Samson, Tragodeia Nova* (1547) and Marcus Andreas Wunstius's *Simson, Tragodeia Sacra* (1604) stage the gouging, while Vicenzo Giattini's *Il Sansone: Dialogo per Musica* (1638) portrays Samson hiding his disfigured face whenever he is in public. Why, then, does Milton represent his protagonist without such deformity? One reason is for Milton to identify himself with his protagonist, at least in terms of their countenances. In her 1934 study of the poet's blindness Eleanor Brown points out that the early modern term for his eye disease was *gutta serena*, which denoted "all blindness in which the eye retains a normal appearance."[20] Milton alludes to the malady in *Paradise Lost* 3 when he states that "So thick a drop serene hath quenched their orbs" (25). And in his penultimate sonnet, "To Mr. Cyriak Skinner Upon His Blindness," Milton declares that his eyes are "clear / To outward view, of blemish or of spot" (1–2). In addition, Milton composed *Defensio Secunda* in part to refute Alexander More's charge that he, Milton, was "'a monster, dreadful, ugly, huge, deprived of sight" (YP 4:582–83), pointing out, among other things, that his eyes "have as much the appearance of being uninjured, and are as clear and bright, without a cloud, as the eyes of men who see most keenly."

Such a link between Milton and his dramatic protagonist might seem to reinforce biographical readings of the tragedy, which have, of course, been quite common for centuries. Indeed, the biographical approach is often adduced to counter claims that *Samson* is a true play. I contend, however, that this method is often deployed uncritically, overemphasizing parallels between the author and protagonist (unhappy marriages, frustration at their fellow citizens, etc.) and downplaying salient dissimilarities (radically different causes for their blindness, Milton's reconciliation with Mary Powell, and so on). It is also worth remembering that in *An Apology Against a Pamphlet*, Milton warns against identifying dramatic characters with their authors (YP 1:880). Perhaps the most compelling refutation of a facile application of the biographical method is performance of the drama, whether physical or in the mind's eye. In this regard, Terence Spencer's review of a 1951 dramatization bears witness to the absence of any external justification or explanation needed to account for Samson's character:

> It was noticeable, too, how unobtrusive during the performance was that "personal element" which inevitably seems important to the reader. The pathos of blindness was Samson's not Milton's. The expressions of misogyny were a natural result of Samson's experience and did not necessarily reflect Milton's disappointments. . . .

> In brief, the impression from this performance was that the play was
> written with far more dramatic objectivity than is commonly sup-
> posed by readers.[21]

Thus, envisioning, or witnessing, Samson as a character in his
own right alleviates the necessity for relying on the import of biographical details.

Hence, while the biographical explanation of the eyeballs' ren-
ovation is interesting, I shall concentrate on their dramatic function in the play, especially the ways in which Milton may have
intended for his prisoner's relatively normal facial appearance to
offset his degradation, which is graphically conveyed in his rags,
despairing body language, filth and chains. Indeed, for the Chorus
and Manoa the last-mentioned item constitutes one of the most
scandalous elements of the captive's present condition, for it underscores his regression from a one-man army whose fighting prowess
once "Made arms ridiculous, useless the forgery / Of brazen shield
and spear" (131–32), to a hostage fettered in links fashioned of
that same metal. Stanley Fish, Laura Knoppers, and Dennis Kezar
argue that the prisoner's appearance is shocking, even moribund.
While I agree with them to some extent, I contend that his squalor
is attenuated by his eyes and the fullness and vigor of his hair.[22]
As noted, making Samson's countenance look normal renders
Dalila's ongoing physical attraction to him plausible.

Do the intact eyes constitute a sign of divine favor? They might
in theory, but in fact, none of the characters regards them as such,
although the presence of the eyes inspires Manoa to tell Samson
that God might miraculously restore his eyesight. There is, after
all, a precedent for such a marvel in the fact that God answered
one of Samson's prior supplications, for relief from thirst after battle by causing a fountain to well up from dry ground (581ff.).
Similarly, keeping early modern optics in mind, we can imagine
God causing a new "fountain," fresh light to be spent, springing
from the dry ground of the captive's eyes. Samson rejects this hope,
yet the Chorus reiterate it after the prisoner has been taken to the
temple (1527–28). Such a restoration, particularly when Samson is

in Dagon's temple, would constitute an unequivocal sign of God's blessing, but of course it does not happen.

IV. The "Rousing Motions" and Samson as True Prophet

Is there, then, any other evidence of Samson being the recipient of divine approval? I believe there is, in the effect of the "rousing motions"; these motions, he claims, "dispose / To something extraordinary my thoughts," and compel him to go to the temple just after refusing to do so in the previous scene (1382–83). They imbue Samson with the power of prophecy, an ability that is confirmed by spectacle in the Dagonalia. The "rousing motions" section is, of course, one of the most contested of the tragedy, particularly in the terrorism debate. Wittreich, quoting James Holstun, has succinctly summarized the controversy: "whether . . . those 'rousing motions' come from within or from above — that is now the pressing matter."[23] Yet because they are invisible to readers, the motions cannot be analyzed directly; instead, we must evaluate them in terms of their effects, which are visible in the play's spectacle.

In an influential essay, later incorporated into *How Milton Works* (2001), Stanley Fish argues that there is no objective correlative indicating that the protagonist has indeed been compelled by God rather than his own design. In Fish's fideistic reading, one of the tragedy's primary insights is that "no firm — that is, external — basis for action exists in this world," and declares that while "Samson *hopes* that the thoughts stirring within him are prompted directly by God (rather than being merely permitted by him), . . . short of an angelic visitation . . . he must rely, like all men, on his best lights." Fish also states that the difficulty of interpreting the motions is compounded if we turn to previous moments in the play, "for what we find is that the status of Samson's inward promptings (to marry, first, the woman of Timnah, then Dalila) has already been a topic of discussion in a way that is decidedly unhelpful . . . when he later reports on the 'rousing motions' . . . there is no way to be confident that those motions correspond to some communication that is occurring between him and God."[24]

Similar doubts about Samson's claims of divine inspiration are frequently raised by the revisionists, who often compare him to Oliver Cromwell; like Samson, Cromwell (mistakenly) followed his own "rousing motions" to wreak havoc on the innocent. Wittreich, for instance, quotes contemporary accounts of the Protector's eyes sparkling before the Battle of Dunbar, as if possessed by "a Divine Impulse," and roaring with laughter just prior to the Battle of Naseby for the same reason.[25] Just so, Derek Wood offers the Cromwell-Samson comparison in his 2001 book *"Exiled from Light": Divine Law, Morality, and Violence in Milton's* Samson Agonistes.

Yet Anthony Low, who reviewed Wood's study, refutes the Cromwell-Samson link:

> Although the action of the play remains in the natural world, God's choosing of Samson is amply confirmed by objective evidence. Although many Puritans conjectured that Cromwell's remarkable string of victories implied providential design, nothing he did exceeded human abilities. That is not true of Samson. Cromwell had nothing like Samson's God-given strength. . . . Great soldier that he was, he could never have killed a thousand men in one day with an ass's jawbone.[26]

Even so, a revisionist might concede that the rousing motions are genuine, and perhaps admit that the first act of Samson's performance is characterized by clearly miraculous feats of strength, while still arguing that he ceases to be divinely motivated the moment he tells the crowd "Now of my own accord such other trial / I mean to show you of my strength, yet greater" (1643–44). Wittreich, for instance, discusses the phrase "of my own accord" at length, adducing examples from Milton's prose to argue that the phrase "always seems to imply *without prompting from anyone, or provocation by any external authority.*" He also contends, "Strength comes to Samson as a gift from God, but how that gift will be used — or abused — is determined by Samson himself." In his view, Milton's protagonist misuses his potency in his final deed, although God intervenes and overrides the deed somewhat by "sparing some of those Philistines from the slaughter."[27]

The problem with this line of argumentation is that it pays attention to the prisoner's words without sufficient consideration of the physical context, which, as noted, indicates that Samson is exhausted from his initial exploits and is, nonetheless, contemplating a far more difficult task, one seemingly beyond even his own remarkable powers. That he subsequently receives the ability to perform that task despite these obstacles indicates that "of my own accord" signals something quite different from a cessation of obedience to God.

A better understanding of the phrase is provided by Alan Rudrum, who is more sensitive to the dramatic context. He remarks that Wittreich's argument "has not won general acceptance," and notes, "A basic problem is that he takes the phrase ['of my own accord'] at face value, as if it were embedded in omniscient author commentary rather than in a dramatic narrative. Samson is under no compulsion to reveal his intentions to his enemies."[28] John Leonard concurs, noting, "the antithesis is between Samson's own deeds and the Philistines' *commands* (1640), not between Samson's will and God's."[29]

Wittreich also cites John 11:49–52 to indicate that the Bible clearly differentiates between those who are inspired by God and those who act on their own will. In this passage, the high priest Caiaphas predicts that Jesus will die for the Jewish nation. The narrator then remarks, "He did not say this on his own, but being high priest that year he prophesied that Jesus was about to die for the nation."[30] However, John 10:18 provides a counterexample, for there Jesus claims that he has the power to lay his life down "of my own accord," then immediately follows this by asserting that "I have received this command from my father" (10:18b; RSV). Second, both the Chorus and Manoa rejoice when they hear what Samson has done; his father, in particular, emphasizes that there is nothing in the Messenger's news about the catastrophe that would elicit contempt, dispraise, or blame for his son's actions (1723–24), and, as we saw, Manoa claims that God was "not parted from him, as was feared, / But favoring and assisting *to the end*" (1719–20; my emphasis). Manoa also predicts that the Jewish community will judge the event as completely praiseworthy: valiant Jewish youths and virgins will come to Samson's tomb to pay homage to his memory. While both Manoa and the Danites do say some patently incorrect things throughout the play, the fact that they regard Samson's feats in the temple as nothing but admirable suggests that this is how Milton intends his audience to view them as well. As Roy Flannagan puts it, "Toward the end [of the tragedy], Manoa and the Chorus do seem to speak Miltonic truth or, as Michael Spiller puts it, they 'speak in an authorial fashion, and guide us to the delight that accompanies wisdom.'"[31]

Are there, however, any indications in the drama *other* than these speeches that either confirm or refute the putatively divine origins of the "rousing motions"? Spectacle helps to answer this question, especially if we consider what the prisoner predicts about his performance at the festival, and the visual representation of the Dagonalia itself. Because the Miltonic Samson has clearly recovered all, or nearly all, of his former potency, he is heavily guarded in the temple. By contrast, as both the biblical narrative and all other early modern versions of the tale have it, the captive is a weak version of his former self, and his foes are celebrating precisely for that reason. In fact, in all the non-Miltonic accounts, no small part of the celebration is devoted to humiliating the once powerful man by forcing him to clown for the spectators. The sense of him being made a spectacle, a laughing-stock, is evident in all ancient versions of Judges 16:25, including the Hebrew (Masoretic), the Greek (Septuagint, both the Alexandrine and Vatican codices), and the Vulgate. Paul Sellin, discussing the Hebrew rendering of 16:25, notes that

> the initial sentence of verse twenty-five tells why the Philistines ordered Samson to be brought before them: Call Samson, they commanded . . . "that he may sport for us." . . . The next sentence

of this verse offers a second clue to Samson's action, but in stating
that Samson in fact did — or began to do — what was commanded
of him, the Masoretic text shifts to a verb (*va-y-tsa-chek*). . . . The
shift does not seem to depart radically from the meaning of the first
verb, but of the two, the latter carries a stronger connotation of laughter, or of causing laughter *by being ridiculous — i.e., "Samson
caused them to laugh"* — than the first.[32]

Of all modern translations, the Geneva Bible (1611) is perhaps
closest to the ancient Hebrew discussed here. The Authorized
Version reads at this point, "And it came to pass, when their hearts
were merry, that they said, Call for Samson, that he may make us
sport. And they called for Samson out of the prison house; and he
made them sport." As the Geneva translators have it, however, the
Philistines said, "Call Samson, that he may make us pastime," and,
in the second half of the verse, that he became "a laughing stocke
unto them."

Other versions of the story feature his humiliation prominently.
Josephus, for instance, notes that "they sent for Samson, and he
was brought to their feast, that they might insult him in their cups."[33]
The other early modern Samson plays are particularly emphatic
about his humiliation. Hieronymus Zieglerus's *Samson, Tragoedia
Nova* (1547) depicts a Philistine prince forcing the prisoner to
dance for the crowd:

> Dance on, Dance on.
> Skip in your wonted style, your Hebrew fashion.
> Sing, O musicians, to the harp, and play,
> And we shall watch a judge of Israel
> Dance trippingly.   (2.4–8)

Marcus Wunstius's *Simson, Tragoedia Sacra* (1600, 1604) represents
the prisoner being handed a lyre and forced to sing; it also shows
a group of young men tearing his hair and beard, pulling on his ears
and nostrils, and joking about his blindness (act 4). The nuntius in
Theodore Rhodius's *Simson* (1600) notes that the crowd demanded
that the captive "sing a song about your love affairs, / Your famous
exploits, or your Hebrew God!" (act 5). In Vincenzo Giattini's *Il*

Sansone: Dialogo per Musica (1638), Delilah brings the prisoner's shorn hair into the arena and holds it aloft: "Behold the symbol of his conquered strength, / The sign of thy power, behold the hair!" (part 2). And in Joost van der Vondel's *Samson, of Heilige Wraeck, Treurspel* (*Samson, or Holy Revenge*, published in 1660) — a work that Milton almost certainly knew, according to Watson Kirkconnell[34] — the captive is led by the nose into the arena. Men in the crowd offer him honeycomb and dare him to eat it, to see if its sweetness matches that of the honey from the lion's carcass. They also crown him with oak leaves and invite him to dance in front of the altar, at which point he sings for them, accompanied by a harp.

Milton's Samson fears precisely this sort of degradation. He refuses the Public Officer's initial summons by claiming that he will be mocked by his foes as they compel him to "sport with blind activity" and "make a game of [his] calamities" (1328, 1331). Just so, when the Officer presses him, Samson again refuses, believing that they will make him "their fool or jester" (1338). True, his situation is more complicated than those of his biblical and Renaissance counterparts, for the fact that he possesses much, if not all, of his former power lends a certain plausibility to the Officer's invitation. That is, the Philistines know that their captive is capable of impressive physical deeds, so they are able to make the initial summons sound sincere. But Samson senses that any such performance will be undercut by mockery and derision, and of course he has had direct experience with such treatment. Again, his foes might have had the word "Fool," or at least the letter *F,* scrawled on his forehead when he was in prison, and when the Chorus first approaches, Samson fears that his enemies have returned to afflict and insult him — after all, this has been "their daily practice" (114). Manoa, too, worries that his son will be compelled to do "things unseemly" (1451), and thus decides to forego the Dagonalia. Given such awareness of his foes' cruelty, Samson nonetheless agrees to go to the temple, compelled by the rousing motions.

In order to evaluate the authenticity of the motions a novel approach is required. I turn to the significance of the fact that the promptings imbue the captive, albeit temporarily, with genuinely prophetic power. Upon feeling the motions Samson remarks, "If there be aught of presage in the mind, / This day will be remarkable in my life / By some great act, or of my days the last" (1387–89). Roy Flannagan interprets line 1387 to mean, "If the mind has any prophetic power"[35] and commentators frequently note the irony of the prisoner's words here, that he will, in fact, carry out his great act on a day that will also be his last. One probable source for the irony, adduced by Flannagan and several other editors, is Sophocles's *The Women of Trachis* (1169–72), where Heracles realizes that an oracle that earlier forecasted either death or freedom from toil in fact meant both, since at death his labors cease.[36] However, an important element of this source that may also have influenced Milton has gone unnoticed. In Sophocles's tragedy, the oracle and Heracles are separate characters, but in Milton's play, Samson himself becomes an oracle, at least for a time. The fact that both terms of his prediction come true authenticates this oracular role, for there is no way he could have accurately forecasted either event apart from supernatural assistance.

Some revisionists claim that the motions assure Samson that he will have an opportunity to execute a plan he has been mulling over before the motions come to him, namely, the destruction of the temple. Thus, the motions are seen as a kind of logical consequence of what he has already been plotting, and are thus not necessarily divine. Burns's refutation of this claim is convincing, as he notes, first, "Wittreich surmises that Samson has some program to execute his revenge, [Irene] Samuel believes he goes knowing 'he can deal death,' Burton J. Weber thinks that through the 'rousing motions' God tells Samson he is to go on a military mission, and William Kerrigan says, 'Samson knows what to do in the theater. He leaves the stage with the scheme in mind.'" Burns then refutes these speculations by pointing out that "none of these readings satisfactorily explains what plan a blind man could have to hurt his enemies," and I would add that Samson fully recognizes that his enemies have complete control over him. He is escorted into the temple by a small army of heavily weaponed guards, so it seems extremely unlikely that he would contemplate making a single unexpected move. (Even suicide would be impossible under these circumstances, as long as the Philistines were determined to keep him alive.) To the claim that the captive might nonetheless have a plot in mind, Burns responds, "When he challenged Harapha to a single combat, bold as that was, Samson was careful to specify that it be fought in a narrow place to reduce the giant's advantage of vision . . . but what could be planned in an arena?" Burns also cites Albert Labriola's insight that "Since the feast of Dagon is repulsive to Samson, going there is not a natural instinct that can be mistaken for a divine command."[37] In sum, the fulfillment of Samson's prediction that he will either execute some great act or that this day will be his last is quite impressive, because again, there is no way he himself can bring about, unaided, either term of the prophecy. Hence, the motions would seem to have moved him to genuine prophecy.

Moreover, I would argue that they allow him to foretell three events, not just two. The third claim is one that might seem incredible, given the Philistines' treatment of him thus far, namely, that in the Dagonalia he will not comply with anything "scandalous" (1409), and that the Chorus will not hear anything "dishonorable, impure, [or] unworthy / [of] Our God, our Law, my nation, or myself" (1424). This claim has not received the scholarly attention that the two other, more explicitly prophetic ones have, yet I regard it as true prophecy because, like the others, he simply cannot execute it in his own power. Until now, he has had no reason to expect anything other than humiliation and jeering in the arena, and to assert that he will not be at all mocked seems painfully naïve.

And yet, the forecast is confirmed in the Dagonalia, thus underscoring Samson's status as a real prophet. Not only does he die *and* perform an act that is "great" in his compatriots' eyes, he executes a performance that is as honorable and pure as he prophesies it will be. Having been washed and dressed in "state livery," the prisoner walks into the temple surrounded by a formidable cohort of heavily armed soldiers, at which point the people cheer Dagon for making "their dreadful enemy" their captive (1622). Not once, however, is he compelled to play the clown; instead, Samson executes without challenge "incredible, stupendious" feats of strength that awe his captors (1627). At no point does anyone in the crowd offer insults or catcalls. Dalila does not come down to hold his hair aloft, nor do any young men pluck his hair or beard. No lyre is thrust into his hand, nor does he sing or dance. He is even granted the courtesy of heaving, pulling, drawing, and breaking objects that can be grasped "without help of eye" (1625), instead of being made to grope for them while crawling around on stage. In short, none of the cruelties heaped on all the other Samsons, biblical and otherwise, are meted out to Milton's protagonist; hence, the captive's dignity and honor remain fully intact. The fact that he accurately predicts such an unlikely outcome as well as his death and his final act confirms that the motions are truly divine, and that a miracle has occurred in the play.

Such an account differs sharply from most other interpretations of Samson's final actions, many of which argue that he plays the fool in the temple. These readings are frequently buttressed by references to Bakhtin's theory of the carnivalesque, and argue that the prisoner is God's holy fool, toying with his foes to subvert the established order. Arnold Stein apparently initiated this interpretation in his 1957 study *Heroic Knowledge,* declaring that when the protagonist enters the theater and performs his feats, "finally the ridicule is faced and mastered in a total victory of patience. The internal anguish at folly, the writhing over the external indignity — they have hindered him and they have helped him, but now he is purged of his folly, for he has accepted it and the consequences entirely. . . . He has been the Athlete of God and failed. Now he is the Fool of God and succeeds."

In like manner, Paul Sellin contends that the captive becomes "an object of ridicule" upon entering the arena, in part because of the state livery his enemies clothe him in: "[Milton's] description of Samson's dress is a wonderful touch for indicating the vindictiveness of the Philistine taunting." Following Stein, William Kerrigan argues that "Before an audience of Philistines . . . Samson plays fool to the Philistines," and suggests that the nuntius uses the term "horrid spectacle" (1542) to express his shock at the prisoner's humiliation. More recently, in a 1998 essay, Elizabeth Sauer declares that "rather than refusing to play the fool . . . Samson deliberately assumes this role. . . . The comic and parodic elements [in the scene] include . . . the descriptions of Samson sporting before and with the Philistines and of Samson's performance of the jester's part." And Norman T. Burns's 1996 article on the tragedy claims that "Samson's athletic performance at the Dagonalia contradicts his commitment to do nothing unworthy or dishonorable there." As evidence, Burns cites the roar of the crowd when they see the prisoner in "state livery," which Burns sees as a sign that Samson has fallen in "with the state's plan to 'magnify' Dagon by crediting him with having made the people's 'dreadful enemy their thrall.'" Anna Nardo's 1989 article "'Sung and Proverbed for a Fool': Samson As Fool and Trickster" is more attentive to the text when Nardo remarks that in the tragedy "We never see the foolish acts recorded in Judges," yet both her title and her opening claim, that "Samson is a fool — in the Judges story and in Milton's *Samson Agonistes*," precisely miss the point: because he does not clown for his enemies, Samson is not a fool.[38] Sellin's and Burns's contention that the livery somehow embarrasses the prisoner is not persuasive either, especially when these fresh clothes are contrasted with the grimy, shredded rags he wore prior to donning these clothes. Also, wearing a servant's clothes may be humbling, but not necessarily humiliating, especially when any potential mortification is more than offset by the imposing image of the soldiers who accompany him. He may be dressed as a servant, but both the soldiers and the crowd regard him with deadly seriousness. In sum, the spectacle of the Dagonalia proves that Samson does not look ludicrous when he enters, and that his exploits of strength are anything but foolish. Regarding him as a buffoon, however, not only neglects the spectacular items in the Messenger's speech, it also sets up a substantial contradiction between the play and its prefa-tory epistle, which censures contemporary tragedies for "inter-mixing comic stuff with tragic sadness or gravity." Critics sometimes argue that Harapha can be interpreted comically, since he is a kind of pompous Braggadochio figure, and they may have a point, but proving that Milton made the same error with his protagonist is much more difficult to establish.

One possible objection to my claim that the motions bestow gen-uine prophetic ability on Samson is that he seems to be prophetic even before the advent of the motions. For instance, speaking to his father early in the drama, Samson states that God will soon vin-dicate himself against Dagon:

> [God], be sure,
> Will not connive, or linger, thus provoked,
> But will arise and his great name assert:
> Dagon must stoop, and shall ere long receive
> Such a discomfit, as shall quite despoil him
> Of all these boasted trophies won on me,
> And with confusion blank his worshippers.   (465–71)

Upon hearing it, Manoa grants him prophetic status:

> With cause this hope relieves thee, and *these words*
> *I as a prophecy receive;* for God,
> Nothing more certain, will not long defer
> To vindicate the glory of his name
> Against all competition.   (472–76; my emphasis)

Not only is Samson's prediction startling, given the Philistines' utter dominance over Israel at this point in the tragedy; it also comes true. Roy Flannagan glosses "stoop" as "'Bow down' or 'submit,' but with the prophetic implication of 'fall on his face.'"[39] Whether we take "fall on his face" (1) to foretell an event that takes place after Samson's death, where Dagon's statue falls down and is beheaded, overwhelmed by the power of the Ark of God, next to which the Philistines unwittingly placed the statue (1 Sam. 5); or (2) to the fact that Dagon's statue in the temple effectively stoops when Samson brings down the roof on it and on Dagon's votaries; or (3) both, the remark constitutes an authentic prediction.

One might also adduce lines 598, where Samson prophesies that he will "shortly be with them that rest"; lines 1265–67, where he predicts of the Philistines that "because their end / Is hate, not help to me, it may with mine / Draw their own ruin who attempt the deed," thus appearing to forecast the collapse of the temple; and line 1347, where he tells the Hebrew Officer, who claims to be "sorry" about what Samson's refusal will lead to, "Perhaps thou shalt have cause to sorrow indeed." Flannagan suggests that line 1347 "may be prophetic of the downfall of the temple of Dagon."[40] In sum, the rousing motions might seem not specifically tied to any new endowment of prophecy. I contend, however, that they are analogous to the second gift of physical strength bestowed on Samson; that is, he may well be prophetic throughout the play, yet the motions instill in him a fresh, heightened sense of prophecy, one that he himself recognizes as such when he refers to it as "presage in the mind" (1387).

The characterization of Samson as prophet does not appear in the biblical narrative or in early modern dramatic analogues, yet it is precedented, in part, by Josephus. Scholars have noted a Josephan influence on the Harapha episode, where Samson defends himself against the giant's charge that he is a "murderer" (1180) for killing 30 men of Ascalon, then awarding their garments to a group of other Philistine men who had helped, first, to celebrate his wedding, then to solve a riddle the groom posed them. Samson responds by claiming that the co-celebrants were not sincere but in fact spies who had come to watch him while pretending to be his friends. Milton gets this detail not from Judges but from *Antiquities of the Jews* (5.8.6). Presumably, Milton added this information to make Samson's general animosity toward the Philistines more understandable since the episode with the spies made him believe that all Philistines were "set on enmity" (1201) against him, and thus Samson did not hesitate to use "hostility" against them whenever possible (1202–03).

Whether or not Samson's self-defense is compelling, the important point remains that Milton's depiction of Samson as a prophet may also be Josephan, for the historian notes that under his parents' care "[Samson] grew apace; and it appeared evidently that *he would be a prophet*, both by the moderation of his diet, and the permission of his hair to grow" (146; my emphasis). William Whiston cautions that "Here, by a *prophet*, Josephus seems only to mean one that was born by a particular providence, lived after the manner of a Nazirite devoted to God, and was to have an extraordinary commission and strength from God for the judging and avenging his people Israel, without any proper prophetic revelations at all."[41] Yet even if Whiston's caveat is true, Milton still could have interpreted Josephus's use of the term "prophet" in the more traditional sense, and employed it as such in the tragedy.

V. The Terrorist Interpretations: Final Considerations

I conclude my account of the rousing motions by considering both Feisal Mohamed's recent *PMLA* article, "Confronting Religious Violence: Milton's *Samson Agonistes*," which complements my own interpretation in certain respects, and two responses to that article by Joseph Wittreich and Peter C. Herman, also published in *PMLA*. Given the prominence of Mohamed's essay — it was the lead article in an issue devoted to terrorism and literature — and the fact that it engages the work of John Carey, perhaps the most influential of the revisionist critics, I shall discuss it in some detail.

Mohamed begins by reviewing Carey's controversial discussion of the play in the *Times Literary Supplement*, published a year after 9/11, in which Carey argues that Samson's actions are reminiscent of the terrorist attacks on New York and Washington, D.C. For instance, Carey states that "the similarities between the biblical Samson and the hijackers are obvious. Like them he destroys many innocent victims, whose lives, hopes and loves are all quite unknown to him personally. He is, in effect, a suicide bomber, and like the suicide bomber, he believes that his massacre is an expression of

God's will."[42] For Carey, the solution is to recognize that while his protagonist believes that he is God's scourge Milton does not, and in fact "holds up for our excoriation his portrait of the Danite Chorus celebrating Samson's murder of the Philistine lords." Mohamed counters this by arguing that Milton *approves* of Samson's actions by depicting him as commendable, citing "a preponderance of evidence pointing to Samson's heroic status," and by reading the drama in terms of how some of the author's friends, especially Henry Vane and Henry Lawrence, forged a definition of "spiritually justified militarism": "The role of the Saints as Lawrence defined it is to avoid the worldly snares with which they are surrounded and to rely on 'God and his Holy Spirit,' who 'has married us to himself in holiness and righteousness,' and thus to embrace the spiritual peace offered by the gospel. This inner peace will paradoxically . . . justify the Saints in their militarism."[43] Mohamed also cites Blair Worden's contention that the tragedy is partly a tribute to Vane, and remarks that "we would expect [the poet] to conform to the brand of sainthood defined in the spiritualist discourse especially important to Milton in his later years." Thus, Mohamed declares that the rousing motions constitute "the immediate divine illumination residing entirely outside the events with which we are presented. Samson must calm the human impulses that led him astray [previously] and follow the divine 'impulse' that is the guide of the Saint." Moreover, the motions, as well as the subsequent action at the temple, are clearly differentiated from the merely "fleshly, rational concerns of [the] three major dialogues [between Samson and his visitors]."[44]

This characterization of the motions as divine is consistent with my own, and I too believe that the poet regards Samson's actions as praiseworthy. However, while Mohamed historicizes the motions externally, in terms of seventeenth century spiritualist discourse, I argue that they are justified within the text, since they result in a miracle of prophecy. Moreover, I take issue with the way Mohamed expands on a common revisionist critique, namely, that despite his claims to be led by God, Samson's final exploit constitutes a slaughter of many innocent people. Mohamed also sees the action in these terms, adding that Milton "downplay[s] the human cost of Samson's triumph" by "marginalizing the humanity of nonadherents — just as he did in his satisfaction over the beheading of Charles, in his triumphalism over Cromwell's Irish slaughters, and in his advocacy in the final days of the republic of military suppression of the 'inconsiderate multitude['s]'" desire for monarchy.[45] He thus argues that the Miltonic Messenger's brief speech on the catastrophe "seems designed not to grant the Philistines the status of human beings" (336). Hence, Milton is able to regard Samson as admirable since his victims are not fully human.

I contend that the tragedy's denouement has the opposite effect, since it humanizes in surprising ways the prisoner's enemies, and more significantly, hints that a number of them may be spared. I do not propose to offer a full-scale theodical reading of the catastrophe, and I recognize that current scholarship tends to emphasize the drama's inscrutability and uncertainty.[46] Nonetheless, it is worth mentioning a few examples that may constitute Milton's attempts to justify and restrict the violence entailed by Samson's final exploit.

One is the Messenger's description of Dagon's temple, which has an arched roof and a semicircular shape, a design that allows for two types of spectators, seated and standing. The former are, of course, the elite of Philistia, the latter its commoners. At least some of the vulgar are thus able to escape relatively easily when the pillars fall, since there is nothing over their heads to crush them. By contrast, Judges describes the building as a house "full of men and women," and notes that "all the *lords* of the Philistines were there; and there were upon the roof about three thousand men and women, that beheld while Samson made sport" (16:27; my emphasis). Rubens and other painters — as well as Wunstius's and Rhodius's tragedies — depict the people on the roof perishing along with those below, but in fact the biblical narrator remarks that when Samson pulls down the pillars, "the house fell upon the *lords*, and upon all the people that were *therein*" (16:30; my emphases), leaving open the possibility that some of those on the roof could have escaped death somehow, perhaps by jumping off. Editors often claim that Milton's preservation of the vulgar is an innovation, but in fact he may be expanding on this hint in the text. Hence, it is possible that the vulgar who are saved in the tragedy number as many as 3,000, based on the Judges text.[47] It is also conceivable in the play that the prisoner's guide is able to escape, for when Samson grasps the pillars he seems to be standing on the edge of the semicircle; hence the guide might have easily stepped aside and avoided the falling columns. It may also be significant that Manoa and the Chorus are confident of retrieving Samson's body relatively easily (1727–30), which would make sense if it was near the edge of the fallen edifice rather than deep inside of it.

Similarly, and unlike any other Samson tragedy, it may be that Milton preserves not only the vulgar, but also would-be spectators who are still making their way to the temple when it is destroyed. Shortly after the protagonist exits, his father enters and tells the Chorus that "the city rings" with news of Samson's upcoming performance (1449), and "numbers thither flock" (1450). His use of the present tense suggests that people are still on their way to the temple when the catastrophe strikes, for little more than 20 lines later, Manoa hears the first "noise or shout" from the temple crowd (1472), and less than 30 lines after that first shout, he and the Chorus perceive the noise of the falling pillars and the screams of the crowd (1508 et passim). Hence, it is possible that not all of the Gaza citizenry is in the temple when it comes down. Further evidence that some may still be at home is suggested by Manoa's remark,

> I have attempted one by one the lords
> Either *at home,* or through the high street passing,
> With supplication prone and father's tears
> To accept of ransom for my son their prisoner.
>
> (1457–60; my emphasis)

Manoa also provides a plausible explanation for why some lords would still be at home at this point: While two-thirds of them are either spiteful, desiring further punishment of the captive, or venal, open to selling "both God and state" (1465) for their purposes, the remnant seem to be good men, "generous far and civil" (1467) and open to ransoming the captive. Also, the latter third differ markedly from the first group of lords, who "most reverenced Dagon and his priests" (1463), and who would have been eager to go to the celebration. Moreover, the other main motive for attendance — to see Samson humiliated in the arena — would also be less attractive to the third group, who earlier "confessed [to Manoa] / They had enough revenged, having reduced / Their foe to misery beneath their fears" (1467–69).

It is true that one of the first things the Messenger tells Manoa and the Chorus is, "Gaza yet stands, but all her sons are fall'n / All in a moment overwhelmed and fall'n" (1558–59), and he refers to the temple as "the edifice where *all* were met to see him" (1588; my emphasis). However, these lines do not necessarily mean that all the lords were present, for the nuntius is speaking quickly and generally at this point, and any precise distinctions about who was there and who was not might seem out of place. Surely Milton's intent at this point was to create a dramatic climax for the nuntius's speech, and the use of "all," whether correct or not, enables him to do so.

Another possible objection to the suggestion that the humane lords are spared is that Milton emphasizes their benevolence simply to make Manoa's attempt to ransom his son plausible. In Judges and the other Samson plays, Manoa is long dead by this point in Samson's life, and there is no mention made of any ransom. However, providing a reasonable motive for Manoa's quest is not inherently at odds with the intimation that some of the good lords may not be killed.

In any case, proving who is present and who absent at the catastrophe is impossible, given the lack of evidence, and would seem to constitute yet another example of the uncertainty that for many scholars characterizes the play. However, whether they do survive matters for the legitimacy, or lack thereof, of Samson's final feat.

By referring to that action as one of "mass murder," Peter Herman agrees with Mohamed's assessment of it as an act of "savagery."[48] Herman also puts his finger on why the question is significant by asking, rhetorically, "Are the generous and civil Philistines, who have had 'anough' revenge, as worthy of death as those who continue to desire Samson's humiliation? Does the simple fact of one's identity as a Philistine condemn one, however much or little one contributes to either Samson's degradation or the war between the Israelites and the Philistines?" Again, though, it is possible that those worthy Philistines may not have perished. In fact, Herman himself concedes that "not all . . . of the 'More generous far and civil' are . . . caught up in the slaughter."[49] Furthermore, if Milton was willing to spare the vulgar, he might also have been prepared to show that some of the lords were preserved.

I also contend that Milton goes to some lengths to emphasize that those who were clearly killed were not the innocent, but rather, the corrupt Philistine leaders, its "Lords, ladies, captains, councellors, or priests" (1653). As becomes clear in the Dalila episode, these are the very persons who violate the "law of nature, law of nations" (890) by setting Dalila and Samson, husband and wife in Milton's version, at odds. In doing so, Samson argues, they ceased to be true rulers and became tyrants, "an impious crew / Of men conspiring to uphold their state / By worse than hostile deeds, violating the ends / For which our country is a name so dear" (891–94). Thus, their deaths in the catastrophe would appear to be justified, from Milton's perspective at least.

Again, my aim here is not to provide a full theodical interpretation, but simply to adduce a few examples to suggest the author's potentially theodical intent. In sum, it is possible that Milton attempted to preserve his hero's moral purity, not by suggesting that those he killed were inhuman, but by intimating that the catastrophe was a comparatively limited action directed against those who fully deserved it, and by sparing the innocent. Wittreich's comment on the preservation of the vulgar in the tragedy can also be applied to the possible preservation of the humane lords: "In

Samson Agonistes . . . Milton's God . . . exemplifies not retributive but distributive justice."[50] Moreover, the contention mounted by John Carey, Herman, and Wittreich, that Milton critiques Samson's final action, may not be far off the mark; the author may well have been repulsed by the notion of an indiscriminate massacre, and thus attempted to render a justified and more restricted depiction of it. Whether or not modern readers find such a representation convincing or palatable, the mere possibility that Milton offers it to readers is significant and deserving of further study.

VI. *Dalila, Spectacle, and the Critical Stalemate*

Dalila's entrance is widely acknowledged to be the tragedy's most theatrical moment. Yet critics tend to focus almost exclusively on her subsequent debate with Samson. Such a response makes sense, for both speakers present highly compelling arguments, yet if we attend solely to the characters' words while ignoring or slighting their physical appearances, we come away with the impression that the scene ends in a stalemate. However, when the dispute is considered in relation to the spectacle a clear outcome emerges.

Their argument centers on the issue of Dalila's motive for betraying Samson. He accuses her of acting out of greed for gold (389, 831, 958, and 1114–15), and in fact, represents himself as cuckolded by gold: he tells Manoa that Dalila was "vitiated" by gold (389), a term John Leonard glosses as "corrupted, with overtones of 'to deflower or violate a woman.'"[51] Samson also remarks that the scent of gold caused her to conceive "her spurious firstborn, treason against me" (391). The fact that she is paid in gold contrasts with the Judges narrative, for according to 16:5, the Philistine leaders gave her silver to tempt Samson. Increasing the type and possibly the amount of money Dalila receives for her efforts is one of Milton's key alterations.

Dalila counters Samson's accusations by declaring that "It was not gold, as to my charge thou lay'st, / That wrought with me" (849–50). Rather, she claims, it was the magistrates and princes of her country who pressured her to betray Samson, to the point that she realized that "to the public good / Private respects must yield" (867–68). Samson responds by undermining her claims to patriotism and zeal. First, he declares that her service to her country was mistaken, since the men who goaded her to betray her own husband were actually violating "the law of nature, law of nations" (890).[52] In doing so, they proved themselves "an impious crew / Of men conspiring to uphold their state" (891–92) and were thus not worthy of her obedience. He then dismisses her argument that she was impelled by religious ardor, since "gods unable / To acquit themselves and prosecute their foes / But by ungodly deeds, the contradiction / Of their own deity, gods cannot be" (896–99). He concludes this section by labeling her professed motives as "false pretéxts" (902).

Again, both speakers' cases are presented with such conviction that it can be very difficult to decide who is telling the truth. Dalila might very well have acted out of patriotism: initially reluctant, she might have become avid for her task when she realized how it would serve Dagon. The gold could have been granted to her as a reward, not an incentive, for the betrayal. Some critics defend her on grounds such as these, although they usually focus on what she says. William Empson, for instance, probably the most influential of Dalila's supporters, remarks that her speeches are "greatly to her credit. . . . It is entirely credible that she betrayed Samson to her relations to save him for her love from the monstrous folly of his political programme." Similarly, James W. Tupper's 1920 *PMLA* article, which seems to have initiated the arguments in favor of Dalila, concludes that "The very fact that Dalila should betake herself to the prison where Samson is confined and beg his forgiveness when the other Philistines are celebrating the victory of Dagon should predispose us in her favor." D. C. Allen labels himself as one of the "advocatus Dalilae," defending her on the basis of her oral argument. And while Anthony Low does not exculpate Dalila, he is sympathetic to her, and he too concentrates primarily on what she says.[53]

I contend that Milton suspected that her speeches would tempt readers to believe her protestations of innocence, and thus included a detailed physical description of Samson's former wife to forestall such a reaction. Here is the choral description of Dalila's approach:

> But who is this, what thing of sea or land?
> Female of sex it seems,
> That so ornate, bedecked and gay,
> Comes this way sailing
> Like a stately ship
> Of Tarsus, bound for th' isles
> Of Javan or Gadier
> With all her bravery on, and tackle trim,
> Sails filled, and streamers waving,
> Courted by all the winds that hold them play.
> An amber scent of odorous perfume
> Her harbinger, a damsel train behind;
> Some rich Philistian matron she may seem,
> And now at nearer view, no other certain
> Than Dálila thy wife.
> *Sam:* My wife, my traitress, let her not come near me.
> *Chor.* Yet on she moves, now stands and eyes thee fixed,
> About t' have spoke, but now, with head declined
> Like a fair flower surcharged with dew, she weeps
> And words addressed seem into tears dissolved,
> Wetting the borders of her silken veil.   (710–30)

The Danites' description begins with an extended simile likening her to a "stately ship of Tarsus." Editors frequently gloss this image as a symbol of pride, citing Psalm 48:7 "(Thou breakest the ships of Tár-shish with an east wind") and Isaiah 23:1 ("Howl, ye ships of Tár-shish.") Less often noted is the fact that ships associated with that ancient city also symbolized great wealth. For instance, in cataloging King Solomon's riches, the narrator of 1 Kings states that the king "had at sea a navy of Tár-shish . . . once in three years came the navy of Tár-shish, bringing gold, and silver, ivory, and apes, and peacocks" (10:22). Similarly, in Isaiah 60:9 God declares that "the isles shall wait for me, and the ships of Tár-shish first, to bring . . . their silver and gold with them." Bruce M. Metzger, editor of *The New Oxford Annotated Bible*, notes that such ships were proverbial for their ability to make long voyages.[54]

It seems, then, that the ship image is intended to suggest not only Dalila's pride but also her wealth. Her riches are evidenced as well by her silken veil, her perfume, and her damsel train, which consists of young women who carry the hem of her dress. Since such trains were usually characteristic of royalty, Milton seems to be conveying here a tremendously inflated self-regard on Dalila's part, and the cumulative impression of her entrance, according to the Danites, is that of a *"rich* Philistian matron" (my emphasis).

A mere line or two at this point in the tragedy, telling rather than showing that she enters gorgeously attired, would not have served Milton's intent, for I believe that he wished to figure her greed as vividly and fully as possible. He did so by showing her as a would-be Cleopatra, decked out in the finest, most expensive dress, accompanied by a retinue fit for a queen, and adorned with enough perfume to carry her presence some distance away. By employing spectacular means to manifest such prodigality, Milton shows — well before she speaks — that Dalila was driven by gold-lust, her protestations to the contrary notwithstanding. He had almost certainly used this same strategy in *Paradise Lost,* when introducing Belial:

> On the' other side up rose
> Belial, in act more graceful and humane:
> A fairer person lost not Heav'n; he seemed
> For dignity composed and high exploit:
> But all was false and hollow; though his tongue
> Dropped manna, and could make the worse appear
> The better reason, to perplex and dash
> Maturest counsels.   (2.108–15)

Readers of the epic who pay attention to these lines are well-armed against Belial's seductive proposal.

Returning to the tragedy, Parker claims that the damsel train "serves no dramatic purpose,"[55] but this seems precisely wrong, for by swelling the scene of her approach, either carrying the dress or at least visually extending it, the damsels underscore Dalila's self-importance. The young women may also help to evoke the choral description of Dalila's exit: "She's gone, a manifest serpent by her sting / Discovered in the end, till now concealed" (997–98). Although the characterization of Dalila here seems primarily figurative, it may be suggested to them by the sight of her walking away followed by her train, who follow her, one assumes, in single file. Elsewhere, the Danites voice similarly figurative descriptions: In addition to their initial characterization of Dalila and her ladies-in-waiting as a vessel, they refer to the approaching Harapha as a "storm" (1061). Also, the representation of Dalila's exit might have been provided to remind any reader still in thrall to her deceptive rhetoric that she is not to be trusted. In sum, awareness of spectacle is essential to an understanding of Dalila's motives, for it serves to manifest what is otherwise concealed by her noble-sounding self-defense. However, as long as critics fail to visualize Dalila and evaluate her dispute with Samson abstractly, they will continue to regard the debate, erroneously, as a draw.

VII. *Spectacle in the Harapha Scene*

The Harapha episode is regarded by some expositors as the most important in the play. Parker deems it "the heart of the drama," and D. C. Allen regards it as "the hinge of the tragedy."[56] While it has not occasioned as much controversy as Samson's regeneration or the Dalila scene, the episode has been criticized on two points, both related to Milton's preface to the tragedy. The first is what might be called its perceived implausibility. Merritt Hughes, for instance, suggests that for many readers "Samson's triumph over Harapha seems too easy," Max Beerbohm remarks that "Harapha's refusal to tackle Samson [is] one of the [play's] crowning absurdities," and Theodor Siebert regards the entire scene as a poetic wish-fulfillment on the poet's part.[57] Moreover, if Harapha is indeed a serious warrior, yet turns down a fight with his country's chief enemy, has not Milton violated one of the virtues extolled in the preface, namely, "verisimilitude," a sense of probability or realism? Also controverted is the giant's nature: if he is a comic braggart, does this fact not contradict the epistle's censure of the intermixing of tragic and comic figures?

As I shall demonstrate, at least one item of spectacle in the scene has been misconstrued at times, first by an influential production of the tragedy, and later by at least two well-known Miltonists. This error may have likewise given rise to the mistaken impression, mentioned by Hughes, that Samson's victory here is effortless. In order to fully understand the error and its impact, it is first necessary to consider the scene as a whole. When the Chorus first see Harapha approaching, they tell the prisoner to

> Look now for no enchanting voice, nor fear
> The bait of honeyed words; a rougher tongue
> Draws hitherward, I know him by his stride,
> The giant Hárapha of Gath, his look
> Haughty as is his pile high-built and proud.   (1065–69)

While the giant's walk identifies him, his purpose for visiting is initially unclear to the Chorus, although less mystifying than Dalila's appearance was at first:

> Comes he in peace? what wind hath blown him hither
> I less conjecture than when first I saw
> The sumptuous Dálila floating this way:
> His habit carries peace, his brow defiance. . . .
>   His fraught we soon shall know, he now arrives.   (1070–73; 1075)

Various items of spectacle are furnished here: Harapha is known for his large gait, which is, apparently, excessive even for a giant. He is neither armed nor dressed for battle, for Israel is not at war with Philistia, nor is he seconded by a squire. Still, his haughty demeanor seems belligerent since his body is referred to as a "high-built," a "pile . . . proud," and the choral adjectives indicate his sheer size. Interestingly, the term "pile" can denote a large building or edifice in the way Milton uses it to refer to Pandaemonium (*PL* 1.722), as well as a heap of stones.

The fact that Samson arrives in civilian clothing, unseconded, matters because it makes Harapha's refusal to fight him far more plausible and renders the entire scene more complex than many take it to be. If he were armed at this point, it would be evident that the giant was spoiling for a fight, and he would quickly assent to the prisoner's challenge to do so. Instead, when he first comes upon Samson, Harapha explains that he has come not to "condole" the captive's misfortunes, but rather to see if his appearance somehow explains the astonishing rumors he has heard about Samson's exploits in battle, particularly the fight in which Samson killed one thousand Philistines at Rameth-Lehi using a donkey's jawbone. He finds it difficult to believe that such a man could have inflicted so much damage with this paltry weapon, telling him that had he (Harapha) been present at Rameth-Lehi, Samson would "soon [have] wish[ed for] other arms" (1096). Harapha then claims that he will survey each of the captive's limbs, apparently in order to uncover the secret of his strength, such as a massive right arm. He seems to move closer to him at this point to begin sizing up his arms and legs, which prompts Samson to state that "the way to know [my strength] were not to see but taste" (1091). Leonard glosses "taste" as "explore by touch, put to the proof,"[58] and it is clear that the Hebrew is challenging him to grapple in a duel. This summons, the first of three, catches Harapha off guard, for he admits that he assumed that chains and slavery had tamed Samson (1092–93). He points out that no duel is possible anyway since they are not on a battlefield or at a tournament, and because the prisoner is blind.

Samson is not satisfied with these demurrals, of course, and presses him: "Boast not of what thou wouldst; have done [on the battlefield], but do / What then thou wouldst; thou seest it in thy hand" (1104–05). He tells him here, in essence, "You can fight now, using your hand as a weapon"; presumably he is proposing that they wrestle or box. That the giant now understands him is clear from his reply: "To combat with a blind man I disdain, / And thou hast need of much washing to be touched" (1106–07). That is, he recognizes that Samson has asked him to take part in some sort of hand-to-hand combat that will require them to make physical contact with one another. Again, he refuses. In an apparent concession to the giant's adherence to chivalric protocol, Samson then extends another invitation:

> let be assigned
> Some narrow place enclosed, where sight may give thee,
> Or rather flight, no great advantage on me;
> Then put on all thy gorgeous arms, thy helmet
> And brigandine of brass, thy broad habergeon,
> Vant-brace and greaves, and gauntlet, add thy spear
> A weaver's beam, and seven-times-folded shield.   (1116–22)

These suggestions, if carried out, would allow the two disputants to conduct something resembling a traditional duel. Instead of having to engage with the prisoner in a wrestling match, Harapha would not need to touch Samson since they would vie in a sword-staff fight, yet even under such conditions, Harapha will not fight.

How are we to account for his unwillingness to do so? Harapha's reluctance stems from the astonishing visual discrepancy presented to the visitor: On the one hand, he sees a blind, filthy, chained prisoner, considerably smaller than he. Furthermore, the captive is not wearing a scrap of armor or carrying the slightest weapon. On the other hand, Samson hurls challenge after challenge at the giant and extends to him every concession he might require for a proper fight. Harapha therefore rightly suspects that something unusual is afoot, and answers Samson's mock of his armor by claiming that the prisoner would "durst not disparage glorious arms / Which greatest heroes have in battle worn" unless he were using some sort of black magic or charm (1130, 1134–35).

Samson denies the charge, of course, and continues to badger his bewildered visitor. The giant still puts him off, however, on the grounds that the captive is on death row and is thus not a worthy opponent for him. In exasperation, Samson cries out, "Cam'st thou for this, vain boaster, to survey me, / To descant on my strength, and give thy verdict?" (1227–28). He then dares him to "Come nearer, . . . / But take good heed my hand survey not thee" (1229–30). It seems clear, then, that Harapha has been standing apart from the prisoner, just out of reach, and that Samson now begins lunging for him. Samson defies him yet again, telling him to "bring up thy van," (1234), that is, to start fighting, and notes that while his (Samson's) "heels are fettered," his "fist is free" (1235). When the giant declines once more Samson issues his final threat: "Go baffled coward, lest I run upon thee, / Though in these chains, bulk without spirit vast, / And with one buffet lay thy structure low" (1237–39).

This threat causes Harapha to exit in disgrace. As he storms out, the Danites sneer that "His giantship is gone somewhat crestfall'n, / Stalking with less unconscionable strides, / And lower looks, but in a sultry chafe" (1244–46). The image of his leaving "crestfallen" indicates that he has now lowered his unhelmeted head; he is also taking somewhat smaller steps than he did on entering the scene, and his looks are "lower," which means, I suspect, that his gaze seems less arrogant. He is also manifestly angry, blushing with rage and embarrassment. This exit shows what is, perhaps, not quite clear in their argument, namely, that Samson's accusations of cowardice against Harapha are true — the giant is visibly shamed, not just irritated. Still, I take issue with those who characterize Harapha as fundamentally comic, a braggadocio or a Plautean *miles gloriosus.*[59] I contend, instead, that the scene presents an accomplished warrior who has read the situation correctly and acted accordingly. Granted, Harapha's refusal is craven and worthy of contempt, but also understandable, for he realizes that if he consented to fight his death would likely be the result. Hence, Milton has it both ways: Harapha is not inherently comic, even though he is humiliated in the encounter, yet his exit is logical, as well as ignoble.

It is also important to note that the scene's blocking helps to energize what could become nothing more than a long argument. Paul Sellin's claim that the translation of "agonistes" as "a combatant in the Olympic Games" is somewhat problematic since there is no literal contest in the play,[60] yet Milton suggests this rendering by showing Samson as one who is as combative as possible against a reluctant opponent. The episode, perceived correctly, is tense, and nearly violent — Harapha circles the captive warily, while Samson clenches his fist and perhaps takes a swing or two at the hostile visitor. Samson's eventual victory over the giant is achieved without actual conflict, but the way he bests Harapha resonates with the physicality of his former triumphs. For the description of Harapha exiting "crestfallen" functions both as a literal reference to his declined head and an evocation of Samson's former exploits, when he "soiled [the Philistines'] . . . crested helmets in the dust" (141).

In closing, Beerbohm's dismissal of the scene, noted earlier, makes more sense when we consider that the performance he witnessed was directed by William Poel for the Milton Tercentenary (1908). Poel had Harapha seconded by several squires and, presumably, depicted him as well armed. Conversely, the victory is far more convincing if we see the giant as wearing mufti and unaccompanied. Poel was not the only one to characterize the giant in this fashion. A *PMLA* article by Barbara Lewalski claims that Harapha is "heavily armed" in the scene; just so, in a *JEGP* essay, John Steadman characterizes the interaction between the captive and the giant as "an encounter between a physically handicapped 'hero of faith' and a Philistine giant in full armor." Other scholars, including Thomas Kranidas and Derek Wood, may make the same mistake.[61] Granted, these appear to be minority assessments, and both *The Riverside Milton* (edited by Roy Flannagan) and the 1990 Oxford edition of Milton (co-edited by Jonathan Goldberg and Stephen Orgel) annotate line 1073 ("his habit carries peace") as indicating that the giant is unarmed. Even so, Poel's production was the first major staging of the tragedy, and relatively well attended; moreover, it clearly influenced at least one spectator (Beerbohm) to regard the scene as unpersuasive. And of course, Lewalski and Steadman are eminent Miltonists, and normally very careful readers, so one wonders if other readers — whether scholarly or not — similarly neglected line 1073, and then, like Beerbohm, found the episode implausible.

VIII. *The Chorus of* Samson Agonistes: *Gender and Movement*

The Chorus in *Samson Agonistes* is one of its most-discussed features. Nearly all interpretations focus on what the Danites say, and to what extent they function as reliable guides to the action. As with the commentary on Dalila, what is missing from these debates is a consideration of what the Chorus looks like and how it moves. I believe that their costumes and motions are as important as their words, and that a greater awareness of these items helps offset two charges often leveled at the work, to wit, that it is both static and misogynist.

As I shall demonstrate in the next chapter, producers often tend to cast the Chorus as a group comprised of both men and women. The desire for inclusivity was and is commendable, but it departs from the text, which specifies that the Danites are all men, "Brethren and men of Dan," as Manoa calls them (332). They are also referred to in the play's Argument as "friends and equals of [Samson's] tribe"; Leonard cites *OED* B 1c to annotate "equals" as "people of about the same age." The similarities in age between the members of the Chorus may contribute to the prisoner's impression that they walk with "joint pace" (110), that is, with no one getting ahead or lagging behind. It may also evoke his (mistaken) impression that his foes have returned to torment him, if his tormentors tended to be soldiers moving in formation. The ages and gender of the Chorus also help to explain what are perhaps the tragedy's most problematic lines. After Dalila exits, the Danites declare that

> God's universal law
> Gave to the man despotic power
> Over his female in due awe,
> Not from that right to part an hour,
> Smile she or lour.   (1053–57)

Too often, what is overlooked here is the dramatic situation, which is that a number of Samson's friends and neighbors — all of them men of his age — are seeking to console him. Their speech is not what Milton himself thought (in fact, he stated that wives who

excel their husbands in competence should take the lead in marriage), nor even necessarily what Samson thinks, but rather, a comment that is believable considering the source. It does not differ
that much from, say, a group of men at a bar, comforting a thwarted
male friend by pronouncements about "how women really are."
To read the passage without considering the gender and ages of
the speakers, however, is to ignore the dramatic context of these
lines.

The Danites' gender also helps to reinforce their status as self-
appointed guardians of Samson. At times they seem to encircle him;
indeed, while the tragedy does not offer a curtain, they almost
function like a human discovery space. For instance, when Manoa
enters, he does not see his son until they say, "As signal now in
low dejected state, / As erst in highest, behold him where he lies"
(338–39). And at line 725, Samson urges them not to let Dalila come
near him, although she approaches too quickly for them: "Yet on
she moves, now stands and eyes thee fixed" (726). In like manner,
when Samson leaves for the Dagonalia he tells them, "Brethren
farewell, your company along / I will not wish, lest it perhaps
offend them / To see me girt with friends" (1413–15), intimating,
perhaps, that they instinctively surround him as he prepares to leave.

Is there any suggestion that the Chorus also exhibit dancelike
or formal actions? In his entry for "Chorus" in *A Milton Encyclopedia,* John Huntley argues that "There are [for the Chorus] no cues
for patterned or dancelike motion, it being more *coro stabile* than
mobile."[62] Yet the tragedy's prefatory epistle is somewhat equiv-
ocal on this matter. Here is Milton's full comment on the chorus:

> The measure of verse used in the chorus is of all sorts, called by the
> Greeks monostrophic, or rather *Apolelymenon,* without regard had
> to *strophe, antistrophe,* or *epode,* which were a kind of stanza framed
> only for the music, then used with the chorus that sung; not essen-
> tial to the poem, and therefore not material; or being divided into
> stanzas or pauses, they may be called *Allaeostropha.*

At first, he seems to admit the possibility of some sort of turning
(strophe) when he employs the term "monostrophic," which

indicates one change of direction. He then revises this by invoking "apolelymenon," a Greek term meaning "freed," that is, liberated from the obligation to make such a change of direction. Yet he does not fully dismiss the notion of Strophe, but instead alludes to the inclusion of Allaeostropha, that is, "of irregular strophes." The tragedy itself seems to hint at formal motion on the part of the Danites. Perhaps most significant in this regard are the two semichoruses that start at line 1669. This typographical division may also imply a physical separation within the group. Choral divisions appear in several Greek tragedies, including one of Milton's favorites, *Alcestis*. Near the beginning of that work, at line 76, the Chorus enters, then divides into two sections that address one another. Hence, if the Danites are in patterned, formal motion at the end of the play, it seems possible that they are in motion earlier as well.

In *The Riverside Milton,* Roy Flannagan offers the intriguing observation that the 1671 text indents line 300, which begins the second stanza of the choral speech, "Just are the ways of God"; the indentation, he argues, "indicates choral movement."[63] He says this, perhaps, because the indentation introduces a stanza that, if not metrically identical to the previous stanza, contains the same number of lines as it (seven), thus paralleling, somewhat, the strophe and antistrophe of a classical play. Moreover, in the 1671 text there are 16 other indented lines of which all but three are spoken by the Danites; the remaining lines belong to Samson.[64] While none of these indentations, other than line 300, set off stanzas of identical length, some of the stanzas are of similar size, such as lines 1046–52 (seven lines) and 1053–60 (eight lines). These nearly identical stanzas might also be intended to loosely imitate strophe and antistrophe. In this regard, it is worth noting that Milton's "*Ode to Rouse*" (1645), a deliberate imitation of a Greek chorus, clearly indicates strophe and antistrophe, yet while some of its stanzas are precisely the same length, others are only approximately so. He also uses the same term employed in the tragedy's preface, "apolelymenon," at the end of "*Ode to Rouse*" to explain what he has done: "The meters are determined partly by correlation, and they are partly free [apolelymenon]." Conversely, the three indented lines spoken by Samson divide up portions of his speeches. He certainly is not dancing at lines 617 and 633, but rather, lying dejectedly on the mound. Yet William R. Parker contends that this moment constitutes a "stage lyric," a moment not uncommon in Greek drama, in which a character will sing a lyrical monody, a kind of solo that is answered by a choral ode. And line 1640 simply differentiates Samson's speech from the narrative preceding it.[65]

The Choral movement, both formal and informal, is significant because it alleviates one of the central charges leveled at the play, to wit, its static quality. If fully registered, these motions vary the work's texture and pacing. As I will later show, productions of the tragedy have tried to offset its long speeches and apparently inert scenes with various expedients, including, in one version, casting a girl and a boy as part of the Chorus, and having them skip and cavort while the rest of the Chorus intoned their odes. In another, the personae mounted a pyramid-shaped figure and regrouped in varying configurations throughout the performance.[66] Such efforts were, perhaps, provocative, but unnecessary, given the hints about motion buried in the text. To date, no production I know of has realized such hints, but if they did, the play might come off as less immobile. However, it would be wrong to extend this point too far, since formal choral movement is, at most, latent. In a sense, it corresponds to the play's five-act structure, which is not marked, but rather implied by the prefatory epistle's comment that "It suffices if the whole drama be found not produced beyond the fifth act." Following that comment, certain editors and critics, such as Parker, Low, and Leonard, have provided plausible line divisions corresponding to a five-act pattern in *Samson*.

IX. *Acoustics of the Tragedy*

One final staging feature merits attention, namely, the sounds of the Dagonalia crowd. True, acoustic effects might not seem to fit

into the category of *opsis,* but they are nonetheless integral to performance, and, like visual effects, the responsibility of the *skeuopoios*
or one of his assistants. Milton's deployment of acoustic effects
underscores the tragedy's performative quality.

There are three references to the sounds of the spectators in the
drama: at line 16, when Samson seeks shelter from the "popular
noise" of the crowd, which is apparently loud enough to drive him
to a quiet spot; Manoa's questioning of the Chorus, when he asks
them, "What noise or shout was that? it tore the sky," and their
reply, "Doubtless the people shouting to behold / Their once great
dread, captive, and blind before them, / Or at some proof of strength
before them shown" (1472–75); and Manoa's registering of a second noise:

> *Manoa:* I know your friendly minds and — O what noise!
> Mercy of Heav'n what hideous noise was that!
> Horribly loud unlike the former shout.
> *Chorus:* Noise call you it or universal groan
> As if the whole inhabitation perished;
> Blood, death, and dreadful deeds are in that noise,
> Ruin, destruction at the utmost point.
> *Manoa:* Of ruin indeed methought I heard the noise,
> O it continues, they have slain my son.
> *Chorus:* Thy son is rather slaying them; that outcry
> From slaughter of one foe could not ascend.
>
> (1508–18)

Several things are interesting in these passages. The first is that by
having Samson register the noise of the crowd in the opening
speech, Milton may be implying that the noise continues softly
throughout the play. This way the noise would not disrupt the on-
stage action, yet it would be loud enough to remind the audience
of what is transpiring off-stage. Moreover, the continuance of the
noise may also serve to occasion remarks such as Manoa's procla-
mation to Samson that the Dagonalia is marked by "Great pomp,
and sacrifice, and praises loud" (436). Another notable fact is that
the crowd's roar at the entrance of their prize captive, and their

subsequent groan, are unlike anything in Greek drama, which usually has only one audible character off-stage. By contrast, the roar in Milton's play comes from a group of 3,000 spectators on the temple roof, in addition to an unnamed number of audience-members within the building. Moreover, the voices all sound as one: their initial cry is interpreted as a "noise or shout" (1472), and Manoa says that "it tore the sky" (1472). Also, it is called a "universal groan" (1511), and, in fact, at one point Manoa thinks that it is Samson alone who is crying out, a mistaken but plausible impression that the Chorus corrects. In other words, these shouts are not like the cheers or boos commonly heard at sporting events; rather, they are much more integrated, which fact serves to emphasize the essential unity of the crowd, as well as to showcase the unified catastrophe which only the Dagonalia could provide.

FIVE

Intended for the Stage?

SAMSON AGONISTES IN PERFORMANCE

The year 2000 marked the centenary of an important but overlooked milestone in Milton studies, namely, the first staging of *Samson Agonistes* by William Poel. While many scholars may be aware of isolated productions of the tragedy, the extent and variety of its stage history is perhaps less well known. The work was successful as a dramatic reading throughout the eighteenth and nineteenth centuries, yet it had never been attempted on the boards until Poel's landmark production. That event ushered in a range of performances throughout the twentieth century, with nearly every decade offering several dramatizations. At least 15 of these were full-dress affairs mounted in theaters or theatrical settings; others included partially staged dramatic readings, a radio version, and a one-man rendition of the play.[1]

It is important now to assess what light, if any, a century of production has shed on our understanding of *Samson*. For instance, do the various performances tend to confirm or refute Milton's statement in the tragedy's prefatory epistle that it was "never intended" for the stage? Moreover, such deliberation may show that these productions secured a position for *Samson* in the theater canon.

I. *Pre-1900 Stagings*

First, however, a word on the prehistory of the tragedy's productions. In 1671, Milton published *Samson*, along with the prefatory epistle; with several exceptions, for the next 225 years readers took seriously his remark that the drama was not meant for the stage. The few pre-1900 stagings have been ably surveyed by Alwin Thaler and his succinct account of them can be summarized briefly. Luigi Riccoboni, an Italian playwright and stage historian, visited England and seems to have been familiar with Milton's work. In 1717 he composed a French version of *Samson* that was presented in Paris. In 1739 his compatriot Jean-Antoine Romagnesi followed suit, mounting a rhymed adaptation of *Samson* for the same venue. Meanwhile, approximately seven editions of the tragedy had appeared in England by 1722. In that year, Bishop Atterbury approached Alexander Pope about dividing it into acts and scenes for the stage, and expressed the hope that *Samson* could be acted by the King's Scholars at Westminster.[2] Atterbury's subsequent confinement to the Tower apparently scuttled this idea; Pope himself never mentions it. I would add that David Erskine Baker lists *Samson* in his *Companion to the Playhouse* (published in 1764), and observes that he had met a certain (unnamed) gentleman who had altered the work "so as to render it fit for the stage," and who planned to mount it in or around 1741–42. If this intention was ever realized, no record of the performance is extant. By contrast, *A Masque at Ludlow Castle* was not only staged in 1634 but also frequently adapted for the boards throughout the eighteenth and nineteenth centuries. Moreover, theatrical versions of *Paradise Lost, Lycidas, L'Allegro,* and *Il Penseroso* were also produced often during this period.[3]

How are we to account for the near-total lack of staging of the tragedy for over two centuries, an interval in which Milton's other works were performed regularly? Some would-be producers may have been put off by the drama's long speeches and relative lack of physical action, although as we have seen, some were not. Another obstacle to staging *Samson* may have been the popularity of George F. Handel's oratorio *Samson,* which is substantially based on Milton's tragedy. Handel and his librettist Newburgh Hamilton tagged Milton's blank verse to provide airs for the singers. For instance, Samson's great lines "O dark, dark, dark, amid the blaze of noon, / Irrecoverably dark, total eclipse / Without all hope of day" (80–82) were rewritten as follows:

> Total eclipse! No sun, no Moon!
> All dark amidst the blaze of Noon!
> O glorious light! No chearing Ray
> To glad my Eyes with welcome Day!

In addition, Hamilton eliminated the Public Officer and invented a new character, namely, Micah, a Jewish woman. Nonetheless, he and Handel retained the original's basic plot structure.

The oratorio was composed in the early 1740s; it premiered on February 18, 1743, and was performed seven more times that year, twice in 1744, twice in 1820, three times in 1853, and seven times in 1869. Single performances were offered in 1754, 1755, 1772, 1777, 1825, and 1829, and it continued to be mounted throughout the 1900s. Even today, Handel's *Samson* is offered every few years or so; moreover, it has been recorded as recently as 1996, for Coro Records.

Part of the oratorio's initial success seems to have stemmed from its dramatic qualities as much as its musical ones. Handel, in fact, apparently presented it as an alternative to traditional theater, for he realized he was competing against that genre as well as Italian opera. Hence, he produced *Samson* at Covent Garden Theater and employed three well-known actresses to sing in it. Katherine Clive, also known as "the indomitable Pivy," and one of the most popular comic actresses of the time, was contracted for Dalila's part. Her singing ability was criticized by some; Horace Walpole, for instance, remarked that she had no voice whatsoever. Yet Handel seems to have valued her acting talents more highly than her voice. Mrs. Cibber, daughter-in-law of the laureate Colley Cibber,

and rival with Clive for the part of Polly in *The Beggar's Opera,*
played Micah, while subsequent productions featured the lovely —
and scandalous — Anne Catley, a well-known stage beauty.[4]

The tendency to present this oratorio as a semitheatrical event
continues up to the present, where operatic versions of Handel's
Samson are not difficult to find. These partly dramatic productions
may have functioned in effect as musical "stagings" of Milton's
tragedy throughout the 1800s and 1900s. Hence, traditional enactments of *Samson Agonistes* may have struck prospective producers as superfluous. According to Winton Dean's authoritative study
of Handel's oratorios, *Samson* was begun in the fall of 1741; Handel
then traveled to Dublin to oversee the premiere of *Messiah.* He
returned to England in 1742, and *Samson* was produced the following
year. Given Handel's fame, it is possible that news of his upcoming oratorio about Samson was leaked to the Dublin public. If so,
the Dublin theater producer mentioned in Erskine Baker's
Companion to the Playhouse might have scrapped his plans to
mount the work (in or around 1741–42) so as not to compete with
the composer. Others might have experienced a similar reluctance.[5]

II. *William Poel's Production and Its Successors*

William Poel (1852–1934), however, had no such qualms. Poel was
a theater producer whose mission was to recover the original conditions of the Elizabethan stage. Thus, his players often wore
Elizabethan style costumes and spoke rapidly, with few pauses for
business; moreover, they were lit from the top and the front, not
from footlights. Although Poel specialized in Shakespeare, he also
directed *Faustus, Everyman,* Jonson's *Sejanus,* and *The Bacchae.*
Robert Speaight, Poel's biographer, speculates that Poel added
Samson to his other productions because "there was an affinity
[between Poel and Milton] which was both ethical and prophetic . . .
[Poel] asked of the drama that it should elevate; he was not content that it should merely entertain."[6]

Poel's *Samson* was notable for two reasons: Not only is it the
first theatrical production of the drama on record, it also literally

set the stage for at least three subsequent stagings. His version of the tragedy was acted twice in 1900, then six more times in 1908 for the Milton Tercentenary. The most striking facet of Poel's production was its blocking. Despite Milton's single stage direction, "before the prison at Gaza," as well as Samson's own description of sitting on a mound near the prison (3–5), Poel featured the actors on a series of steps with the protagonist seated in a chair at the top of a kind of elevated platform, where he remained until the catastrophe. The characters continually regrouped throughout the play, with Samson staying at the apex of this pyramid and the supporting persons below him at the other points of the triangle.

Reviews varied considerably. The critic for the *Morning Post* was highly complimentary, claiming that the show was "one of the most important that lies in the power of our times to give." Other critics also praised it, including the normally caustic reviewer of *The Referee*. Max Beerbohm, however, panned the dramatization, as did the anonymous reviewer of *The Academy*; both critics felt that the work was essentially autobiographical and unfit for the stage. The latter singled out Poel's handling of the Chorus as especially problematic.[7]

Poel's production remained essentially unchanged when it was encored in 1908 for the Milton Tercentenary. Beerbohm censured the production for casting Ian MacClaren to play Samson; he felt that this actor's average build and soft-spokenness disqualified him for the part. He was also critical of the Chorus's entrance, claiming that it "destroyed all aesthetic illusion, and [sent] us . . . into paroxysms of internal laughter," primarily because, in his term, the Danites "ululated" while approaching the prisoner.[8] In reviewing the 1908 staging, the anonymous critic of the *London Times* echoed Beerbohm by censuring Poel's handling of the chorus: "If women are chosen to play the chorus they should not be allowed to twitter like starlings." (Poel's chorus was comprised of men as well as women.) In general, however, he was complimentary:

> This great tragedy is superb in the study; what of it on the stage? [Its] action is not such as to carry the spectator along with anything like excitement, nor such as to offer him scenes, groupings, changes

which will interest or delight the eyes. Everything . . . depends, in fact, upon the language, that majestic Miltonic language. And in the last issue that means, of course, that everything depends upon the elocution of the actors. In that respect the audience was, on the whole, remarkably well served.

Following this remark, the reviewer praised the actors' declamation, then commended Poel's blocking, noting that the stage composed of steps "worked well" and allowed all spectators to see the protagonist clearly. In addition, C. E. Montague, drama critic for the *Manchester Guardian,* noted that "to an uninformed spectator it looked as if [Poel] had every one of his groupings painted to a finish in his mind and then transferred it, touch by touch, to its place on a purple background, all under the strong influence of Italian medieval and Renaissance theories of pictorial design." Montague likened this pyramidal arrangement to Raphael's well-known *School of Athens* and other classic paintings. For him, Poel's dynamic production solved what he regarded as the chief problem for spectators of the tragedy, namely, its static quality.[9]

Nugent Monck, Poel's one-time stage manager and a cast member of several Poel dramatizations (though not of *Samson*), went on to become a producer in his own right.[10] In 1938, he supervised a staging of the tragedy. Like his mentor, Monck was attracted to *Samson* for its moral and religious content, and he too attempted to offset its static nature, although in different ways. Monck's production, set in Norwich's Maddermarket Theatre and acted by the Norwich Players, distributed choral speeches among the Danites so that they sometimes spoke in turn, sometimes together. He also assigned portions of Samson's opening monologue to the boy who brings him on-stage. Andrew Stephenson, reviewing the show for *Theatre Arts Monthly,* remarked, "This substitution of dialogue for monologue was dramatically an improvement." Monck also divided the drama into two halves, opening the second with a flourish of music that underscored Dalila's entrance. As did Poel, Monck relied on a painterly set: Stephenson noted that "[Monck] first considered [the tragedy] in terms of Rembrandt. Here, too, was solemnity, grandeur, brooding darkness, flashes of light," although he also contended that "the Maddermarket stage is too small to achieve Rembrandtesque lighting effects and the costumes and settings approached an austere kind of Tiepolo decoration." In many respects, Monck followed the text faithfully; for instance, Samson was costumed with long hair and chains, and Dalila was accompanied by her maidens. He did, however, cut the play heavily. Monck's production elicited high praise from Stephenson:

> The second half opened with . . . the superb entrance of Dalila and her attendants, surely one of the most elaborately prepared entrances in all drama. . . . From there on the play gains dramatic force. The speech in which the Messenger describes Samson's heroic end is overpowering and the rest of the poem is one of the supreme achievements of the human mind. It lost nothing of its mystery and peace and consolation on the stage.[11]

Poel's influence was also evident in Nevill Coghill's 1951 Oxford production, which was got up in the quadrangle of All Souls' College, since it too featured the Chorus in seventeenth century garb. (Incidentally, this performance was the third time Coghill directed the tragedy.) The *London Times'* reviewer applauded the enactment and complimented both the costuming and Coghill's ability to exploit the impressive architecture of the "great quadrangle of All Souls," which suggested the battlements of Gaza. Another staging that same year, directed by Ruth Spalding (the first of two women to supervise a staging of the tragedy; Phyllis Look is the other), seemed equally indebted to Poel. It took place at Milton's former parish, St. Martin-in-the-Fields, and was mounted at the front of the church on a small, raised stage erected at the chancel entrance. As in Poel's staging, the personae frequently regrouped into varying configurations, apparently to offset the limitations of the small stage. This blocking decision opened up enough space to include what is often omitted in performance, to wit, Dalila's maiden train. One of this production's interesting — and in light of the terrorist interpretation, prescient — departures from the text was to costume Samson in flowing, Mideastern robes and to have him turbaned.

Commenting on Spalding's production, the reviewer for the *London Times* noted that the drama "is a tragedy which acts well only at rare moments"; he added, nonetheless, "for all the weaknesses of the stagecraft the poem brought to the stage makes a curiously deep impression." In contrast, Terence Spencer, whose review appeared in the *Seventeenth Century News,* claimed that "what was surprising was that the play seemed to reveal so much skilled stagecraft. . . . Certain quiet moments in the play, which probably leave little impression on most readers, emerged as startlingly important in the emotional intensity of the play." In like manner, Dwight Durling praised Coghill's production. He remarked that "although Milton did not write *Samson* for the stage, it is a splendid acting vehicle, intensely dramatic. . . . The final scene . . . gains great power in presentation."[12]

Coghill's All Souls' dramatization was not the only notable production within an academic setting. The *London Times* also covered the Guildhall School's 1955 performance, which was directed by George Bartenieff, an American student. The reviewer remarked, "it deserves to be seen by those who are inclined to doubt the effectiveness upon the stage of Milton's poem, which it proves in the simplest of terms." This observer noted that Samson appeared "stand[ing] . . . eyeless, enchained, and most imposingly Hebraic." The set consisted of two sand-colored pillars suggesting the prison, and despite the fact that Dagon's temple is off-stage in the text, this production's backdrop featured the temple, distant but visible, surrounded by the houses of the Gaza citizenry. It also offered a musical score to emphasize changes of mood, as well as a drum-roll to intensify the Messenger's extended speech.[13]

Sir Michael Redgrave's 1965 production came out of his experience as a teacher at the Cranleigh School, where, in 1933, he supervised a staging of the tragedy. The 1965 dramatization starred the six-foot-three-inch actor and was deemed "inconclusive" by the *London Times,* which found it lacking in "barbarity" and overly naturalistic, in part because of the Chorus's delivery of their lines, which were usually spoken by single members instead of in unison. The costumes were elaborate and text-based: Dalila and her maidens resembled Cleopatra and her retinue, while Redgrave's Samson appeared with very long, unkempt hair, an extremely frayed tunic, and intact but lifeless eyes.[14]

Unlike Redgrave's fully outfitted dramatization, William Shaw's 1979 production for the Le Moyne Forum on Religion and Literature was in reader's theater format; the four actors wore black and white clothing and held loose-leaf folders. Nonetheless, it included theatrical elements such as lighting changes, stage movement, props (chairs and platforms), and entrances and exits.

The audience for this performance, which was the main feature of the Le Moyne Forum, consisted primarily of Milton scholars, most of whom found the dramatization a success. Anthony Low, for example, remarked, "*Samson* is an actable play and gains something when put on stage. The interplay of the speeches, the curve of emotional development, the balance of ritual pattern and idea against human character are, as with other plays, all more cogent when seen and heard than when merely read." Lawrence Hyman commented that "seeing the actors on stage allowed me to respond more directly to the emotional situation than I do when I read the play," and Shaw concluded that the production "[demonstrated] vividly the theatricality of *Samson* and its potential for success on stage."[15]

The Yale Drama School performance, enacted in 1985, was in full dress; it reflected Poel's influence by having the protagonist on a raised platform, on center stage. In some respects it was faithful to the original text: Samson was chained at the ankles, and his eyes were darkened with makeup to suggest his blindness. Curiously, however, he was costumed in a white tunic, and his hair and beard were short. Dayton Haskin, who reviewed the production for *Milton Quarterly*, observed that it was "acted valiantly," and remarked that it "elicited from the [company] an evident passion and enthusiasm." While critical of the actor playing Samson, who "had a part that was beyond [his] abilities," Haskins praised Holly Felton's portrayal of Dalila and noted that "the final scene . . . was especially well done."[16]

The most recent major dramatization was in 1998, in East Halifax (England), by the Northern Broadsides Company, a group of Yorkshire-based actors, and was well-received by both the poet Tom Paulin, who covered it for the *Times Literary Supplement*, and by Jeremy Kingston, who reviewed it for the *Halifax Times*. The performance was mounted deep in the basement of a former mill and opened with Samson pushing an enormous gray millstone in a circle. The collapse of the temple was apparently quite impressive: the edifice, which was designed to represent a Drury Lane theater, fell onto the stage when it was destroyed. According to Paulin, Barry Rutter's Samson displayed an appropriately "muscly litheness" and wore a brown loincloth. Near the end of the performance, the Philistine Officer removed the loincloth, washed Samson's naked body, then clothed him in purple silk.

Perhaps most interesting is the way this production dealt with one of the major obstacles to performing *Samson*, to wit, its lengthy speeches. Instead of resorting to measures adopted by previous dramatizations (e.g., cutting lines, or splitting them up among various speakers, or keeping the speakers in perpetual movement), Rutter's company relied on gesture and delivery alone to put the speeches across. Paulin adduces two examples of this approach:

> On the page, "dark, dark, dark, amid the blaze of noon" [line 80 of Samson's 114-line monologue] reads as a brilliant movement from the three opening strong stresses to the security of iambic metre. By contrast, Rutter's delivery makes "blaze" anguished, dominant, tragic, and triumphant. . . . When [Ishia Bennison's Dalila] recounts how Jael drove a nail into the sleeping Sisera's temples, Bennison's stabbing right hand makes explicit the implied gesture of Milton's poetry.

Similarly, Kingston points out that Rutter prefaces Samson's "rousing motions" speech (1381–89) with a deft hesitation, followed by an easing of his frown. Kingston sums up the staging by deeming it a "convincing achievement," one that "makes me feel the work deserves an airing more often than once in a generation." In like manner, Paulin concludes his warm appraisal by stating that the Northern Broadsides's version "lifts [*Samson*] into the canon of English drama."[17]

Are Kingston and Paulin right? Readers and critics will disagree on this question, of course; some will concur, others will argue that *Samson* entered that canon well before Rutter's company mounted it, and still others will contend that the tragedy is and always will be unstageable. Having examined most of the major full-dress performances, I think that the tragedy can be effective in the theater. Of the enactments discussed here, most were well received, some quite enthusiastically, and the few that earned mixed reviews can be accounted for. For instance, the critic who faulted Redgrave's dramatization for lacking barbarity seems beholden to the view that Samson is a terrorist: He refers to him as "the Israelite butcher," and was, therefore, disappointed by this production's tone of "civilized neurosis." But this critic seems to make no room for other perspectives. It seems that he would have been receptive to Redgrave's production only if the entire cast had been characterized by the "blinding ferocity" he praises in Daniel Massey's playing of the Hebrew Messenger. Similarly, the negative reviews of Poel's dramatizations by Max Beerbohm and the *London Times* critic may be explained, in part, by Poel's decision to cast a Chorus comprised of men and women actors, and to have the protagonist sitting in a kind of throne throughout the performance, rather than slumped in the dirt in front of the Gaza prison. Whatever Poel gained from these innovations may have been at the expense of dramatic realism. It is also worth noting that Beerbohm left one of the 1908 performances early, before the catastrophe, so his negative review is not fully authoritative. More, his diatribe is offset, in part, by two admiring critiques of the 1908 show, discussed earlier.[18]

It is arguable that some of these enactments succeeded because of their novel production values rather than any intrinsic dramatic merit in the text. As noted, Rutter's staging featured an unusual setting, actors with broad Yorkshire accents, and full, on-stage nudity (Samson's). In addition, the celebrated sculptor Sir Anthony Caro designed the sets. Undoubtedly, these factors helped make the production a success, but both of the show's reviewers praised its traditional dramatic features as well, such as the actors' delivery, gestures, and movements. Thus Paulin's review states, "Although the drama has often been seen as a piece of academic classicism, a poem rather than a playscript, Milton's lines and the characters he created achieve real dramatic presence. . . . Ishia Bennison's Dalila gives real depth to [the character]; [she] becomes living, breathing, seductive . . . [Dave Hill's] Manoa, in a manner that is both credible and touching, reacts to the news of Samson's death."

And, of course, novel staging does not guarantee a successful outcome. It must accord with at least the spirit, if not the letter of the text in order to work. For instance, the Yale School's enactment seems to have been less convincing than it could have been in terms of Samson's characterization, perhaps because the prisoner's costuming contradicted Milton's lines. The director's decision to present Samson in a white tunic, with both short hair and short beard, was bold yet problematic. The play's frequent references to the prisoner's copious locks must have seemed incongruous, and Manoa's hope — based on his son's visibly abundant, regrown hair — that Samson's eyes would also be restored (581–87), must have come off as odd in performance.

Others, however, find *Samson* fundamentally unstageable, at least without a departure from the text. Beerbohm, for instance, contended that "even an ideal performance of [*Samson*] would be tedious; there is in it no dramatic quality whatsoever; Milton was out to edify, not to thrill."[19] And we have seen how various productions have had to contend with the work's long speeches, lack of stichomythia, and relative absence of physical action. Such nonstage elements raise the possibility that Milton set out to write what is, in effect, a closet drama.

We will never know his precise intentions, but I think that Milton's disclaimer about staging is not categorical. For one thing, it seems unlikely, perhaps even impossible, that Milton could have written a closet drama, given his ties to the commercial stage. Such early connections to the commercial theater may have influenced Milton as he created his first two dramas, *Arcades* and the Ludlow masque, both of which were written for performance. What is more, as we saw, the ideas for tragedies set down in the Trinity manuscript contain numerous stage directions. It also seems telling that the model for *Samson* is not Seneca, whose plays were almost certainly not produced, but Greek tragedy, which, as Milton well knew, was staged for the Athenian populace. In sum, the links between Milton and the physical stage were too strong for him to write a play that ignores staging concerns.

The other factor that causes me to regard Milton's disclaimer as being limited to the Restoration stage is the abundance of directions embedded in the text. While scholars are only now beginning to recognize the presence and significance of these cues, theater producers and actors have responded to them, and to the play's latent theatricality, for over a century. The fact that *Samson* has inspired numerous and successful productions, far more so than any traditional closet drama — indeed more than many traditional plays that closed after a performance or two — suggests that Milton did indeed keep staging in mind as he composed the tragedy.

Six

Conclusion

Milton's Achievement as a Dramatist

Having considered the major critical stages of Milton's growth as a dramatic artist, we are now in a position to examine patterns and connections that have emerged, and to assess his achievement as a dramatist. I have already considered the impressive progress he demonstrates between the writing of *Arcades* and *A Masque at Ludlow Castle*. In the first work, he evidences his mastery of both entertainment and masque structures, including the lavish praise characteristic of the court masque. Within a year or so of completing *Arcades*, Milton was offered another commission to compose a second masque. Instead of creating a second, straightforwardly laudatory piece, however, he crafted a longer, richer work that artistically retards and complicates the masque's progressive structure. The dramatic representation of the Egerton children's "hard assays" in and through the Ludlow woods renders the Attendant Spirit's closing compliment far more compelling than the unearned flattery that concluded the typical masque.

Although a juxtaposition of the rudimentary *Arcades* alongside the Ludlow masque serves to highlight his growth as a dramatist, Milton was still in his apprenticeship when he finished *Comus*. Because of this, I noted characteristics of the masque that show his inexperience. For instance, in *Comus* the exposition of the villain's heritage is spoken first to the audience by the Attendant Spirit (46–77), then essentially repeated at lines 520–30, a repetition that slackens the masque's pacing. A seasoned dramatist would have found a way to include such exposition without hindering the play's momentum, and indeed, Milton does just that in *Samson Agonistes.*

Published in 1671, nearly 30 years after the Ludlow masque, the tragedy was probably also composed late in Milton's career. Hence, it is separated from his early engagement with drama by several decades, yet basic motifs link it with these works. For instance, both *Arcades* and *A Masque* constitute approaches to seats of state, by the Arcadians in the first case, and the Egerton children in the second. Likewise, Milton deployed the same image of a group approaching an illuminated throne in both *Arcades* and in *Paradise Lost,* book 10. In a similar manner, the tragedy consists of a series of approaches by Samson's visitors as he sits, not on a throne, of course, but on a mound near the prison. This structural resemblance is underscored by the fact that when the Danite Chorus declare "This, this is he" (115) they nearly echo the Arcadian nymphs and shepherds, who remark, twice, "This, this is she" as they walk toward the Countess Dowager (5, 17). Also, both groups are astonished by the incongruity between what they had been told about their subjects and what they actually see before them: the Arcadians, because the Dowager is even more resplendent than they had heard, and the Danites, by the shocking disparity between their memories of the former judge and the bedraggled figure sitting next to the mill.

Milton's views of tragedy also seem to have remained essentially unchanged from the 1640s to the 1670s, for his remarks on the subject in *The Reason of Church-Government* (1642) are quite similar to the tragedy's prefatory epistle. Both documents praise Sophocles and Euripides as exemplary playwrights; both stress the importance of catharsis in the body politic; both extol the Calvinist commentator David Pareus, as well as his remark that Revelation constitutes an instance of biblical tragedy; and both censure playwrights who introduce vulgar personages into their plays. To be sure, there are differences as well, such as in the epistle where Milton admits Aeschylus to the inner circle of Greek dramatists he most esteems. Also, he claims that *Samson Agonistes* is "never intended" for staging, while *RCG* speaks of producing "doctrinal and exemplary" theater. Still, the tragedy preserves many implicit stage directions in its dialogue. Milton's penchant for embedding such cues stems from his work on the Ludlow masque, for it too was intended to evoke spectacle in the minds of its original audience through the characters' speeches.

Milton's early drama also influenced *Samson* both thematically and imagistically. For instance, the distinction between love and lust central to the Ludlow masque resurfaces in the Sodom sketch, wherein Milton envisaged the two visiting angels debating with the Sodom citizenry about the difference between these impulses. The heated agon between Dalila and Samson also seems indebted to this argument. Similarly, *A Masque* and the tragedy both figure their villains as Circean: Comus's mother and chief influence is Circe, of course, and Samson denounces Dalila's "fair enchanted cup, and warbling charms" (934) as well as her "sorceries" (937). And in both works, the protagonists are capable of bringing down the roof on the heads of their enemies.

Perhaps most importantly, *Samson* solves many of the problems that mar the early dramatic works and sketches. For instance, at one point in the Ludlow masque the Lady speaks the following lines:

> Was I deceived, or did a sable cloud
> Turn forth her silver lining on the night?
> I did not err, there does a sable cloud
> Turn forth her silver lining on the night. (221–24)

She voices this question when she is lost in the woods, cut off from her brothers, and thirsty — an easy target, it would seem, for Comus and his sparkling glass of liquor. Yet the gravity of her peril is undercut by this faintly comic repetition, which may have been provided to cue a stagehand to shine a light on the speaker. By contrast,

Samson is free of such awkward reiteration. Furthermore, the tragedy's single lighting effect, which consists of the sun rising while the captive walks away from the prison, is conveyed effectively when he remarks "here I feel amends, / The breath of heav'n fresh-blowing pure and sweet, / With day-spring born" (9–11).

Milton also deploys exposition more skillfully in the tragedy than in the masque. As we saw, at the opening of *Comus*, the Attendant Spirit tells the audience about the villain's lineage, his penchant for offering his glass to weary travelers, and the resulting disfigurement afflicting those who imbibe (46–77). Virtually the same information is presented later in the masque when the Attendant Spirit, now in the guise of the kindly shepherd Thyrsis, tells the two brothers about Comus (520–30). By contrast, even though certain events from Samson's life — the angel's descent at his birth, his exploits in battle, and the revelation of his secret to Dalila — are recalled by him and others throughout the tragedy, the recollections are varied, emphasizing different aspects of each event. Thus, on first viewing Samson in front of the prison, both the Chorus and Manoa remark on the difference between his current state in prison and his former glory, yet the Chorus specifically recall at least three extraordinary deeds from Samson's past — his barehanded killing of a lion, his dispatching of 1,000 Philistine soldiers at Rameth-Lehi, and his seizure of the Gaza city gates (125–49). Manoa, by contrast, alludes more generally to his son's past exploits without repeating the specific information already voiced by the Chorus. In like manner, although Samson repeatedly refers to his betrayal by Dalila, each time he emphasizes a different facet of that event.

Other problems encountered in the Trinity manuscript sketches are also solved in the tragedy. Samson is on-stage from the very start of the play, so Milton does not have to fill up the time with other characters speaking until he appears, as is the case with Adam and Eve's arrival in "Adam Unparadised." Moreover, the tragedy's catastrophe rectifies some of the difficulties encountered in the TMS sketches. As demonstrated, when outlining the Sodom play, Milton vacillated between presenting the falling fire and brimstone directly and narrating the conflagration. He also seems to have had trouble finding a convincing nuntius figure; an avenging angel who had just performed the deed might have inspired terror when relating the event to the audience, but it is difficult to imagine him evoking pity as well. Also, the actual Sodom catastrophe might have taken several hours, a fact that could be difficult to convey on stage. In *Samson*, however, the catastrophe is narrated in a remarkably vivid manner by a human — and thus sympathetic — nuntius. As this messenger recounts the fall of Dagon's temple, he indicates that Samson brought down the temple in a matter of a few seconds, killing himself and the Philistines almost instantly. Thus, the catastrophe in *Samson* is far more effective because it is unified and rapid.

Milton's towering reputation as the greatest modern epic poet began to be established relatively early, starting with encomiums by Marvell, Dryden, and "S. B." (probably Milton's friend Samuel Barrows), published in the 1688 Folio edition of *Paradise Lost*. Despite the attacks of the Miltonoclasts in the early twentieth century, that reputation has remained intact. By contrast, his achievement as a dramatist has not even been considered, let alone celebrated. That achievement is difficult to assess in large part because Milton only wrote one full-length tragedy and cast it in a neoclassical form that has never been very popular with English-speaking readers. Nonetheless, in the tragedy's prefatory epistle, he invites posterity to evaluate *Samson Agonistes* when he remarks that those "will best judge [it] who are not unacquainted with Aeschylus, Sophocles, and Euripides, the three tragic poets unequalled yet by any." Commenting on this line, Joseph Pequigney remarks that "while [the three Greek playwrights] have not been matched, the word 'yet' indicates that they can be. Their primacy is acknowledged — and challenged."[1] I would add that in the preface Milton may have been countering Ben Jonson, whose tribute to Shakespeare, initially published in the First Folio, placed the Bard above Aeschylus, Sophocles, and Euripides (lines 33–34).

Did Milton surpass his Greek models? William R. Parker believed he had matched them, and Watson Kirkconnell asserts that *Samson* "may fairly challenge most of the surviving dramas of Athens' greatest period." Yet the prefatory epistle intimates a larger claim. Pequigney explains that that assertion was based on Milton's sense of moral and spiritual superiority vis-à-vis the Greek playwrights:

> If the "very critical art of composition" superlatively exercised by [the three playwrights] and expounded by Aristotle . . . could be mastered and then used with the advantage "over and above of being a Christian," used to inculcate true instead of their false religion, to present a "divine argument" from Scripture instead of their pagan ones . . . the resulting tragedy would be incomparable, aesthetically on a level with those "anciently composed" and . . . surpassing them doctrinally.[2]

In the current day, of course, Milton's claim to moral superiority would not be universally accepted. Is it possible, then, along with Parker and Kirkconnell, to evaluate his achievement from a purely aesthetic standpoint? Perhaps, although that too is difficult, given the considerable erudition required for such a task, in that one would have to know all the Greek plays in the original language in order to make such judgments.

Even so, there remains a less daunting standard of comparison by which to assess Milton's achievement, one closer to home. It is true that neoclassical tragedy was never popular in England, but it was for a time in France, and one French playwright in particular may be profitably compared with Milton. I refer to Jean Racine (1639–99), who shares a number of similarities with the English poet. Near contemporaries, both men were allied with reformist religious movements, Milton with the Puritans, Racine with the Jansenists. Both tried to convince adherents of their respective parties of the moral and educational value of the theater, Milton most notably in *The Reason of Church-Government* and Racine in his preface to *Phèdre* (1677):

> I have composed [no other work] where virtue has been more emphasized than in this play. The least faults are punished in it. The mere

thought of crime is here regarded with as much horror as crime itself. . . . Such is the proper aim that any man who works for the public should cherish. . . . It would be desirable that our works should be as solid and as full of useful instruction as those of [the Greek playwrights]. It would perhaps be a way of reconciling tragedy with a number of persons renowned for their piety and their doctrine.[3]

What is more, both men composed short dramas intended to be acted by children. In fact, Racine's *Esther* resembles *Comus* in that it constitutes a three-act musical play, and commences with the descent of Piety, who, like the Attendant Spirit, resides in heaven. It was first staged in 1689 by the schoolgirls of Saint-Cyr, a lycée for daughters of insolvent noblemen. Both writers, moreover, were haunted by Euripides' story of Alcestis, as is evidenced by Milton's final sonnet, and by the fact that Racine started, then destroyed, a play based on the Alcestis myth. Also, Racine's preface to *Iphigénie en Aulide* (1674) weighs in on early modern debates over line attributions in *Alcestis*. Milton's annotations of Euripides evidence a similar concern for accurate speech assignment. Like *Samson Agonistes*, Racine's final play, *Athalie* (1691), combines a biblical plot (taken from 2 Kings 11 and 2 Chron. 23–24) with a neoclassic form. Suggestively, the Trinity manuscript plans indicate that for a brief period of time Milton considered writing a tragedy on the Athalie plot. Both *Samson* and *Athalie* feature choruses, and both present the main characters voicing double-edged prophecies.[4] As well, the climax of each tragedy involves an outsider entering the precincts of the temple.

True, there are significant differences as well between the two men. Racine's devotion to the Sun King, Louis XIV, contrasts with Milton's fervent antimonarchism, and Racine was a devout Catholic, his Jansenism notwithstanding, while Milton was highly critical of the Roman church. Furthermore, the Jansenists were sometimes accused of being Calvinists, while Milton, of course, was an Arminian. Even so, such differences are more than offset by the numerous and striking similarities between these two writers.

Curiously, they have seldom been discussed in relation to one another, which makes a brief account of them worthwhile.[5] I will concentrate on two Racine tragedies: the deliberately Euripidean *Phèdre*, which revises its Greek source (*Hippolytus*), and *Athalie*. *Phèdre* was Racine's last secular tragedy. In it he created what many regard as the finest female dramatic role ever. The title character displays a depth of passion and force that outstrips Euripides' characterization of Phèdre. Racine did so, in part, by altering the original, as he explains in the play's prefatory epistle, where he points out that he intended to make Phèdre "less odious than she is in the tragedies of the Ancients, where she herself decides to accuse Hippolytus. I consider slander too mean and too black to put into the mouth of a princess, who otherwise evinces such noble and virtuous feelings."[6] He thus decided to have Phèdre's egregious nurse Oenone present the accusation, with the result that Phèdre arouses considerable pity as well as terror.

Like Racine's Phèdre, Milton's Dalila is also passion-haunted, and also Euripidean, though not as obviously. Parker compares Dalila to Helen in *Trojan Women*, for several reasons: both women have deceived their husbands; both come back to visit them; both appear before them richly costumed; both try to justify themselves; and both attempt to touch their wronged spouses at the end of their interviews with them.[7] Still, while Dalila is an impressive figure, a worthy antagonist of Samson and one who evokes sympathy from some readers, she does not surpass any of Euripides' female protagonists. At most, one might say that her characterization is as compelling as some of the Euripidean heroines. Hence, it would seem that Racine has outdone Milton in this category.

It is harder to assess *Samson* as a whole in relation to the ancients, partly because of its biblical plot. This is where Racine's achievement may also be of assistance, given his interest in neoclassical scriptural tragedy, as in *Athalie*. This play is considered by some to be Racine's greatest drama, though most, including myself, prefer *Phèdre*. While *Athalie* is excellent, its plot lacks an equivalent of the extraordinary catastrophe in Milton's *Samson*.

In *Athalie*, Racine follows the biblical narrative closely. According to 2 Kings 11, even though Athalie, the usurping queen of Judah, attempted to wipe out David's royal line by killing all of his seed, she did not slay one of the king's sons, Joas, who was saved by Josabeth, wife of the High Priest Joad, and secretly brought up in the temple at Jerusalem. The climax of both biblical narrative and play occurs when, according to 2 Kings 11:12, Joad "brought forth [Joas] and put the crown on him . . . and they made him king, and anointed him; and they clapped their hands, and said, God save the king." When Athalie hears the noise of the insurrection she comes in to see what is afoot in the temple, at which point everyone else rejoices (again), trumpets sound, and she tears her cloak in anguish at the sight of the one who has supplanted her. Joad then orders her to be seized and killed outside the temple.

Racine alters this account by making the revelation of the new king to Athalie more intimate, yet also more dramatic. In the play, she enters the temple because she has been lured there by the promise of receiving King David's long-hidden treasure, which she mistakenly thinks consists of gold. In a stunning disclosure, Joad draws aside a curtain, showing the actual treasure therein — Joas, the lone surviving son of the Davidic line. Athalie is forced to view the child, who is her grandson through her son Ochosias (Ahaziah, in English), and is about eight years old. Upon viewing the tell-tale dagger marks where she ordered him cut years before, she is crestfallen: "It is [Joas]. Useless to deny it! / I recognize the spot where I had him struck" (5.5.1770–71). She then curses the young king, at which point Joad orders her removed and slain.

This denouement is intellectually compelling, particularly in the way it exploits unity of place. As George Steiner remarks, "In the end she does invade the sanctuary itself and finds that she has entered a deadly trap. There is no retreat from God's presence. . . . It is a marvelously expressive design. Unity of place acquires a double significance: it is both a convention of the neoclassic form and the prime motive of action. In *Athalie* . . . a place of sanctuary is preserved against the incursions of violence."[8] Still, the play's nearly bloodless coup and its happy ending seem anticlimactic, less affecting when compared to the extraordinary catastrophe in *Samson*

Agonistes. Indeed, it is possible that Milton eventually decided not to write a tragedy about Athalie precisely because of its comparatively subdued ending, for as described previously, he apparently was looking for narratives involving large-scale calamities. To be fair, the Samson stories might have struck Racine as overly simple, unanswerable to his complex, demanding aesthetic. Nevertheless, if my remarks on *Athalie* do that tragedy at least partial justice, it would seem that *Samson Agonistes* holds its own when compared to Racine's play. If so, one could argue that while the overall dramatic achievement of Milton is not as impressive as Racine, who composed twelve plays, four of them (*Phèdre, Bérénice, Iphigénie en Aulide,* and *Athalie*) masterpieces, Milton at least equaled his French counterpart in the genre of biblical, neoclassical tragedy.

In closing, while Milton's reputation as an epic poet was established very early, it has taken two centuries for scholarship to recognize the significance of his theological views. Those views continue to be vigorously debated, of course. Similarly, while his tragedy was published in 1671, its status as a play did not begin to emerge until William Poel's inaugural production of it in 1900. As with his theology, then, Milton's accomplishment in drama may take time to absorb. If so, I suspect that that process will prove worthwhile, and will result in a richer, better balanced picture of one of our most illustrious writers.

Appendix

Stagings, dramatic readings, and adaptations of *Samson Agonistes*, arranged (where known) by date and type, auspices, director/producer and/or company, and number of performances.[1]

1717	French adaptation by Luigi Riccoboni. The Italian Theatre, Paris.
1739	*"Samson" Mit en Vers*. French adaptation by Jean-Antoine Romagnesi. The Italian Theatre, Paris.[2]
1739	Dramatic Reading, Earl of Shaftesbury's home. G. F. Handel, accompanist.
1743–present	Oratorio by G. F. Handel and Newburgh Hamilton. Covent Garden Theatre. Multiple performances.
1900	Full Staging. Premiered April 7 at the Lecture Theatre, Victoria and Albert Museum; repeated shortly after at St. George's Hall. William Poel. 2 performances.
1908	Full Staging. Revival of 1900 show in honor of Milton Tercentenary. Lecture Theatre, Burlington Gardens; Memorial Hall; Farringdon Street; Whitworth Hall (Manchester University); Bedford Corn Exchange; New Theatre (Cambridge University). 6 performances. William Poel.
1921	Princeton University.
1925 (?)	Produced in Birmingham (U.K.). Stuart Vinden.[3]
1930	Queen Elizabeth Grammar School, Wakefield. Two performances.

1930 (?)   Boar's Hill Theatre. John Masefield.[4]

1930   Full staging. Gardens of Exeter College (Oxford), Dramatic Society. Nevill Coghill.[5]

1933   Full Staging. The Cranleigh School, Guildford (U.K.). Michael Redgrave.[6]

1935   "The King-Maker": One-act radio drama, BBC.

1936   Full Staging. Tewkesbury Festival. Nevill Coghill.[7]

1938   Full Staging. Maddermarket Theatre, Norwich. Nugent Monck, Norwich Players.

1950 (?)   Full Staging (?). African Production.[8]

1951   Full Staging. All Souls' College, Oxford. Nevill Coghill. 5 performances (?).

1951   Full Staging. St. Martin-in-the-Fields. Ruth Spalding, The Rock Players. Approximately 20 performances.

1955   Full Staging. The Guildhall School. George Bartenieff. 2 performances.

1956   Ludlow Festival, Wales. 2 performances.

1957   Full Staging (?). Phoenix Theatre Group, Birmingham (U.K.).[9]

1959   Full Staging (?). Dartmouth College.

1960 (?)   Hillbarn Theatre, San Mateo, Calif.[10]

1961   Full Staging. Harrow County School. Harrow Dramatic Society.[11]

1961   "Visionary Recital." Balletic adaptation for two dancers. 54th Street Theatre, New York, N.Y.; revived in 1962 under the title *Samson Agonistes* at the Broadway Theatre. Score by Robert Starer. Created by Martha Graham, who also danced the role of Delilah.[12]

1964 (?)   Dramatic Reading, Tufts University Chapel.[13]

1965   Full Staging. Arnaud Theatre, Guildford. Sir Michael Redgrave.

1967   Sound Recording. Dir. Peter Wood. Perf. Michael Redgrave, Faith Brook, Daniel Massey. LP. Caedmon Records.

1971   Dramatic Reading. University Theater, Southern Illinois University. Tercentenary of first publication of *Samson Agonistes*. Stella Revard.

1973   Staged version, Poland.[14]

1978   Partial Staging. St. Andrew's Episcopal Church, Ann Arbor, Mich., Frank L. Huntley, The Saint Andrew's Players.[15]

1979   Reader's Theater. Le Moyne Forum on Religion and Literature, Syracuse, N.Y. William P. Shaw.[16]

1980   One-man Show. Edinburgh Fringe Festival.

1982   Full Staging (?). University of Ottawa. Dennis Danielson.

1984   Full Staging. Chalfont (U.K.). Parish church (?).[17]

1985   Full Staging. Yale Drama School. Phyllis Look. 3 performances.

1994   *Samson Agonistes: Libretto for Bass Voice and Choir.* Matthew Power, composer; Michelene Wandor, librettist. Hillingdon (U.K.) Church.

1998   Full Staging. East Halifax (U.K.). Barry Rutter, Northern Broadsides Company.

1999   Full Staging. Fringe Festival: Minnesota Community Theater, Plymouth Congregational Church, Minneapolis, Minn.

2003   Dramatic Reading. German Evangelical Church (New York, N.Y.). Nancy Bogen, The Lark Ascending Company. 2 performances.[18]

2003   Dramatic Reading. 92nd Street Y (New York, N.Y.). Bryn Mawr College. Robert Scanlan, The Lark Ascending Company. 2 performances.

2003   Partially Staged Dramatic Reading. Southeast Renaissance Conference, Beaufort, S.C. Roy Flannagan.

Notes

Notes to Introduction

1. Coleridge and James Russell Lowell are quoted in Anthony Low, *The Blaze of Noon: A Reading of* Samson Agonistes (New York: Columbia University Press, 1974), 2–3; George Steiner, *The Death of Tragedy* (New York: Knopf, 1961), 232; Watson Kirkconnell, *That Invincible Samson: The Theme of* Samson Agonistes *in World Literature with Translations of the Major Analogues* (Toronto: University of Toronto Press, 1964), viii; and William R. Parker, *Milton's Debt to Greek Tragedy in* Samson Agonistes (New York: Barnes & Noble, 1969), 250.

2. For these assessments, see Frank Magill, *Critical Survey* (Englewood Cliffs, N.J.: Salem Press, 1985); Frederick Link, *English Drama* (Detroit: Gale Research Company, 1976); William Adams, *Dictionary of English Literature* (Detroit: Gale Research Company, 1966); Clarence L. Barnhart, ed., *The New Century Handbook of English Literature* (New York: Appleton-Century-Crofts, 1967); Arthur Pollard, ed., *Webster's New World Companion to English and American Literature* (New York: World Publishers, 1973); Fredson Bowers, ed., *The Dictionary of Literary Biography*, vol. 58 (Detroit: Gale Research Company, 1987); and Ian Ousby, ed., *The Cambridge Guide to Literature in English* (Cambridge: Cambridge University Press, 1988). Alfred Harbage's description can be found in his *Annals of English Drama, 975–1700: An Analytical Record of All Plays, Extant or Lost, Chronologically Arranged and Indexed by Authors, Titles, Dramatic Companies, &c.*, rev. S. Schoenbaum (Philadelphia: University of Pennsylvania Press, 1964), 225.

3. "Theoretics or Polemics?: Milton Criticism and the 'Dramatic Axiom,'" *PMLA* 82 (December 1967): 505–15.

4. For his comments on *Comus*, see Samuel Johnson, *Lives of the English Poets*, ed. George B. Hill, vol. 5 (New York: Octagon Books, 1967), 230; and *Rambler*, vol. 3 (London, 1796), 162, for his discussion of *Samson Agonistes*.

5. Milton's poetry is quoted from *John Milton: The Complete Poems*, ed. John Leonard (New York: Penguin Books, 1998).

6. See Anthony Low, "Milton's *Samson* and the Stage, with Implications for Dating the Play," *Huntington Library Quarterly* 40 (1977): 313–24; quotations, 313, 317.

7. Robert Hume, "The Aims and Limits of Historical Scholarship," *Review of English Studies* 53 (August 2002): 399–422; quotation, 416.

8. Margot Heinemann, *Puritanism and the Theatre: Thomas Middleton and Opposition Drama under the Early Stuarts* (Cambridge: Cambridge University Press, 1986), 19, notes that the Earls of Leicester and Walsingham served as patrons to both Puritans and actors. The Third Earl of Pembroke, Shakespeare's patron, was also a leader of the Puritan group in James I's government, while the Fourth Earl of Pembroke, joint dedicatee of Shakespeare's First Folio, was a parliamentarian during the civil war. Bulstrode Whitelocke, Keeper of the Great Seal during the Interregnum, frequented the Blackfriars, and during the Protectorate persuaded Cromwell to allow opera to be performed. Another Puritan, Sir Thomas Barrington, owned a copy of the First Folio. The Earls of Essex and Warwick, two leaders of the parliamentarians, employed the playwright Arthur Wilson, and Peter Sterry, Cromwell's chaplain, loved and quoted Shakespeare's works. See also Laura Knoppers, *Puritanism and Its Discontents* (Newark: University of Delaware Press, 2003).

9. References to Milton's prose are to *The Complete Prose Works of John Milton*, 8 vols. in 10, ed. Don M. Wolfe et al. (New Haven: Yale University Press, 1953–82), and are designated as YP, with volume and page numbers given parenthetically in the text.

10. See Herbert Berry, "The Miltons and the Blackfriars Playhouse," *Modern Philology* 89 (May 1992): 510–14; and Timothy J. Burbery, "John Milton, Blackfriars Spectator?: 'Elegia Prima' and Ben Jonson's *The Staple of News*," *Ben Jonson Journal* 10 (2003): 57–76.

11. William Hazlitt, *Complete Works*, ed. P. P. Howe, vol. 5 (New York: AMS Press, 1967), 230; and Roger Wilkenfeld, "Theoretics or Polemics?: Milton Criticism and the 'Dramatic Axiom,'" *PMLA* 82 (1967): 505.

12. Terence Spencer, "*Samson Agonistes* in London," *Seventeenth Century News* 9 (September 1951): 35.

13. Derek Wood, "*Exiled from Light*": *Divine Law, Morality, and Violence in Milton's* Samson Agonistes (Toronto: University of Toronto Press, 2001): 20–21. J. Martin Evans is quoted in Alan Rudrum's review article, "Milton Scholarship and the Agon over *Samson Agonistes*," *Huntington Library Quarterly* 65 (2002): 465–88; quotation, 463. Joseph Wittreich's comment appears in Wood, "*Exiled from Light*," 21.

14. Francis Peck's surmise is set forth at length in his *New Memoirs of the Life and Poetical Works of Mr. John Milton* (London, 1740): 265–428. William R. Parker, *Milton: A Biography* (Oxford: Oxford University Press, 1968), states that the translation is "not [Milton's] work" (2:836). For a more recent account of the attribution controversy, see Stephen Berkowitz, ed.,

A Critical Edition of George Buchanan's "Baptistes" and of Its Anonymous Seventeenth-Century Translation "Tyrannical-Government Anatomized" (New York: Garland, 1992): 105–59.

15. Robert Hume, "Texts Within Contexts: Notes Toward a Historical Method," *Philological Quarterly* 71 (1992): 69–100; quotation, 80. The project forecasted by its subtitle is more fully developed in his article, "The Aims and Limits of Historical Scholarship," cited in note 7. Elizabeth Sauer's "The Politics of Performance in the Inner Theater: *Samson Agonistes* as Closet Drama," in *Milton and Heresy*, ed. John Rumrich and Stephen Dobranski (Cambridge: Cambridge University Press, 1998), 200, a critique of Fish's notion of interpretive communities, is akin to Hume's. She argues, "For Fish, the essentially authoritarian community imposes meaning on ahistorical textual determinacy." Sauer also contends that Fish does not "adequately problematize the relationship between reader and text, precisely because he dehistoricizes it and posits an authoritarian reading community."

16. See Gordon Campbell, "Shakespeare and the Youth of Milton," *Milton Quarterly* 33 (December 1999): 95–105.

Notes to Chapter One, "Milton as Spectator, Reader, and Editor of Drama"

1. Harris Fletcher, *The Intellectual Development of John Milton*, vol. 1 (Urbana: University of Illinois Press, 1961), 431; *John Milton, Poet and Humanist: Essays by James Holly Hanford* (Cleveland: Press of Western Reserve University, 1966), 224; Denis Saurat, *Milton, Man and Thinker* (New York: Dial, 1925), 7; T. H. Howard-Hill, "Milton and the 'Rounded Theatre's Pomp,'" in *Of Poetry and Politics: New Essays on Milton and His World*, ed. P. G. Stanwood (Tempe, Ariz.: Medieval and Renaissance Texts and Studies, 1997), 95–120; quotation, 120; and Roy Flannagan, *The Riverside Milton* (Boston: Houghton Mifflin, 1998), 107. Cook and Gurr both claim that at age 12 Milton attended a performance at the Fortune Theatre. See Ann Cook, *The Privileged Playgoers of Shakespeare's London, 1576–1642* (Princeton: Princeton University Press, 1981), 131; and Andrew Gurr, *Playgoing in Shakespeare's London* (Cambridge: Cambridge University Press, 1987), 199.

2. For representative statements of the first group, see Gurr, *Playgoing in Shakespeare's London*, 199; Richard Hosley, "Elizabethan Theatres and Audiences," *Renaissance Drama Supplement* 10 (1967): 14; Campbell, "Shakespeare and the Youth of Milton," 99; Mary Ann Radzinowicz, *Toward Samson Agonistes: The Growth of Milton's Mind* (Princeton: Princeton University Press, 1978), 12; Flannagan, *The Riverside Milton*, 179; Fletcher, *Intellectual Development of Milton*, 431; and Walter

MacKellar, *The Latin Poems of John Milton* (New Haven: Yale University Press, 1930), 16, 194.

Opposing views are presented by Douglas Bush, *A Variorum Commentary on the Poems of John Milton* (New York: Columbia University Press, 1970), who remarks that "it seems likely that [Milton] is describing plays he has read rather than plays seen in London theatres, though he writes as if he had been an actual witness" (1:50). Also, Leonard, *John Milton: The Complete Poems*, observes that "Although Milton speaks as a spectator, the details [recounted here] recall Greek and Roman, rather than English, drama" (943 n. 27). In like manner, Parker, *Milton: A Biography*, observes that while "Drama receives considerable emphasis in the 'Elegia Prima.' . . . Milton seems not to distinguish between the 'well-trod stage' and the well-thumbed page" (1: 31). See also Jonathan Goldberg and Stephen Orgel, eds., *John Milton* (Oxford: Oxford University Press, 1990), 789; John Shawcross, ed., *The Complete English Poetry of John Milton, Arranged in Chronological Order with an Introduction, Notes, Variants, and Literal Translations of the Foreign Language Poems* (New York: New York University Press, 1963), 6–7; and Howard-Hill, "Milton and 'Theatre's Pomp,'" 120.

3. Harbage, *Annals of English Drama*, notes that Aeschylus was not staged in England until 1663. Performances of Euripides were given in 1543, 1550, 1558, 1579, and 1602, while Sophocles was mounted in 1543, 1564, 1581, and 1649 (293). It is possible that Milton witnessed Latin comedies at Queen's or Trinity College; his own college, Christ's, discontinued these performances in 1568. See Alan H. Nelson, ed., *Records of Early English Drama: Cambridge*, 2 vols. (Toronto: Toronto University Press, 1989), 2:713.

4. Parker, *Milton: A Biography*, 1:31.

5. See Berry, "Miltons and the Blackfriars," 511, 513; and Campbell, "Shakespeare and the Youth of Milton," 103.

6. Gurr, *Playgoing in Shakespeare's London*, 85.

7. I am quoting from Leonard's translation in *Milton: The Complete Poems*, 515.

8. William Cowper, *Milton's Earlier Poems: Including the Translations by William Cowper of those written in Latin and Italian* (London: Cassell, 1909), translates the lines as follows: "here my books — my life — absorb me whole. / *Here too* I visit, or to smile or weep / The winding theater's majestic sweep" (29; my emphasis). Shawcross, *Complete English Poetry of Milton*, believes that Milton does not refer to physical attendance at a theater, pointing out that the opening phrase of line 27, "Excipit hinc fessum," need not indicate a literal transition. His translation reads as follows: "For I am permitted to dedicate my free time to the gentle muses, and books — my life — transport me entirely away. Here the display of the curved theater captivates me, when wearied" (6–7). The majority of

translators, however, interpret *"hinc"* (an adverb meaning "from this," or "hence") as implying an actual move from study to playhouse.

9. Berry, "Miltons and the Blackfriars," 510.

10. For references, see Flannagan, *The Riverside Milton*, 179; Hosley, "Elizabethan Theatres and Audiences," 14; John Carey and Alastair Fowler, *The Poems of John Milton* (London: Longman, 1968), 789; Leonard, *John Milton: The Complete Poems*, 515; Gurr, *Playgoing in Shakespeare's London*, 199; Shawcross, *Complete English Poetry of Milton*, 6–7; Campbell, "Shakespeare and the Youth of Milton," 103; Berry, "Milton and the Blackfriars," 510; Goldberg and Orgel, *John Milton*, 889; and Hughes, *Milton: Complete Poems and Major Prose*, 9. Caroline Perkins gave me her translation in an email message of January 16, 2002.

11. John Orrell, "The Private Theatre Auditorium," *Theatre Research International* 9, no. 2 (1984): 79–93. I am indebted to Andrew Gurr for bringing Orrell's article to my attention.

12. Leonard, *John Milton: The Complete Poems*, 943.

13. Ibid., 943; Bush, *Variorum Commentary on Milton*, 45; Gurr, *Playgoing in Shakespeare's London*, 56. According to Gurr, prohibitions against play performances during Lent were seldom enforced. He lists several official dispensations granted against the prohibitions by William Herbert, the master of revels, in the 1620s. See Gurr, *The Shakespearean Stage, 1574–1642* (Cambridge: Cambridge University Press, 1970), 56.

14. Harbage, *Annals of English Drama*, 122; C. H. Herford, Percy Simpson, and Evelyn Simpson, ed., "Stage History of the Plays," in *Ben Jonson*, 11 vols. (Oxford: Clarendon Press, 1925–52), 9:251.

15. Ben Jonson, *The Staple of News*, ed. Devra Rowland Kifer (Lincoln: University of Nebraska Press, 1975), xxii. All references to the play are taken from volume 6 of Herford and Simpson, *Ben Jonson*.

16. Ben Jonson, *The Staple of News*, ed. Anthony Parr (Manchester: Manchester University Press, 1988), 49.

17. Ibid., 49–50.

18. Levin's comments were offered in an email message to me on March 11, 2002.

19. In his 1791 edition of Milton's poetry, Thomas Warton initiated what became a long-standing editorial tradition of adducing the lawyer in George Ruggle's neo-Latin play *Ignoramus* as the source for the one delineated in *Elegia Prima*. Staged in 1615 at Cambridge for King James, *Ignoramus* was first published in 1630 and, as Douglas Bush, *Variorum Commentary on Milton*, points out, remained popular in print. Bush also observes, however, that "even if Milton had a manuscript copy, his description does not fit Ruggle's burlesque lawyer, who spouts shreds of legal Latin but does so in this private role of pedantic lover and butt" (51). No classical comedy offers a lawyer who becomes rich on a ten-year case.

20. Tragedies that were staged by the King's Men, possibly at Blackfriars

from the period 1620–26 include *The Double Marriage*, by John Fletcher and Philip Massinger (1620); Massinger's *The Duke of Milan* (1621); Thomas Middleton's *Women Beware Women; Osmond, the Great Turk* (1622), whose author is unknown, and whose text is no longer extant; and *The Roman Actor*, by Massinger (1626). Two other tragedies, now lost, that may have been performed by the King's Men include *The Fatal Brothers* and *The Politic Queen, or Murder Will Out*, both by Robert Davenport, in 1623. See Harbage, *Annals of English Drama*, 110–22.

21. Milton's depiction of "an unfortunate youth [who] leaves joys untasted, and is torn from his love to perish and be mourned" might correspond to Orgilus in *The Broken Heart*. His lady-love Penthea is taken from him and given to another. After Orgilus murders her husband (Bassanes), he bleeds himself to death on stage, an action that elicits grief from the on-stage witnesses as well as, no doubt, from the theater audience.

22. Pete Ure, "A Simile in *Samson Agonistes*," *Notes & Queries* 195 (1950): 298. For Hughes's reference, see his *Milton: Complete Poems and Major Prose*, 568 n. 714. Leonard's note appears in his *John Milton: Complete Poems*, 930.

23. G. M. Young's observation was first printed as "Milton & Harrington," *Times Literary Supplement*, January 9, 1937, 31.

24. Parker, *Milton: A Biography*, 99; Flannagan, *The Riverside Milton*, 65.

25. Flannagan, *The Riverside Milton*, 70.

26. See Gerald E. Bentley, *The Jacobean and Caroline Stage* (Oxford: Oxford University Press, 1968), 7:79, 98, 112.

27. For the references to Henry Todd, C. B. Cooper, and G. C. Moore Smith, see Bush, *Variorum Commentary on Milton*, 2:773–74.

28. Bentley, *Jacobean and Caroline Stage*, 5:986–87; Parker, *Milton: A Biography*, 1:71.

29. See *Poetical and Dramatic Works of Thomas Randolph*, 177.

30. Wotton's letter is quoted in Flannagan, *The Riverside Milton*, 121.

31. Bush, *Variorum Commentary on Milton*, 2:774; Parker, *Milton: A Biography*, 2:817.

32. Bush, *Variorum Commentary on Milton*, 2:298.

33. Bentley, *Jacobean and Caroline Stage*, 1:83.

34. Stephen Dobranski, "Milton's Social Life," in *The Cambridge Companion to Milton*, ed. Dennis Danielson (Cambridge: Cambridge University Press, 1999), 1–24; quotation, 5; Barbara Lewalski, *The Life of John Milton: A Critical Biography* (Malden, Mass.: Blackwell, 2000), 58, 60. See Charles Osgood, "Milton's 'Elm Star-Proof,'" *Journal of English and Germanic Philology* 4 (1903): 374; Parker, *Milton: A Biography*, 1:81.

35. Lewalski, *Life of John Milton*, 60.

36. Goldberg and Orgel, *John Milton*, 179.

37. Howard-Hill, "Milton and 'Theatre's Pomp,'" 105.

38. Goldberg and Orgel, *John Milton*, 179.

39. Wright is quoted in Gurr, *Playgoing in Shakespeare's London*, 143–44.

40. Arthos, *Milton and the Italian Cities* (New York, 1968), 78. See also Parker, *Milton: A Biography*, 1:170. For Milton's quote, see YP 1:334.

41. Harbage, *Annals of English Drama*, 167, 178, 205.

42. Flannagan, *Riverside Milton*, 407; Leonard, *Milton: Complete Poems*, xii; *The Norton Anthology of English Literature* (New York: W. W. Norton, 2000), 1:446. See Robert L. Ramsay, "Morality Themes in Milton's Poetry," *Studies in Philology* 15 (1918): 123–58.

43. Samuel Adkins and Maurice Kelley, "Milton's Annotations of Euripides," *Journal of English and Germanic Philology* 60 (1961): 638.

44. Ibid., 686.

45. John Hale, "Milton's Euripides Marginalia: Their Significance for Milton Studies," in *Milton Studies*, vol. 27, ed. James D. Simmonds (Pittsburgh: University of Pittsburgh Press, 1991), 24, 25–26, 29. See also his discussion in *Milton's Languages: The Impact of Multilingualism on Style* (Cambridge: Cambridge University Press, 1997), 74–80.

46. Heinemann, *Puritanism and the Theatre*, 19.

47. This censure is quoted in the introduction to *The Masque of Blackness* in *Norton Anthology of English Literature*, 1295.

48. Ethyn Kirby is quoted in Parker, *Milton: A Life*, 337.

49. Harbage, *Annals of English Drama*, 304–05; David Kastan, *Shakespeare after Theory* (New York: Columbia University Press, 1999), 226.

50. Campbell, "Shakespeare and the Youth of Milton," 103.

51. Annette Flower, "The Critical Context of the Preface to *Samson Agonistes*," *Studies in English Literature* 10 (1970): 417–23.

52. Castlevetro is now perhaps best known for expanding Aristotle's remark that most tragic plots occur within 24 hours into the rule of the three unities.

Notes to Chapter Two, "Mastering Masque, Engaging Drama"

1. Cedric Brown, "Milton's *Arcades*: Context, Form, and Function," *Renaissance Drama* 8 (1977): 245–74.

2. While *Arcades* was written in the 1630s, the exact year of performance is disputed. All we know for certain is that it was not staged in 1631, since the Earl of Castlehaven was hanged (for sexual crimes and suspected popery) in April of that year. I assume that it preceded *A Masque*, and while the sequence cannot be proven, it seems likely, given that *Arcades* comes first in both the Trinity manuscript and in the 1637, 1645, and 1673 editions of Milton's poems. Furthermore, the Earl of Bridgewater

would probably have been more inclined to commission Milton to write a full masque if he had first seen the young writer's ability displayed in a smaller, masquelike work such as *Arcades*. Parker, *Milton: A Biography*, suggests it was performed in either 1629 or 1630, stating that "The strong Jonsonian influence on 'Arcades' has persuaded me to bring it as close as possible to 'On Shakespeare' (1630) and the 'Epitaph on the Marchioness of Winchester' (1631), which are among the first of Milton's poems to exhibit this influence" (758). William Hunter Jr., "The Date and Occasion of *Arcades*," *English Language Notes* 9 (1973), has proposed a performance date of May 3, 1634, the eve of the countess's seventy-fifth birthday (46–47); David Masson suggested 1633 or 1634, and Herbert Grierson, 1630 or 1632.

3. Herford and Simpson, *Ben Jonson*, 128.

4. Leonard glosses "state" (line 14) as "canopy," citing *OED* 20b.

5. See A. S. P. Woodhouse, *A Variorum Commentary on the Poems of John Milton* (London: Routledge and Kegan Paul, 1972), 531; and Brown, "Milton's *Arcades*," 267.

6. Leonard, *John Milton: The Complete Poems*, 650, and Goldberg and Orgel, *John Milton*, 753.

7. Parker, *Milton: A Biography*, 1:83.

8. One possible exception is Ben Jonson's "An Entertainment of King James and Queen Anne at Theobald's," in Herford and Simpson, *Ben Jonson*, 7:154–58, which, despite its title, is far more like a masque than an entertainment. Because it was staged indoors it apparently offered a dramatic discovery of "the Lararium, or seat of the household gods" (155).

9. See John Demaray, *Milton and the Masque Tradition* (Cambridge, Mass.: Harvard University Press, 1968).

10. Lewalski, *Life of John Milton*, 77.

11. Parker, *Milton: A Biography*, 1:131; Lewalski, *Life of John Milton*, 77.

12. See John Summerson, *Inigo Jones* (Harmondsworth: Penguin, 1983), 50.

13. *The Complete Masques of Ben Jonson*, ed. Stephen Orgel (New Haven: Yale University Press, 1969), 114.

14. Quoted in Stephen Orgel and Roy Strong, *Inigo Jones: The Theatre of the Stuart Court* (Berkeley and Los Angeles: University of California Press, 1973), 84.

15. Orgel, *The Jonsonian Masque* (Cambridge, Mass.: Harvard University Press, 1965), 82–83.

16. Flannagan, *The Riverside Milton*, 126.

17. Aurelian Townshend, *Poems and Masks*, ed. E. K. Chambers (Oxford: Clarendon Press, 1912), 119.

18. William Shakespeare, *The Tempest*, ed. Frank Kermode (London: Methuen, 1987), 93–102.

19. George William Smith Jr. contends that in the twentieth century a relatively widespread sense that *Comus* was a failed drama led to a new focus on its themes and ideas. This new approach was perhaps best characterized by A. S. P. Woodhouse, "The Argument of Milton's *Comus*," *University of Toronto Quarterly* 11 (1941): 46–71. Similarly thematic readings remained popular in the second half of the twentieth century, although they were eventually displaced by new historicist approaches. Notable recent considerations of dramatic issues relevant to *Comus* include Stephen Orgel's "The Case for Comus," *Representations* 18 (Winter 2003): 31–45, which attempts to exonerate Comus (the character) from the traditional view that he is a villain; Martin K. Doudna, "'Nay, Lady, Sit': The Dramatic and Human Dimensions of *Comus*," *ANQ: A Quarterly Journal of Short Articles, Notes, and Reviews* (Fall 1995): 38–44, which reads the Lady's famous rebuttal of Comus within the dramatic context of the masque performance; and Michael Wilding, "Milton's 'A Masque Presented at Ludlow Castle, 1634': Theatre and Politics on the Border," *Milton Quarterly* 21 (December 1987): 35–51. Wilding's purpose is to show how the ambiguities of the theatrical genre enabled Milton to risk offering political criticism without endangering himself.

20. Cedric Brown believes that the Bridgewater manuscript (*BMS*) is not authoritative, arguing that its cuts were made by someone other than Milton. William B. Hunter, John Shawcross, and Flannagan disagree that a censor was involved, and Hunter uses *BMS* as the foundation for a reconstructed performance version. See Flannagan, *The Riverside Milton*, 115–16, for a brief discussion of the debate.

21. C. S. Lewis, "A Note on *Comus*," *Review of English Studies* 8 (1932): 170–76, cites as evidence passages such as portions of the brothers' conversation (384 and 409), the last line of the Lady's song (242), the Elder Brother's reply to Thyrsis (605 and 608), the omission of the image at line 847 ("and often takes our cattle with strange pinches"), the alterations in the concluding song (975 et passim), and the substantial addition, starting at lines 779, of the Lady's proposal to expound on the doctrine of virginity, and Comus's reply. Most of the changes, Lewis admits, are "minute ones" (175), but the addition of lines to the debate between Comus and the Lady is considerable, and regarded by him as "the most important single addition made in the composition of *Comus*" (174).

22. Flannagan, *The Riverside Milton*, 116.

23. References to the Bridgewater and Trinity manuscripts are from *A Maske: The Earlier Versions*, ed. S. E. Sprott (Toronto: University of Toronto Press, 1973); quotation, 58.

24. Ibid., 59.

25. Ibid., 134.

26. Lewis, "A Note on *Comus*," 174.

27. See Flannagan, *The Riverside Milton*, 638 n. 176.

28. See Leonard, *John Milton: The Complete Poems*, 845–46.

29. Ibid., 846.

30. See *PL* 1.592–94, 5.708–09, and 7.131–32.

Notes to Chapter Three, "Problem-Solving in Milton's Biblical Drama Sketches"

1. Regarding the question of when the plans were probably begun and finished, Harris Fletcher, *John Milton's Complete Poetical Works Reproduced in Photographic Facsimile* (Urbana: University of Illinois Press, 1945), remarks that "the outlines and subjects begin just after what is rather obviously a fair copy in the making of 'Lycidas.' . . . That would point to a date from the position in the manuscript as it now exists of almost any time soon after 1637 or 1638 for the earliest material. . . . The pages are followed by a page containing the date 1645 connected with *Sonnet XIII*. . . . [R]oughly, the material on these . . . pages was probably written thereon between 1637 and 1645. . . . An absolute terminal for any material on these pages in question would be afforded by his total blindness in 1652" (2:14). Fletcher extends the date to 1652 because many of the entries seem to have been rewritten or changed by Milton after he first set them down. The plans, especially the Fall sketches, are frequently included in editions of Milton's works. See, for example, *The Student's Milton*, ed. Frank Patterson (New York: Appleton-Century-Crofts, 1933), 1128–34; Flannagan, *The Riverside Milton*, 310–11; and the Scolar Press reproduction of the Trinity manuscript in John Milton, *Poems, Reproduced in Facsimile from the Manuscript in Trinity College, Cambridge, with a Transcript*, ed. William A. Wright (Menston, England: Scolar Press, 1972), 34–40. To facilitate ease of reading, I have corrected and modernized spelling in the longer TMS excerpts. Page citations in the text are to the Scolar Press edition.

2. See, for example, James Holly Hanford and James G. Taaffe, *A Milton Handbook* (New York: Meredith Corporation, 1970), 150–54; John Demaray, *Milton's Theatrical Epic: The Invention and Design of* Paradise Lost (Cambridge, Mass.: Harvard University Press, 1980), 3–20; Allan H. Gilbert, "The Cambridge Manuscript and Milton's Plans for an Epic," *Studies in Philology* 16 (1919): 172–76; and J. Milton French, "Chips from Milton's Workshop," *English Language Notes* 10 (1943): 230–42. Michael Lieb considers the Sodom material in relation to *Paradise Lost* in "Cupid's Funeral Pile: Milton's Projected Drama on the Theme of Lust," *Renaissance Papers* 34 (1972): 29–41. The dating of the sketches has been taken up not only by Fletcher (see previous note), but also by David Masson in *The Life of John Milton: Narrated in Connexion with the Political, Ecclesiastical, and Literary History of His Time* (New York: Peter Smith, 1946), 105–21, and

in John M. Steadman's article, "Milton's Dramatic Plans," in *A Milton Encyclopedia*, ed. William B. Hunter Jr. (Lewisburg, Pa.: Bucknell University Press, 1979), 2:168–70.

3. William R. Parker, "The Trinity Manuscript and Milton's Plans for a Tragedy," *Journal of English and Germanic Philology* 34 (1935): 225–32, sums up the basic questions at stake: "[TMS] indisputably proves Milton's early interest in writing a tragedy. . . . What form would such a tragedy have taken? Are Verity and many others justified in saying that 'any drama composed by Milton about 1641–1642 would have been cast in the self-same mould whence issued *Samson Agonistes*'? Was Milton, at this time, interested in writing a Greek tragedy in English?" Some critics concur with A. W. Verity's assessment. Masson, in *The Life of John Milton*, for instance, claims that "the form of the *TMS* plays . . . should be that of a Tragedy with a chorus, after the ancient Greek model, and the hesitation seems to have been mainly as to the subject for such a Tragedy" (2:105). Ida Langdon, *Milton's Theory of Poetry and Fine Art* (New York: Russell & Russell, 1965), maintains that the outlines "uniformly show an intention to follow Greek models" (98). Also, J. H. Hanford, "The Dramatic Element in *Paradise Lost*," *Studies in Philology* 29 (1917), remarks that "[Milton's] plans for drama show that he contemplated only tragedy on severely classical lines" (179).

4. See Steggle, "Milton's Masque and Euripides," 18–36.

5. In the biblical account, Jeroboam's son Abijah is stricken with a disease. Jeroboam sends his wife in disguise to Ahijah, the oracle in Shiloh, yet Ahijah is told in advance by God that she is coming. When she arrives, the prophet denounces Jeroboam's household for its spiritual unfaithfulness to God, and tells her the child will die. She then returns to Jeroboam, and when she reaches the household, the boy has indeed perished. In Milton's version, by contrast, the queen makes a decision reminiscent of Oedipus's: on "hearing the child shall die as she comes home refuses to return, thinking thereby to elude the oracle" (36).

6. Parker, "The Trinity Manuscript," 228. Parker regards other aspects of the plans as nonclassical, such as their use of personifications and the high number of figures on-stage in certain sketches. Joseph Pequigney, "Tragedy," in Hunter, *A Milton Encyclopedia*, 8:76, echoes that view and adduces nonclassical features such as the masque of evils and the late entrance of Adam and Eve, both of which occur in the Fall outlines. Other features in the plans that are rare or unheard of in classical drama include multiple choruses, an absence of any classical subjects, and a preference for historically true fables. Parker, "The Trinity Manuscript," 232 n. 21, notes, "The *Persae* is the only extant [classical] drama written about an historical subject."

7. Goldberg and Orgel, *John Milton*, 170.

8. The TMS topics frequently cite the name of the protagonist, then

follow it with a Greek, Latin, or English epithet. Examples include "Gideon Idoloclastes" (Gideon the Idolbreaker), "Elisaeus Menutes sive in Dothaimis 2 Reg." (Elisha the Informer, or in Dothan 2 Kings), and "Doeg Slandering." Possible sources for this convention are Greek drama, which offers precedents such as *Oedipus the King* and *Prometheus Bound* — the latter, in fact, may be echoed in the TMS listing "Christ Bound" — and, possibly, Ariosto's *Orlando Furioso* and/or Boiardo's *Orlando Innamorato*. Some listings offer a place name followed by a participle; at least one of these, "Samaria Liberata," is clearly based on Tasso's *Gerusalemme Liberata*, and others may be as well, including both *Paradise Lost* and "Sodom Burning."

9. Low, "Milton's *Samson* and the Stage," 319.

10. John Leonard, *Paradise Lost* (New York: Penguin Books, 1999), xii.

11. Both Aubrey's and Phillips's remarks are reprinted in Hughes, *Milton: Complete Poems and Major Prose*, 1024, 1034–35. Phillips's quotation of the speech substitutes "glorious" for "matchless," the phrase used in *PL* 4.41. Allan Gilbert, *On the Composition of* Paradise Lost: *A Study of the Ordering and Insertion of Material* (New York: Octagon Books, 1966), believes the error is Phillips's, since "glorious" first appears just lines earlier and "its repetition [in Phillips's version] is not according to Milton's habits of echoing words" (17).

12. Peck is quoted in Gilbert, *On the Composition of* Paradise Lost, 17; Gilbert's own quote is also found on this page. For the Voltaire passage, see *The Life Records of John Milton*, ed. J. Milton French (New Brunswick: Rutgers University Press, 1949), 1:379–80. Voltaire composed two versions of this essay; in the first he claims that "Milton pierced through the absurdity of that performance to the hidden majesty of the subject, which being altogether unfit for the stage, yet might be . . . the foundation of an epic poem." Voltaire's assessment was questioned by various poets and critics of the eighteenth century, including Alexander Pope and Samuel Johnson. Others, however, such as William Hayley and William Cowper, accepted it. John Shawcross, "Andreini, Giovanni Battista," in Hunter, *A Milton Encyclopedia*, contends that "the subject matter of Andreini's play and Milton's epic, deriving from the basic Genesis story, is the only point of tangency between the two" (1:47). The lack of specific parallels between the two works would seem to confirm Shawcross's judgment, yet even if Andreini were not a plot source for Milton, he still might have influenced the younger writer simply by inspiring him to write a tragedy based on the Fall.

13. See C. S. Lewis, *A Preface to* Paradise Lost (Oxford: Oxford University Press, 1967), 139–40.

14. Grant McColley, "Milton's Lost Tragedy," *Philological Quarterly* 18 (1939): 78–83.

15. Gordon Teskey, ed., Paradise Lost: *A Norton Critical Edition* (New York: W. W. Norton, 2005), 211.

16. Thanks to my student Megan Basham, whose paper on Satan's characterization in the diffuse epic stimulated my thinking on this question.

17. Gilbert, *On the Composition of* Paradise Lost, 22.

18. French, "Chips from Milton's Workshop," 236; and Lieb, "Cupid's Funeral Pile," 35.

19. Parker, "The Trinity Manuscript," 227; Low, "Milton's *Samson* and the Stage," 318.

20. Another possible source for the outline's multiple choruses could have been furnished by David Pareus's *Commentary on the Revelation,* a work that Milton alludes to in *The Reason of Church-Government,* when he states that "the scripture also affords us a divine pastoral drama in the Song of Solomon, consisting of two persons and a double chorus" (YP 1:815). Pareus was probably referring to the two protagonists of the Song of Solomon, namely, the bride and bridegroom, as well as the maidens accompanying the bride and the "mighty men" who bring in the bridegroom on a litter. Similarly, *The Reason of Church-Government* quotes Pareus's notion that "the Apocalypse of St. John is the majestic image of a high and stately tragedy, shutting up and intermingling her solemn scenes and acts with a *sevenfold* chorus of hallelujahs and harping symphonies" (YP 1:815; my emphasis).

21. Parker, *Milton's Debt,* 152.

22. Ibid., 6.

23. *Aristotle on the Art of Poetry,* ed. and trans. Ingram Bywater (Oxford: Oxford University Press, 1920), 355.

Notes to Chapter Four, "Theatrical Spectacle in Samson Agonistes"

1. Hume, "Aims and Limits of Historical Scholarship," 416.

2. Radzinowicz, *Toward* Samson Agonistes, 15–16; F. T. Prince, "Milton and the Theatrical Sublime," in *Approaches to* Paradise Lost: *The York Tercentenary Lectures,* ed. C. A. Patrides (Toronto: Toronto University Press, 1968), 54; Anne Ferry, *Milton and the Miltonic Dryden* (Cambridge, Mass.: Harvard University Press, 1969), 133, 135; John Shawcross, "The Genres of *Paradise Regained* and *Samson Agonistes,*" in *Milton Studies,* vol. 17, *Composite Orders: The Genres of Milton's Last Poems,* ed. Richard Ide and Joseph Wittreich (Pittsburgh: University of Pittsburgh Press, 1983), 236; John Steadman, "Milton and the Bible," in Hunter, *A Milton Encyclopedia,* 1:161; and Sauer, "The Politics of Performance," 202.

3. Parker, *Milton's Debt,* 143; Flannagan, *The Riverside Milton,* 788; David Loewenstein, *Milton and the Drama of History: Historical Vision, Iconoclasm, and the Literary Imagination* (Cambridge: Cambridge University Press, 1990), 124.

4. While I largely agree with the regenerationist line of argument, I believe it is partly to blame for the failure to see *Samson* as a true play. With the exception of Anthony Low, most regenerationist critics have over-reacted to Samuel Johnson's well-known censure that the play lacks a middle by emphasizing the protagonist's inner renewal at the expense of the work's "physical," exterior elements.

5. See Bywater, *Aristotle on the Art of Poetry*.

6. Flannagan, *The Riverside Milton*, 799.

7. Sauer, "The Politics of Performance," 202. See also Susan B. Iwanisziw, "Conscience and the Disobedient Female Consort in the Closet Dramas of John Milton and Elizabeth Cary," in *Milton Studies*, vol. 36, ed. Albert C. Labriola (Pittsburgh: University of Pittsburgh Press, 1998), 109–22. Iwanisziw argues that Milton's prefatory epistle fails "to observe any indebtedness to the labors of Renaissance closet dramatists such as Fulke Greville and Samuel Daniel, both radical Protestants" (110). Similarly, she suggests that Milton "apparently suppressed references to Cary in his introduction to the drama" (121). But there may not have been any significant debt to register or suppress if Milton was not interested in composing a closet play.

8. Oliver Taplin, *Greek Tragedy in Action* (Berkeley and Los Angeles: University of California Press, 1978), 34.

9. In *The Riverside Milton*, Roy Flannagan cites John Carey's suggestion that Milton's depiction of the building as a theater may have come from George Sandys's 1615 work *A Relation of a Journey* (London: William Barrett), which mentions the ruins of a "theater of Samson" on a hill overlooking Gaza (840 n. 296).

10. These productions were the Guildhall School's 1956 show, whose set featured Dagon's temple in the distance, surrounded by houses, and the 1998 dramatization by the Northern Broadsides Company, which culminated in the collapse of the temple onto the stage.

11. Walton, *Greek Theatre Practice*, 144.

12. The quotation here is from *The Tragedy of Mariam, the Fair Queen of Jewry*, ed. Barry Weller and Margaret Ferguson (Berkeley and Los Angeles: University of California Press, 1994), 69.

13. *Selected Writings of Fulke Greville*, ed. Joan Rees (London: Athlone Press, 1973), 66–67.

14. See Flannagan, *The Riverside Milton*, 815 n. 134, for his mention of this possibility.

15. David Berkeley, "On a Common Error Respecting Samson's Size and Musculature," *English Language Notes* 19, no. 3 (March 1982): 260–62. Adams's and Mollencott's statements are quoted in Berkeley's note. Other critics who misread the protagonist's size include James Holly Hanford, D. C. Allen, Arthur Barker, Carole Kessner, Nancy Hoffman, and Emile Saillens. Flannagan's characterization appears in *The Riverside Milton*,

795; Kerrigan's appears in "The Irrational Coherence of *Samson Agonistes*," in *Milton Studies*, vol. 22, ed. James D. Simmonds (Pittsburgh: University of Pittsburgh Press, 1986), 217–32; quotation, 219.

16. Unless otherwise noted, all biblical quotations are taken from the Authorized Version.

17. Sandys is quoted in Carey and Fowler, *The Poems of John Milton*, 397.

18. References to Sophocles are taken from *Oedipus the King*, trans. David Grene (Chicago: University of Chicago Press, 1942).

19. For a fuller discussion, see my article, "The Representation of Samson's Eyes in *Samson Agonistes*," *English Language Notes* 35, no. 2 (December 1997): 27–32. See also Flannagan, *The Riverside Milton*, 817 n. 158, citation of Carol Bisbee, who confirms that the eyes are intact.

20. Eleanor Brown, *Milton's Blindness* (New York: Columbia University Press, 1934), 22.

21. See Spencer, "*Samson Agonistes* in London," 35.

22. Dennis Kezar, "Samson's Death by Theater and Milton's Art of Dying," *English Literary History* 66 (1999): 295–336, attempts to situate Samson in the tradition of the *ars moriendi*, or "art of dying" literature. He thus overlooks the hopeful elements in the prisoner's appearance, as do Fish and Knoppers. Stanley Fish, "Spectacle and Evidence in *Samson Agonistes*," *Critical Inquiry* 15 (1989): 585, 557–58, later reprinted as "The Temptation of Intelligibility," in *How Milton Works* (Cambridge, Mass.: Harvard University Press, 2001), 435, 440, claims, erroneously, that Manoa and the Chorus cannot look Samson in the face, and argues that the captive presents a "terrible visage . . . with the face and look of Medusa." Similarly, Knoppers, *Historicizing Milton: Spectacle, Power, and Poetry in Restoration England* (Athens, Ga.: University of Georgia Press, 1994), 154, states that the Chorus "see only his misery." I contend that they do look at him and thus find reason for hope, not despair, mainly because of his hair and eyes.

23. Joseph Wittreich, *Shifting Contexts: Reinterpreting* Samson Agonistes (Pittsburgh: Duquesne University Press, 2002), xviii. The terrorist reading of the tragedy seems to have been initiated by John Carey, *Milton* (London: Evans Bros., 1969), 138–46. See also Irene Samuel, "*Samson Agonistes* as Tragedy," in *Calm of Mind: Tercentenary Essays on* Paradise Regained *and* Samson Agonistes *in Honor of John S. Diekhoff*, ed. Joseph A. Wittreich (Cleveland: Press of Case Western Reserve, 1971), 235–57. Both Wittreich's *Interpreting* Samson Agonistes (Princeton: Princeton University Press, 1986) and its sequel, *Shifting Contexts*, extend the terrorist reading, as does Wood's "*Exiled from Light.*" The terrorist interpretation has been disputed by various critics, including Wendy Furman, Low, Philip Gallagher, and Alan Rudrum. Their work, as well as that of Carey, Samuel, Wittreich, and Wood, is discussed in a review article by Alan Rudrum, "Milton Scholarship."

24. Stanley Fish, "Spectacle and Evidence in *Samson Agonistes*," *Critical Inquiry* 15 (1989): 556–87, later reprinted as "The Temptation of Intelligibility," in *How Milton Works*, 416, 419, 453–54. In "Milton Scholarship and the *Agon* over Samson Agonistes," Rudrum counters Fish's claim that the rousing motions are unreliable because earlier instances of such inner promptings of Samson cannot be definitively interpreted:

> In contemplating his marriages, to the Timnian woman and to Dalila, Samson had worked out the difference between marrying "the daughter of an Infidel" because, as he knew from "intimate impulse," it was "motion'd" of God and marrying another because he "thought it lawful from [his] former act" (lines 219–31). His initial refusal to the Officer, followed by "I with this Messenger will go along," after he has begun "to feel / Some rousing motions," indicates precisely that he has learned the difference between breaking the Law for the sake of convenience and doing so because, as "the Argument" to the poem puts it, he is "at length persuaded inwardly that this was from God." (468–69)

25. See Wittreich, *Shifting Contexts*, 270.

26. Low's quotation appears in his review of Wood's book in *Christianity and Literature* 51 (Winter 2002): 287–91; quotation, 290.

27. Wittreich, *Shifting Contexts*, 221, 223.

28. Rudrum, "Milton Scholarship," 476, 477.

29. Leonard, *Paradise Lost*, 940–41.

30. Wittreich, *Shifting Contexts*, 223.

31. Flannagan, *The Riverside Milton*, 787.

32. Paul Sellin, "Milton's Epithet *Agonistes*," *Studies in English Literature* 4 (1964): 137–62; quotation, 144.

33. *The Works of Flavius Josephus, Complete and Unabridged*, trans. William Whiston (Peabody, Mass.: Hendrickson Publishing, 1987), 147.

34. Kirkconnell, *That Invincible Samson*, 179. All quotations from the analogues are taken from this edition.

35. Flannagan, *The Riverside Milton*, 836.

36. Anthony Low labels this species of irony the "irony of alternatives," in which two apparently contradictory results come to pass (*Blaze of Noon*, 77). Along with Joseph Summers, Low cites this and other passages from the drama that exemplify the irony of alternatives, including lines 1637–38, where the nuntius describes Samson "as one who prayed, / Or some great matter in his mind revolved." He concludes that at this point Samson "both chooses freely *and* is led by divine providence" (79; my emphasis).

37. Burns, "'Then Stood up Phinehas,'" 40, 45.

38. Arnold Stein, *Heroic Knowledge: An Interpretation of* Paradise Regained *and* Samson Agonistes (Minneapolis: University of Minnesota Press, 1957), 196; Sellin, "Milton's Epithet *Agonistes*," 157, 150; William

Kerrigan, *The Prophetic Milton* (Charlottesville: University Press of Virginia, 1974), 206; Sauer, "The Politics of Performance," 207; Norman T. Burns, "'Then Stood up Phinehas': Milton's Antinomianism, and Samson's," in *Milton Studies*, vol. 33, *The Miltonic Samson*, ed. Albert C. Labriola and Michael Lieb, 27–46 (Pittsburgh: University of Pittsburgh Press, 1996), quotations, 41, 42; and Anna Nardo, "'Sung and Proverbed,'" *Mosaic* 22, no. 1 (1989): 1–16, quotations, 11, 1.

39. Flannagan, *The Riverside Milton*, 814.

40. Ibid., 835.

41. See *The Works of Flavius Josephus*, 146, and Whiston's note on the same page.

42. Quoted in Feisal G. Mohamed, "Confronting Religious Violence: Milton's *Samson Agonistes*," *PMLA* 120 (2005): 327–40; quotation, 328.

43. Ibid., 328, 329, 333.

44. Ibid., 334.

45. Ibid., 336.

46. Claims for the drama's essential coherence and reasonableness have perhaps been most closely associated with the regenerationist critics, who have sought to answer Samuel Johnson's charge that the play lacks a proper middle by adducing what they regard as the relatively uncomplicated, though unseen, process of the protagonist's moral regeneration. Probably the most influential of these studies is Mary Ann Radzinowicz's *Toward* Samson Agonistes: *The Growth of Milton's Mind* (Princeton: Princeton University Press, 1978). See also Anthony Low, *The Blaze of Noon: A Reading of* Samson Agonistes (New York: Columbia University Press, 1974). More recent critics have become skeptical of the claims about the work's reasonable character, in part because of David Loewenstein's well-known study, *Milton and the Drama of History: Historical Vision, Iconoclasm, and the Literary Imagination* (Cambridge: Cambridge University Press, 1990), which contends that such interpretations "tend to smooth over the jagged emotional edges of Milton's tragedy, not to mention the disturbing images of Samson's vehement iconoclasm" (133). Michael Lieb's 1996 essay, "'Our Living Dread': The God of *Samson Agonistes*," employs Loewenstein's discussion as a starting point in order to explore Milton's term "Our Living Dread" as it is applied to God in the tragedy. Lieb's essay appears in *Milton Studies*, vol. 33, *The Miltonic Samson*, ed. Albert C. Labriola and Michael Lieb (Pittsburgh: University of Pittsburgh Press, 1996).

47. In an email message to me on August 18, 2006, Kathleen Burbery comments on the Hebrew text of Judges 16:27, arguing that it "supports a multiplicity of views of the rulers and the crowd — from seeing the crowd as a unit to seeing it as discrete individuals, from looking at the rulers as cut off from their people to seeing them as representatives of them." She also points out that the contingency of the Hebrew text could indicate that

the total number of spectators, both in the temple and on the roof, is 3,000, or that, in addition to those in the temple, 3,000 others are on the roof watching.

48. Peter Herman, "Milton and Religious Violence," *PMLA* Forum 120 (October 2005): 1642–43; Feisal Mohamed, *PMLA* 120 (October 2005): 1644.

49. Herman, "Milton and Religious Violence," 1642–43.

50. Wittreich, *PMLA* 120.5, 1641.

51. Leonard, *John Milton: The Complete Poems*, 925.

52. It is often claimed that Milton departed from Judges by making Dalila Samson's wife — see, for example, Flannagan, *The Riverside Milton*, 801 — but the biblical narrative does not specify if they were married or not. According to Pseudo-Philo's *Liber Antiquitatum Biblicarum,* a work Milton may have known, she was first a harlot, then his wife (43.5). See Brenda E. Richardson and Norman Vance, "Delilah," in *Dictionary of Biblical Tradition in English Literature,* ed. David Lyle Jeffrey (Grand Rapids, Mich.: Eerdman's, 1992), 193–94.

53. William Empson, *Milton's God* (London: Chatto & Windus, 1965), 219, 220; James W. Tupper, "The Dramatic Structure of *Samson Agonistes,*" *PMLA* 35 (1920): 38; D. C. Allen, *The Harmonious Vision: Studies in Milton's Poetry* (Baltimore: Johns Hopkins University Press, 1954), 89; Low, *The Blaze of Noon*, 123–25.

54. *The New Oxford Annotated Bible with the Apocrypha,* ed. Herbert G. May and Bruce M. Metzger (New York: Oxford University Press, 1977), 432.

55. Parker, *Milton's Debt*, 143.

56. See ibid., 46, and Allen, *The Harmonious Vision,* 91.

57. Hughes, *Milton: Complete Poems and Major Prose,* 535; Max Beerbohm, *Around Theatres* (New York: Greenwood Press, 1968), 531; and Theodor Siebert, "Egozentrisches in Miltons Schreibweise," *Anglia* 54 (1930): 64.

58. Leonard, *John Milton: The Complete Poems*, 934.

59. See, for example, Edith Buchanan, "The Italian Neo-Senecan Background of *Samson Agonistes*" (Ph.D. diss., Duke University, 1952); and Daniel Boughner, "Milton's Harapha and Renaissance Comedy," *English Literary History* 11 (1944): 297–306.

60. Sellin, "Milton's Epithet," 137.

61. For Barbara Lewalski's comment, see "*Samson Agonistes* and the 'Tragedy' of the Apocalpyse," *PMLA* 85 (1970): 1050–62; quotation at 1059; for John Steadman's, see "Milton's Harapha and Goliath," *Journal of English and Germanic Philology* 60 (1961): 786–85, quotation, 795. Thomas Kranidas's introduction to *Samson Agonistes* in *A Milton Encyclopedia* (Lewisburg, Pa.: Bucknell University Press, 1978), 141–64, represents Harapha as "gorgeously-clad . . . strong, healthy, seeing, 'secure,'

circling the blinded ruined man and talking about what might have been" (161). It is not clear if Kranidas thinks that the giant's mufti is gorgeous, or if he has, like Lewalski and Steadman, armed him. The fact that his description echoes Samson's taunting reference to the giant's "gorgeous arms" (1119) points, I think, to the latter possibility. More recently, Derek Wood had described the giant as "a young warrior in all his finery," in *"Exiled from Light,"* 154. Again, it is not clear if he alludes to the visitor's civilian clothes or his armor.

62. See John Huntley, "Chorus," in *A Milton Encyclopedia,* ed. William B. Hunter Jr. (Lewisburg, Pa.: Bucknell University Press, 1978), 44.

63. Flannagan, *The Riverside Milton,* 810 n. 87.

64. The other indentations in the 1617 text include lines 315, 322, 327, 617, 633, 667, 687, 705, 710, 1018, 1034, 1046, 1053, 1287, 1298, and 1640. Lines 617, 633, and 1640 are spoken by Samson, while the rest are uttered by the Danites.

65. Parker, *Milton's Debt,* 108.

66. The first example is from Frank Huntley's 1978 staging in Ann Arbor, Michigan, the second from William Poel's 1900 staging. See chapter 5.

Notes to Chapter Five, "Intended for the Stage?"

1. Details for the performances of *Samson* mentioned throughout this chapter may be found in the appendix.

2. See Alwin Thaler, "Milton in the Theater," *Studies in Philology* 17 (1920): 274–75. The full article appears on 269–308.

3. For a comprehensive account of the staging of Milton's other works during the eighteenth and nineteenth centuries, see Thaler, "Milton in the Theater." Baker's book is *The Companion to the Playhouse; or, An Historical Account of all the Dramatic Writers (and their Works) that have appeared in Great Britain and Ireland* (London: AMS Press, 1966), unpaginated.

4. See Thaler, "Milton in the Theater," 278–79.

5. In discussing the dramatic virtues of Handel's piece, Stella Revard's observation is apt:

> The problems of performing *Samson Agonistes* are much like those of performing Handel's *Samson.* . . . How much staging should an oratorio have? I myself found that the performances of Handel's oratorio that were staged in the 1980s at Covent Garden and at the Chicago Lyric Opera were much more effective than the simple stand-up oratorios that I have seen of the same work. I was at an "unstaged" performance in Albert Hall last summer and felt that musically and dramatically the oratorio was less interesting than when presented with costumes and some staging.

Post to the Milton listserv (Milton-l@richmond.edu), November 3, 2002. See also Revard, "Handel's *Samson*: London 1985," *Milton Quarterly* 21 (March 1987): 28–30.

6. Robert Speaight, *William Poel and the Elizabethan Revival* (Cambridge, Mass.: Harvard University Press, 1954), 157. Speaight was himself an accomplished actor who recorded excerpts from Milton's poetry. See the audiocassette *Treasury of John Milton* (New Rochelle, N.Y.: Spoken Arts). He also starred in *Paradise Lost*, a three-act opera-oratorio by Phillip Rhodes (Louisville: Louisville Orchestra, 1972).

7. Portions of these reviews are quoted in Speaight, *William Poel*, 153–54.

8. See Beerbohm, "Agonising Samson," 531.

9. See the *London Times*, December 16, 1908. Montague's assessment is excerpted in Speaight, *William Poel*, 156.

10. For a brief discussion of Monck's ties with Poel, see Speaight, *William Poel*, 180.

11. Andrew Stephenson, "*Samson Agonistes*," *Theatre Arts Monthly* 22 (1938): 914–16.

12. The *Times*'s review came out on May 8, 1951, on page 17; Spencer, "*Samson Agonistes* in London," *Seventeenth Century News* 9:35; and Dwight Durling, "Coghill's *Samson Agonistes* at Oxford," *Seventeenth Century News* 9 (September 1951): 63.

13. This review appeared in the *London Times* on May 13, 1955.

14. The 1933 production was reviewed in the *London Times* on March 29, 1933 (two earliest editions only), 12. For the *Times*'s account of the 1965 staging, see "Too Little Barbarity in this *Samson*," *London Times*, April 4, 1965, 34.

15. William Shaw's account of the staging, as well as the remarks by Low and Hyman, appear in Shaw's article, "Producing *Samson Agonistes*," *Milton Quarterly* 13 (1979): 69–79.

16. Dayton Haskin, "*Samson Agonistes* on the Stage at Yale," *Milton Quarterly* 19 (1985): 48–52; quotations, 50, 51–52.

17. See Paulin, "The Poet Breaks His Bonds," *Times Literary Supplement* 2 (October 1998): 21, and Kingston, "Good Hair Day," *Halifax Times*, September 18, 1998, 1–2.

18. See Beerbohm, "Agonising Samson," 529.

19. Ibid., 527.

Notes to Chapter Six, "Conclusion"

1. See Pequigney, "Milton's Poetics," in Hunter, *A Milton Encyclopedia*, 6:164.

2. For Kirkconnell's assessment, see *That Invincible Samson*, viii; for Pequigney's comment, see "Milton's Poetics," 164.

3. Quotations of Racine are from *Jean Racine: Complete Plays*, trans. and ed. Samuel Solomon, 2 vols. (New York: Random House, 1967), 235.

4. In 3.7 of *Athalie* the High Priest Joad foresees, respectively, the eventual corruption of King Joas; the death of his own son Zacharie, while serving as High Priest; and the advent of the Messiah. Throughout my discussion of *Athalie* I use the French versions of the characters' names in order to avoid confusing it with the biblical version.

5. For an exception, see Pierre Han's 1971 note, "Vraisemblance and Decorum: A Note on the Baroque in *Samson Agonistes* and *Berenice*," *Seventeenth Century News* 29 (1971): 67–68.

6. Racine, *Oeuvres complètes*, 233.

7. Parker, *Milton's Debt*, 125–28.

8. Steiner, *The Death of Tragedy*, 99–100.

Notes to Appendix

1. In my survey I have tried to include every performance of *Samson* that was substantially reviewed in major English print venues such as the *London Times* and *The New York Times*, as well as those reviewed and/or noted in *Milton Quarterly* and on the Milton listserv.

2. Both Riccoboni and Romagnesi's adaptations are briefly discussed in Thaler, "Milton in the Theater," 275 n. 21.

3. This version is praised by the poet John Masefield in a letter to the *London Times*, May 26, 1930, 15.

4. This production is briefly noted in the *London Times*, May 23, 1930, review of Coghill's production, on page 14. See the following note.

5. Coghill's show was critiqued in the *London Times*, May 23, 1930, 14b.

6. This performance was reviewed in the *London Times*, March 29, 1933 (earliest and second-earliest editions only), 12.

7. Reviewed in the *London Times*, July 24, 1935, 12.

8. This production was praised by C. S. Lewis, according to the drama critic of the *London Times*. This (anonymous) critic notes that the staging witnessed by Lewis was "thrilling," in part because the producer "discovered fierce drum rhythms in the text," with "some passages almost approaching Vachell [*sic*] Lindsay." These comments appear in the *Times*'s review of Redgrave's 1965 enactment.

9. This performance is mentioned in Haskin's account of the Yale Drama School's enactment.

10. This production is mentioned in the Hillbarn's on-line history ("Our History"), available at http://www.hillbarntheatre.org/about/history.htm; accessed February 2, 2004.

11. Reviewed in the *Harrow Observer and Gazette,* March 30, 1961.

12. While Graham's primary inspiration for this ballet seems to have been the Judges narrative, she may have also been influenced by Milton, since the ballet features Samson and (in Graham's spelling) Delilah in a series of agons. Graham studied English literature both in high school and as an adult. Agnes de Mille notes that throughout her career Graham "read prodigiously, and took fire. Her notebooks were choked with quotations from Shakespeare, Milton, and Coleridge." See de Mille, *The Life and Works of Martha Graham* (New York: Vintage Books, 1992), 285. Hence, in retitling this ballet *Samson Agonistes,* it may be that Graham was acknowledging a debt to Milton. It is also worth noting that some of Graham's greatest roles were Clytemnestra, Cassandra, and other women from classical drama, parts that may have instilled in her an appreciation of Milton's Dalila. Thanks to Deborah Hull for assistance on this point.

13. Paul Stanwood took part in this production and briefly described it on the Milton listserv, September 3, 2001.

14. Anthony Low refers to this performance in "Milton's Samson," 321 n. 12.

15. Norman Burns described this presentation on the Milton listserv, September 6, 2001.

16. Shaw discusses this production in "Producing *Samson Agonistes,*" *Milton Quarterly* 13 (1979): 69–79.

17. Burns noted this performance on the Milton listserv, September 4, 2001.

18. John Shawcross attended this presentation and furnished an account of it for me, via email, on May 21, 2003. He points out that "it was the full dramatic poem, apparently the first such dramatic reading; all others have various cuts." Shawcross also noted that "Samson the Terrorist didn't come through to me at all!"

Index